The Girl Who Loved Elvis

The Girl Who Loved Elvis

Susie Mee

PEACHTREE PUBLISHERS, LTD.
Atlanta

The author would like to thank both the Virginia Center for the Creative Arts and the MacDowell Colony, where large portions of the novel were written.

Published by
PEACHTREE PUBLISHERS, LTD.
494 Armour Circle, NE
Atlanta, Georgia 30324

Except for Elvis Presley, all persons represented in this book are fictional, and any resemblance to actual persons, living or dead, is purely coincidental.
A version of chapter 18 was published in Redbook, November 1986.
The title for the sermon on pages 16-17 was suggested by Howard Finster.
Doffing rules reprinted from Trion Facts, August 1, 1973, by permission of Harold L. Peek.

Manufactured in the United States of America

10 9 8 7 6 5 4 3 2 1

Jacket design by Candace J. Magee
Jacket illustration by Richard Hicks
Composition by Ann Walker Pruitt

Library of Congress Cataloging in Publication Data

Mee, Susie, 1938-
    The girl who loved Elvis / Susie Mee.
      p. cm.
    ISBN 1-56145-080-4
    I. Title.
PS3563.E284G57 1993
   813' .54—dc20   92-43511
                                    CIP

This book is dedicated
to the memory of my mother,
Addie McWilliams Baker,
and to all my friends in
Chattooga County.

Chapter One

I'M STANDING IN GRANT'S FIVE & TEN-CENT STORE in Chattanooga. I don't really like five & ten-cent stores much, in fact they make me half-sick. It's the same feeling I get in zoos. But tomorrow's mama's birthday and I'm here to pick out a parakeet to give her for a present. There's not much choice. I can either take the pea-green one with black markings or the aquamarine with yellow markings. But there must be *some* difference between them besides color.

While the saleswoman cleans out its cage, the aquamarine parakeet sets up such a squawking that I can barely hear the music drifting over from the record department nearby. Which is annoying because music is the best thing about Grant's.

"Does it always make that much racket?" I ask.

The saleswoman is wearing a hairnet dyed the same shade as her yellow hair. "Hon, it don't know no better. Wears down your nerves though, don't it?"

"Can it say anything?"

"Not that I've heard."

"I thought parakeets were supposed to talk."

"Listen, birds is like anybody else. They need TLC. Give 'em TLC and they'll tell you their life stories. Keep you up all night." She shuts the cage door and gathers up the soiled papers. You can tell she's taking care that none of the mess gets on her long red nails. Then she goes off, leaving me to make up my own mind about the birds.

I decide to audition them, like my high school English teacher used to do for the school play. Pursing my mouth, I do little crooning noises such as "cheep, cheep, cheep, ooooh, oooh," or "hi, birdieee, hi birdieee"—but these stupid birds don't respond. So I bend closer. At least the pea-green one finally does *something*. It flutters over to the plastic wheel and sticks its head through one of the circles like it's playing hide-'n'-go-seek with me. The other one, the squawker, just sits on its perch staring the way Tessie Scoggins does sometimes through her thick glasses. When mama sees this bird, I bet she'll faint. I bet she'll throw her arms around me and say, "LaVonne, you are the sweetest daughter in the whole world." Well, she won't say that but maybe she'll at least smile. Then, when I finally leave home, she'll have something to keep her company. See? I got it all figured out.

It's at this moment—this same . . . exact . . . moment—that I hear that voice for the first time.

> . . . *s'lonely, babieeeeeee,*
> *s'lonely,*
> *s'lonely. . . .*

Whoever it is sounds just like my daddy used to. Same way of dipping his voice as if he suddenly skipped down a hole and come up on the other side. "A bolt of electricity out of the blue" is how I plan on describing it to Dot. Dot's my good friend. She likes hearing stories. Or I might say, "It was like being bit on the tip of my finger by a parakeet." Because that's what happens.

"What's the matter?" The saleswoman has returned and is now standing close enough for me to detect the strong scent of Tabu.

"That *thing*," I point to the cage, "bit me."

"Huh! All I can say is you must not have been paying much attention." She grabs my finger and examines it, then lets it fall again. "Anyhow, it don't amount to much."

"Well, it's bleeding." I stick it in my mouth and suck on it, the way I used to suck my thumb. (Mama claims I did it till I was fourteen, but that's not true.) I begin backing away.

"Hey! Wait a minute!" the woman calls. "What about the parakeet?"

"Welll. . . ."

The woman's been frowning, but now a sly half-smile flicks across her lips. "Listen, you better take this bird home and check it for parrot fever." Her nails tap out a rhythm on the glass counter.

I think she must be pulling my leg, but I'll play dumb. "Parrot fever! What's that?"

"You know what rabies is in dogs, don't you?" 'Course I do. Couple of years ago, Miz Cowan's dog started foaming at the mouth and the police had to shoot it. "Parrot fever's the same in birds. If you get bit by a parakeet that's carrying it, you might have to take them shots."

"What do I do?" Now I'm curious to see how far she'll go.

"Just keep an eye on it, that's all. If it starts . . . acting weird, then you better see about it. But it don't happen too often, and if it don't, you've got yourself a real nice bird."

"But what if it does?"

"Oh, you can return it. All our birds are guaranteed." She points to a high shelf. "Now, we got two cage sizes. You want the large or the small?"

I say I don't like spending too much for a diseased bird. She says she'll give me a discount on the large cage—because of my finger—and I say okay. She also throws together what she calls the "essentials"—food and water dishes, cuttlebone, birdseed, grit—and tells me about each one. I feel like I'm listening to one of Mr. Baxter's mill lectures. Last of all comes the parakeet. When the saleswoman brings her fingernails close, the bird flutters its wings in terror. Finally, though, she's able to grab it and stuff it into the cage. Then she hands it to me. Holding the cage as far from my body as possible, I pass the counter of socks and men's underwear, the counter with fresh-roasted peanuts and cashews and pecans, pass the striped beach umbrellas that sit beneath a yellow spotlight, cut across to the display for Dr. Scholl's arch supports, pass bottles of mouthwash and lotions for liver spots, turn right to the bobbypins and hairnets and curlers, and right again to dog bones and artificial seaweed until I see the parakeet cages and realize that I've come full circle.

That's when I hear the song again, and this time I follow the beat.

Although it's always crowded,
You still can find some room
For broken-hearted lovers. . . .

Once I get near the record counter, I stop and shut my eyes for a minute so I can hear the music better.

As it winds down, the salesgirl suddenly comes to life. "Isn't he *wonderful?*" she says. Her voice sounds warm and breathy as though it's just come out of a hot oven.

I nod and move closer. "Who *is* he?"

"Don't tell me you never heard of Elvis Presley!"

Have I heard of him? His name sounds vaguely familiar. "I come from Georgia," I say, as if this single fact explains my ignorance. I could add that mostly what I hear is mill gossip.

"He's the biggest thing to hit show business in years," the girl says. "Already been on the 'Milton Berle Show.'" Leaning forward, she says in a more confidential tone, "I heard him in person three weeks ago at Memorial Auditorium, and I tell you, it was something! People screaming, tearing off his clothes." Picking up the record cover, she hugs it close for a second before handing it over. "This picture doesn't do him justice. He just brims over with personality."

3

From the photograph on the back, he even *looks* a little like daddy. Same pompadour wave that has as many swirls to it as the top of a vanilla frosted. The mouth's different, though.

"He has nice lips." I turn the record over.

"You want to buy it? It's eighty-five, plus tax. We only got a few left."

I do some subtracting in my head. Having already spent almost fifteen dollars for the bird, the cage, and a return bus ticket, I have only two dollars and five cents left. That should be enough, unless there's an emergency, and then what's the difference? Might as well die happy. "Yeah, I'd like to."

"You won't regret it." The girl drops the record into a sack. "I played mine so much I wore it out and had to get myself another."

Just then a customer walks up to the other end of the counter and the girl goes over to help him. I hang around examining the record covers. Eddy Arnold . . . Roy Acuff . . . Frankie Laine . . . Jo Stafford. My favorite's Johnny Ray. I just love the way his voice trembles.

Finishing the sale, the girl returns. She has a slight frown on her face as if she's thinking hard. "I'm starting an Elvis Presley Fan Club in this area. Maybe you'd like to do the same in Georgia."

My mind is still back with "Heartbreak Hotel" so at first I don't hear her. Then the words begin to sink in. The head of a fan club. Me! LaVonne Grubbs! Then I think to myself, is she trying to put something over on me, like that woman with the parakeet? "Does it cost anything?"

"Five dollars." I try hard not to look shocked. If you consider that I make exactly $8.65 a night in the spinning room, it's almost the equal of an evening's work. "But for that, you get a beautiful poster of Elvis, a button, official membership blanks, and a monthly newsletter. Look!" Grabbing a printed pad nearby, she tears several sheets off the top. "Why don't you take a form home, and think about it? Here are some extra." Smiling, she nods, and moves away.

With the form in one hand and a bird that might start squawking at any minute in the other, I walk out. The sunlight's bright so I move over to the strip of shade that hugs the buildings. The cage makes people stare. Some even grin. Big grins with white even teeth. Not like the teeth of people I know. Dot Ledbetter, for instance. Dot has a huge gap between her two front teeth, though it doesn't faze her one bit. She claims it's the perfect place for Troy Wiggins to put his tongue when he kisses her and without that space, he wouldn't know what to do with it. The same phrase goes round and round in my brain, making me dizzy. *S'lonely. S'lonely.*

When I reach the Tivoli Theater, I stop for a second. I haven't been inside there since daddy took me that time mama was in the hospital with appendicitis. He said he wanted it to be something I'd remember all my life (was he already thinking about leaving?). And I *have*.

In the lobby, he points out things I haven't even noticed. "LaVonne," he whispers, bending down to my height. "Know what this is?" He leads me over to an orange plant set in a little cubicle. "It's coral. Grows under the sea. And see that?" The hanging vine springs from his fingers as he touches it. "That's seaweed. Isn't it pretty?" daddy asks, taking my hand.

He buys a bag of popcorn, and after the two of us eat it all, he buys another. The theater's like a castle, with painted ceilings and balconies draped in red curtains and lamps in the shape of golden cupids.

Stop daydreaming, I say. (Sometimes I can be as hard on myself as mama.) Move on, move on. In Loveman's windows, I catch a brief glimpse of myself—an eighteen-year-old girl with gold hair that looks darker in the glass. My face, though—except for my green eyes, which are big like mama's—remains a blur. Always did. Even when Gene told me how beautiful I was.

Inside the Greyhound Bus Station, I spy a weighing machine and immediately rush to it, set down the cage, insert a penny, and stand there while the numbers spin. But it's the fortune card I'm waiting for, and when it comes, I turn it around. SOMEONE IMPORTANT HAS JUST ENTERED YOUR LIFE. You may laugh but these cards have never failed me. I just have to figure out what this one means. Preacher Crow once said that people are never really aware what's happening to them until they have the chance to reflect on it. He said reflection's the only way the mind can grab hold of experience. But I could have told him that some things come in lightning flashes.

I buy myself a bag of corn curls and the latest issue of *True Confessions* and settle down to read. The parakeet pecks around in its cage as if it's looking for something, but I ignore it. I start a story called "We Traded Our Baby for a Tractor," but it's too sad. "Car Hop" is better. The boy in it reminds me of Gene. He's trying to get this girl Vickie to do it with him, and the second she gives in, she gets pregnant and has to go away to a Salvation Army home for unwed mothers. Just then, the announcement crackles over the loudspeaker: "South-bound bus leaving in ten minutes on Platform Seven for Rossville, Fort Oglethorpe, Midway, Delphi, Goody, Richville, Armuchee, Rome, Cartersville, Acworth, Marietta, Atlanta, and points south. Platform Seven." Grabbing my stuff, I walk out to the place where the driver's already taking tickets. I'm afraid he'll make trouble about the bird, but he doesn't. A few minutes later, we're heading toward Rossville Boulevard and Highway 27.

I try reading a little more. Then I get to feeling nauseous—I don't know whether it's the motion of the bus or Vickie's baby being born without a hand—so I lean back against the seat and close my eyes.

The next thing I know, the edges of the city have given way to cornfields and pastureland, and the pastureland to woods, and we're passing one of the places where daddy would look for deer. When he spotted one, he'd stop the car and point it out. At first I had a hard time seeing what he saw, but gradually my eyes got trained to it, and I could spot a moving beige splotch behind trees about as quick as he could. Daddy was always fascinated by anything that could disappear without a trace. He used to say that life was just one big vanishing act, and although I didn't understand it at the time, I do now, or I think I do. It's about change and how people and things pass away and never return. It's the same as when he put pennies, dimes, and nickels through a slot in a china bank, and refused to open it once the bank was full. After he left, mama found six banks choked to the brim. She smashed them all against the side of the garage until the ground was littered with coins.

Oh, daddy, daddy. Why didn't you take me with you?

Such thoughts weigh down my eyelids. I shut them again, but don't sleep.

The bus comes to a halt just beyond the Texaco Service Station. Soon as my feet hit the pavement, I light out, cage in hand, toward the mill where the sun has turned the red brick buildings the shade of a rusty nail. If I was conducting a tour the way Mr. Baxter sometimes does for out-of-town visitors, I'd do it this way: I'd say, "Okay, folks, that small building with no windows is the personnel office. You can tell the people who work there because they wear jackets and ties. Next to it is the dye plant with its big vats of steam, then sizing, where the warp threads are treated to make them stronger, then slashing, where, as you might have guessed already, they're cut into long strips. After that comes finishing, where the woven cloth is "cured" and made more durable. The finishing plant is just behind my house. It has three chimneys and the middle one throws out lots of angry smoke. Reminds me of my mama. Next to finishing is the glove mill, where work gloves are cut and sewn together.

"Now, on the left side is the Grey Mill. I don't know why it's called 'Grey,' and nobody else seems to either, not even Mr. Baxter. It's huge. One section's carding, where the raw cotton's combed clean, next roving, where it's broken down into strips, then spinning, where I work, and finally weaving.

"I reckon one of the most interesting things about the town of Goody is that big building at the head of the plaza called the Store, with a capital S. It houses ten different departments. On the second floor, there's the undertaking, where daddy used to work, the furniture store, the ladies' ready-to-wear, and the remnant department. The soda fountain, drugstore, grocery store, meat market, hardware, candy counter, and bank are on the bottom. Way in back's the Goody Café. All of it's owned by the Goody Mills, a company established around 1891 by somebody named J. D. Goody. That's J. D's picture above the Store entrance. Don't you love his long whiskers?

"Now, Goody's dividing line is not a road or railroad track like it is in most towns, but a river—called the Coochee by the Cherokees who used to camp around here. The side of the river we're standing on now is where the mill workers live. It can be divided again into four sections: Wart Town (named for the warts that sprung up—it was believed—from all the frogs in the area), the one closest to the river so it catches the flooding; Snake Town next to it; Pleasant Hill, a bluff rising directly behind the store, where some of the most miserable people in town hang out; and Chimney Road, where I live, a long street starting at the mill and leading past the golf course. As you can tell, it's only a hop and skip from my house to the Store and on to the Grey Mill.

"You can't see the opposite side of the river from here because it's across the bridge. But if you go along Broad Street, you'll bump right into a three-tiered wedding cake. That house belongs to Mr. Fortune, grandson-in-law of the original Mr. Goody and current general manager.

"Have you got it all?

"If you haven't, don't worry about it. This is a town you can't get lost in."

Four times a day—at eight and four, as well as a warning fifteen minutes before—a loud whistle blows, and now, hearing the quarter-till whistle, I break from a walk into a trot.

Panting hard, I reach the Grey Mill and run up the steps into the roving room, where great "cheeses" of thread hang on hooks ready to be taken across to the dye plant. The spinning room beyond—longer, I bet, than even the city block in Detroit where daddy lives—is filled with row after row of big frames.

Last year, when I first started working here, all these machines looked the same, but I sure know their differences now. Some have to do with warping—or the yarns going length-wise—which Mr. Baxter calls "the backbone of the fabric." Others, like the ones in my own section, spin filler yarn. Mr. Baxter always explains that this is the thread that runs crossways and makes the cloth softer because it has less twist to it.

At the place where the sections divide off, I run into Dot Ledbetter. Or I should say, Dot runs into me. She stares at the cage. "LaVonne! You did it! Now I feel ashamed."

"Why?"

"I told Troy you wouldn't have the nerve to make it up to Chattanooga by yourself."

"Once I set my mind about something," I say, holding up the cage in triumph, "I don't let go of it." Secretly, though, I know this isn't true. Just before the bus pulled away, I came *that* close to getting off, and probably would've, too, if the driver hadn't stopped me by yelling, "Sit down!" in such a rough voice that I felt obliged to obey.

Dot bends over. "Oooooo, its wings are so pretty. Wouldn't you just love to have a dress this color?"

"Watch out!" I say. "It bites."

Moving away, I set both the cage and the record down on the middle windowsill where the bird won't catch so much lint, then walk quickly over to my frames to check on whether the spindles are filled and the traveler rings threaded, at one point glancing up just in time to see Grady Fay Owens push the quill buggy into the next aisle.

Since Grady Fay's the doffer on my set of machines, in a sense we're partners. Or have been for the past three weeks, which is when he was hired. I don't know what to make of him. At first glance, he looks soft, as if his body has no muscle or grit to it. But, oddly enough, he's very fast. "Ten to one that boy's gonna make one of the best doffers we've ever had," Mr. Baxter says, as if planning to take odds on it. (He'll bet on *anything*: how long it takes a piece of lint to drift down to the floor, how many days before Shorty Toles wears out his overalls at the knees, the number of gold fillings in Reba Petit's mouth. . . .)

Of course, it could be that he simply feels sorry for Grady Fay because underneath his gruff tone, Mr. Baxter's a big softy. Rumor is, Grady Fay's mama up and left home when he was only eight, and from then on him and his daddy had to fend for themselves. All I know is what I hear from Dot because I've not had more than ten minutes' worth of conversation with him.

He's real tall and not bad-looking, in fact Dot and Tessie both think he's cute. "Clean-cut," they call him, whatever that means. But I like men with a little more swagger to them. Daddy had swagger. And Gene Hankins, the boy I dated in high school, walked around like a banty rooster. Every time he came near me, I felt like my legs couldn't find the ground. "I won't rest till you're mine, LaVonne," he'd whisper, sticking his tongue in my ear. I was right on the verge of it once or twice, too— especially when he was begging me so bad—only mama's voice kept calling me back: "LaVonne, don't do nothing you'll regret." And in church Preacher Crow's always going on about the sinful ways of sex. So I ended up stalling Gene off, although I often think about it, especially when I'm piecing up.

Me and Gene didn't really break up. He got kicked out of school. Because of mama. She made a big fuss about his nasty talk to the principal, and when the principal tried to to speak to him about it, Gene lost his temper and called him and mama every name in the book. He still phones me every now and then—getting one of his buddies to make the call in case you-know-who answers. He always tells me how much he misses me. I miss him, too. He used to say that one day he'd whisk me right out of here. "That'll fix your mama's wagon," he'd laugh. He hates mama. Says she vexed him out of sheer spite. Says she's a witch and would be better off dead. Gene's always mouthing off like that. I don't pay no attention.

It takes my fingers about fifteen minutes to warm up to the speed you need for piecing up—that's picking up the broken threads and twisting them together. After that, I can go pretty fast. Not like in the beginning, when thirteen or fourteen threads'd break at the same time and the bobbins'd get choked up and I'd start crying out of sheer frustration. Then Dot'd come over and put her arm around me. "Just keep your mind on the job, LaVonne," she'd say, "and you'll be alright." Without Dot Ledbetter, I'd never have made it. Mr. Baxter says Dot's a natural manager. He says if she was a man, she'd be running the whole shebang.

Moving along the frame, I hum the tune that I can't seem to get shed of. *"I feel s'lonely I could die."*

When it's time for the supper break, I make a dash for the canteen in order to get there before Mollie Sue Morton sells the two ham sandwiches that she brings over from the Café every night along with the tuna fish and pimento cheese. Ham's my thing. I have it five times a week and sometimes on Sundays. By the time Dot and Tessie Scoggins arrive, I've already finished eating. As soon as Dot sits, she downs a whole dopie. I've never seen anybody with such a thirst.

Fishing a brown paper bag from her pocketbook, Tessie spreads out a tinfoiled package of spareribs. "Y'all help yourselves. I brought 'em from home." Bet she did it to impress Dot. We're in a competition to see whose best friend Dot'll be. Tessie doesn't know it but I'm gonna win.

"Oooo! Those look delicious!" Reba Petit says as she walks up. "Can I try one?" Her short little fingers pluck out the largest piece and she begins gnawing on it. None of us ask her to sit down, but she does anyway.

The canteen's filling up fast. I wave to Shorty Toles and Boley Westbrooks over by the Coke machine. Boley's trying to make it take a Canadian dime. When it refuses, he kicks at it. I don't see Grady Fay anywhere. Wonder if he eats by himself. Marvin Cowan comes over with the news that Pete Hammond got his arm caught in the napping machine. "Half the skin was pulled off. Shoulda seen the blood. Took 'em two hours to get the machine cleaned up." Marvin loves gory stories. He keeps an "accident diary" of all the bad things that happen in the mill. Says he plans on sending it to Mr. Fortune once he gets enough pages.

Finally Dot pushes back her chair. "We better get a move on." Everybody at the table gets up except me. "What's the matter?" Dot asks, putting a hand on my shoulder, which makes Tessie frown.

"Oh . . . " I let out a slow sigh. "Nothing. Guess I'm just wore out from all that bus riding." Which is true, but not the whole truth. The whole truth is, that song started something.

"How about some B.C. powders?"

Usually I refuse because mama claims they eat up your stomach lining. But this time I hold out my hand. "I'll take a few."

Dot gives me five envelopes. "Boley has something stronger if you need it," she says, as if I didn't know. Mr. Baxter calls Boley a walking drugstore.

Reaching the window where the cage is stowed, I peer into it. The parakeet doesn't look very perky. Surely to God that saleswoman was pulling my leg about the parrot fever. If anything happens, it'll be Miz Cowan's fault. Miz Cowan and her son Marvin live across the street. It was her who kept insisting that I get mama a pet. She suggested a dog like that mutt she used to have, but I told her mama didn't want no dog to clean up after. I hit on the idea of a parakeet one night when we saw one on "Arthur Godfrey's Talent Scouts." Mama had a fit over the tricks it did, like taking food from this lady's mouth and saying, "Thank you."

Maybe it's not getting enough air. I crack the window a bit wider. Though it's almost dark, I can still see the river below. The dyes they put into it are a constant surprise: this evening it's like the insides of hundreds of soft-boiled eggs are threading their way to the bottom.

Once I get home, I set the cage on the kitchen table and go over to the stove where a sweet potato pie is laid out. It's so gummy that a whole batch sticks to the roof of my mouth and I have to suck it down.

Tiptoeing into my bedroom to fetch some red Christmas ribbon and an old school tablet, I write, "HAPPY BIRTHDAY, MAMA—LOTS OF LOVE, LAVONNE," and place it against the cage. I'm so tired that I crawl into bed without cleaning any of that big city-Greyhound grit off my face.

A banging noise wakes me up. It comes from the kitchen. Uh-oh, that's a bad sign. I'd stick my head under the pillow but it's too hot, so I pull the sheet up instead. Even when I hear the door open and my name being called, I pretend to be asleep. Mama's onto my tricks though. By the time I raise up enough to open one eye, she's standing beside the bed, holding the bird cage way out like it has a bad smell. Her mouth's all pursed up. "Don't know what gets into you sometimes." The cage still has the ribbon that I put on it last night. Wonder if she's bothered to read the note. "Where'd you get it anyway?"

"Chattanooga."

"Chattanooga! So that's where you went?!" She sniffs and clicks her tongue. "Bet you were with that Dot Ledbetter."

I shake my head. I hate being questioned but she won't leave me alone until I tell her. "By myself."

Her jaw drops. "By *yourself!*"

"I wanted to surprise you." Her face grows a little softer. Bending over, she makes clucking noises through the bars. "Just don't stick your finger in," I say. "Let the bird get used to you first."

"You mean, let *me* get used to *it!* Just one thing more to take care of." She walks to the door in her most uppity manner. "There's two biscuits warming in the oven."

One of mama's biggest pleasures is watching me eat, "putting meat on my bones," as she calls it. "I'm not hungry," I say, and lie there listening to her go on and on about my being too thin, which I'm not. I wait another minute or two. Then, throwing aside the covers, I deliberately shuffle into the kitchen and over to the fridge. "I'll get me a dopie." Nothing gets her goat more than too many dopies.

"Can't live on just that."

Opening a Coca-Cola, I sit at the table sipping, drink half, pour the rest down the sink. She's standing there frowning at me, then she frowns at the bird. I walk over to it. It bobs up and down a few times. Looking better, though. "I got it to keep you company."

She eyes me. "What do I need company for? You planning on going somewhere?"

I shrug. What's the point of starting something? "Where would I go?"

Actually, I could think of lots of places, but they call for money that I don't have. But someday I will. Someday I'll fly right out of here, just like daddy did.

While I'm dressing, mama calls from the kitchen. "I've run out of fatback. You'll have to go to the Store for me."

She doesn't say, "Do you mind" or "please" or nothing like that. But I do it anyway, especially when it dawns on me that I can stop by the post office on the way back. I get the form that the girl in Grant's gave me, then I slip into the living room and sneak a five dollar bill out of the envelope behind the clock. A secret loan. Till payday.

In the Store, I skate over the tiles like I've been doing ever since I was five years old, cross to the soda fountain to see who's there, head on to the meat market where I pay for the fatback, then go out through the hardware and start back.

The post office's in a white frame building that used to be a night watchman's house. I fill in my name and address on the official fan club form and blot it on the big blotter that somebody's written dirty words all across. But the next line stumps me. It wants to know the *name* of the fan club, and this takes some thought. I could call it "The Original Elvis Presley Fan Club," but it's not very original. Or "The Elvis Presley Fan Club of Goody, Georgia"—but that sounds too local. Next to the blotting table are several posters showing the pictures of wanted men.

The poster says they're "real criminals who are armed and dangerous." The word *real* catches my eye. "The Real Elvis Presley Fan Club." I repeat it a couple of times. Though it may not be real right now, it soon will be. I write it down, seal the envelope, and push it through the mail slot. Daddy was always peeking through that slot to see what was happening on the other side. "Once something's in," he used to say, "there's no pulling it out again." Reminds me of Preacher Crow's advice to "cast your bread upon the waters." Well, I've just done that.

Chapter Two

I HEAR BUB'S HORN OUTSIDE, WHICH MEANS IT'S time to go. I'm standing in front of the mirror trying to see if my dress is hanging right. It looks crooked on one side to me, but mama says I must be cross-eyed. She's the expert. Used to sew in the glove mill, till she come in one morning upset about daddy and sewed two of her fingers together. After that she lost the use of a nerve in that hand and had to quit. Then Jake Haygood, daddy's old boss, hired her to make pillows for the caskets. But today's Sunday. She makes a point of never sewing on the Lord's day.

As far back as I can remember, mama and me have spent every single Sunday in Snuffy, which is about six miles south and two miles west. First we attend church, then go on to Grandpa Jess's. He still lives in the old house where mama was born, if you call it living. I call it laziness, because everything in it looks like it's falling apart. Before she died, Grandma Eller would always cook Sunday dinner. Now Mama does it, and carts it over. We don't have a car so we hire Bub's taxi. When Grandpa Jess's sober enough, he drives us back.

I'm supposed to sing a solo number at the church today. Don't think I'm not nervous just because I've done it before. Every time it's like sticking my head through a clothes wringer. Don't know why I say yes. (Well, I do know, too. It seems to make mama proud.)

Bub sits in front of the wheel, chewing his tobacco. I crawl in the back seat, but not without dusting it off first. Even then, I don't lean back.

Mama settles herself and the two bundles of food in front. We drive along Broad Street past the Inn, the hospital, and the tiny Episcopal church Mr. Fortune attends. A lot of the mill bosses go there. I've heard they have no foot washings and hardly sing any songs at all. Can't imagine church without singing. To me, it's the joyful part of "joyful noise."

When we go by the cemetery on the highway, I remember to lick my finger and stamp my hand with it. That's my caution against death. My daddy helped bury people in there. In the family album is an old picture of him decked out in a white suit. He's lounging beside a big spray of glads. Grandpa Jess once said that the daughters of the deceased, and sometimes wives, too, would fall all over themselves trying to stand next to him. He said the only reason daddy worked as an undertaker was so he could dress up and strut around like a peacock. I used to cry when him and mama bad-mouthed my daddy like that.

On the other side of Richville, I catch a glimpse of the mountains. Not real mountains, more like hills. Snuffy's off to the right of the highway as it begins to wind its way up. People are always asking how Snuffy got its name. Grandpa Jess's answer is that it "just happened," the way a stray hound *happens* to be called Spot. But mama says it's on account of Earl's General Store selling more cans of snuff than anybody else in the county, and that it was the Beech-Nut man, bringing in his third load from the truck, who dubbed it Snuffy, and the name just stuck.

Across the road from Earl's is a sign that Preacher Crow painted himself in gold and black letters: CHURCH OF GOD OF THE PROPHECY. Instead of putting his name on the sign as pastor, Preacher Crow—whose hobby is stuffing dead animals—mounted a big black crow and stuck it on top. Some people objected, saying that a black crow was bad luck. Preacher Crow replied that crows had as much of God in them as anybody else, and mama backed him up. 'Course she'd back Preacher Crow in anything. He's her fortune teller, advisor, and healer, all in one.

The church is a wooden building with a tiny steeple and a bell that can be heard clear to Richville when the wind's right. Over the door, four little pink angels float. People used to say that the second one on the left looked like me. But the church's best feature is three arched windows covered with contact paper in a stained glass design. When the sun shines through, it takes your breath away.

Bub pulls off the road. Soon as mama pays him, we get out and he scratches off again, setting up a huge cloud of dust. Mama pulls a kleenex out of her pocketbook and holds it to her nose. "Relying on Bub is a burden the Lord give us to bear," she says, not for the first time.

Inside, the pews are already half-filled. She goes toward the front to sit by Ettie Mae Tucker, but I stay at the back. This is where the members of the Sunshine Choir assemble. There're twelve of us, ten women and two men, Bobby Echols and Calvin Toombs. I hate sitting by Bobby because of all the flies that swarm around his hair tonic. Instead, I ease myself next to Jeanette Teague so we can walk in together. Jeanette is sporting a new hairstyle—turned under and fastened on the side by two clips.

"I like your page-boy," I whisper.

When Pearlie B. Bramlett starts playing the first notes of "Onward Christian Soldiers," it's our cue to begin. Never once have I failed to get goosepimples as we march down the aisle, the eyes of the whole congregation fixed on us. As we enter the choir, Calvin Toombs slips in ahead of Bobby, on the other side of me. Calvin's been trying to get up a quartet to sing at local churches. He's asked me to become a member. At first I said no, but mama thought it was a good opportunity, so I changed my mind.

We bow our heads while Preacher Crow prays. His prayers are always drawn out. The hardest thing about being a choir member is keeping your head bowed and your eyes shut for all that time.

My solo number's coming up. I pray not to forget the words.

Pearlie B. plays the introduction, her fat fingers racing over the keyboard. I make myself glance into the audience so I won't be so nervous. Mama isn't even looking up, she's studying the bulletin. I see Calvin Toombs's wife on the front row as usual. Feel like I might be sick. But then I swallow and plunge ahead.

I've not had much rehearsal so my first notes are a bit shaky. I'll never be able to get through this, I think. But at the beginning of the second verse, I feel myself revving up. Pretty soon I don't even care who's looking and who's not. I just hold my head high and let the words fly right out.

> *I don't know how wide will be that city so fair,*
> *I don't even know how many seats will be there,*
> *I don't know how high will be that mansion of mine,*
> *I only know for sure that Heaven's really going to shine. . . .*

I can tell by the way people are smiling and swaying that the song's going pretty well. Mama sits there glancing around to see how everybody's taking it. When I mess up, she bows her head. She's easily mortified.

> *It's gonna shine, it's gonna shine,*
> *Oh yes, I know it's gonna shine. . . .*

Soon as I sit back down, Calvin leans over. "That's the sexiest song I've heard in a long time."

Sexiest? What's he talking about?

Then Preacher Crow steps up to the pulpit. I try to pay attention, but I'm still feeling pretty high. Now that my nerves are gone, I'd like to do the whole thing again.

Mama's eyeing me. I concentrate harder on Preacher Crow. He's so deliberate about everything: opening the Bible, removing the marker, standing there a minute before saying his first words, as if building suspense. And it does make me sit up. Or is it because Calvin shifts his hips closer?

> Woe unto them that call evil good, and good evil;
> that put bitter for sweet, and sweet for bitter; that put
> darkness for light, and light for darkness. . .

The next song, after the scripture reading, is sung by everybody, which means it's nowhere near as good as the ones the choir sings alone. If only Ettie Mae Tucker didn't pitch the alto part so loud. But she's always showing off in one way or another.

"Beloved friends," Preacher Crow says as he steps back up to the pulpit and leans forward, confidential-like. "I'm going to tell you a true story. This story is called 'The Dark That Was Darker Than Dark.'" I can see mama focused on him like her eyeballs are ready to bust.

"Friends, the dark began with darkness, and I was walking through it, stumbling and groping like a blind man, unable to see my fingers in front of my face."

Out of the corner of my eye, I catch a tiny movement, then feel Calvin's hand sliding next to my thigh. I try to squeeze away, but I'm already as far as I can go without landing in Jeanette's lap. Maybe it's just an accident. Or maybe it's not. I'm reminded of Gene's fumblings that time in the picture show. I put a hand up to my cheek. It feels hot. Is it red, too?

Meanwhile Preacher Crow's voice gets louder and more sing-song. "And I kept on walking, walking, walking, walking, not having any *idea* where I was going, or why. All I knew was that I was stepping over dirt clods and roots and sharp rocks. Then, out of that dark, a hand grabbed hold of me. I tried to pull away, but that hand helt on. I called out, 'WHO ARE YOU? NOW YOU ANSWER ME.' But there was no sound." Stretching out a hand, he grabs a fistful of air. "'Do these cold, clammy fingers belong to a dead man?' I asked myself. And I commenced to feeling around until I come upon a deep hole in the palm, and felt around some more and, sure enough, there was another hole. 'WHO ARE YOU?' I cried out again. And this time the voice answered. It said, 'LEROY CROW, YOU KNOW WHO I AM.'

"I didn't say another word, but friends, I dropped to my knees, still unable in that darkest of darks to make out a single thing." He pauses to take off his glasses. "Then I groped around some more until I come upon a foot standing in that dirt and dust. Well sir, I lifted up that foot, and on the skin was another . . . deep . . . deep . . . hole. I knew then that it could only belong to one man . . . "

"Jesus! It's Jesus!" Ettie Mae cries out, as if she's just solved a riddle that's been stumping everybody.

"Yes, friends, it was Jesus! And I cried out in that darkest of darks. I cried, 'O LORD!' And Jesus knelt right there and pulled me down beside him and I could feel the touch of his hand on my shoulder."

Something's trying to worm its way underneath my thigh. I have a suspicion what those fingers are groping toward. I move forward to get away from them, but it only makes things worse. Trouble is, I halfway like it. Or would if I could shut my eyes and imagine Gene sitting next to me. I'm glad Calvin can't hear my heartbeat because then he would only be encouraged.

". . . and friends, at that moment . . . at that very *second* . . . the darkest of darks changed to the lightest of lights. O, it was a blinding light! And Jesus said, 'How is it? How is it when i call that you don't answer?' and he started walking away, leaving me there in that lightest of lights, crying and praying."

Stepping down from the pulpit into the church aisle—carefully, though, because his glasses are still off—Preacher Crow raises his face to heaven. "'How is it, Lord,' I cried, 'how is it?'" He really screams this out.

I can only see the back of Preacher Crow's head. Am I imagining things, or is it glowing again? I remember that night he conducted a revival service over at Sandy Creek, and me and mama went. I hadn't expected to get so carried away. It was that tic in his eye and that gleam over his head that did it. Suddenly I felt hot all over. When he shouted, "Let the Holy Ghost rise, let the Holy Ghost rise in you!" I knew what the heat was all about, and without saying a word to mama, I stumbled down the aisle to receive His blessing. Mama was so happy that night. "If I never do nothing else," she said, "at least I've led you to Christ." She likes to take the credit for everything.

"How is it?" Preacher Crow yells again. Then he points to the congregation. "How is it, friends, how is it?"

Calvin's fingers inch closer till I hold my breath. What can I do? When Gene tried to touch me in the same place, I let him. But that was different. Thank God, my dress is in between. Can Jeanette guess what my squirming and twisting is all about? Can anybody in the congregation? But every eye seems fixed on Preacher Crow. "How is it?" he repeats over and over, his arms flapping up and down. "How is it?"

I see Ettie Mae Tucker grab hold of mama's hand and ask, in imitation of Preacher Crow, "How is it? How is it?" Pretty soon Lemannuel Hayes takes up her chant, and Calvin, finally moving his fingers away, begins repeating it to the choir members. He gets right up in my face and asks "How is it?" with a kind of smirk. I shoot him the dirtiest look possible.

"Now, friends," says Preacher Crow, "I'm going to ask the Sunshine Choir to give us two more verses of 'Heaven's Gonna Shine.' Everybody join in the chorus. Let's make the words shine out for Jesus."

I am so relieved to stand up! Preacher Crow gestures for me to come forward and lead the song. Since nobody knows any more verses, we just sing the same one over and over.

As usual, people take their time about filing out. They're laughing, talking. Several come up to compliment me on my voice.

I make certain to stay as far away from Calvin as I can, but I feel his eyes seeking me out. Finally I pull mama away—she's talking with Preacher Crow and Pearlie B.—and we set off down the dirt road toward Grandpa Jess's, passing two or three little shotgun houses, all with a parcel of barefoot kids screaming and yelling loud enough to wake up the dead.

We find Grandpa Jess spraddled out on the porch steps, his head resting against a post, the brim of an old felt hat pulled down as far as possible over his eyes. His mouth gapes open.

"Some day a bug's gonna fly right in there," mama says.

"Should I wake him up?"

"Leave him alone. Keeps him outta trouble. Come on. You help me with dinner."

Sighing as loud as possible, I pull back what's left of the screen door. I know what helping means. It means washing all the dirty dishes.

When I walk in the kitchen, sure enough there they are, stacked beside the sink. He hasn't even bothered to scrape them out. Makes me sick. I think of daddy. He didn't come over to Grandpa Jess's house very often, but when he did, he fled right out the back door. That's what I do now. "I'll see what's in the garden," I call back to mama.

Taking off my pumps, I race barefoot through the tall rows of stalks and vines. Above my head, a flock of tiny martins busts out of a hole in one of the gourds Grandpa Jess has hollowed out. I envy them. They can go anywhere they want. I run faster, out of the garden, onto the path that leads to Grandpa Jess's old still. Out of breath, my left side stitching a pain the way it does when you run hard, I stop at a hickory tree that I used to bend over and ride. Now it's too big and so am I.

There's not much left of the still except a couple of half-gallon jugs buried in weeds, and two rusty pipes. When it was operating at full tilt, he had customers all over the county. Usually they'd warn him when the sheriff was on the way, to give him enough time take it apart and stow everything under an old moth-eaten blanket in the cellar. One day, though, he was caught with the goods: twenty-two bottles of moonshine "beautiful as gold dust," as he called it. The sheriff hauled him into jail and fined him fifty dollars, which mama had to pay. When he went before the judge, Grandpa Jess defended himself by saying that he performed a public service, just like a druggist or an undertaker. "Maybe more," he said. The "more" was probably a slap at daddy.

By the time I return to the house—carrying corn, some over-ripe tomatoes, and a handful of string beans, all gathered up in an old croker sack I found—mama's at the stove and Grandpa Jess is standing in the doorway.

"Howdy, LaVonne." Unbuckling his belt, he pulls it a notch tighter and fastens it again. "I was just asking your mama where you's at."

"Your garden's skimpy," I say, setting the vegetables on the table. For a second, I think he might paddle my bottom the way he used to before mama made him stop. Sometimes it was hard to tell paddling from patting.

"Never claimed to be no farmer." He grunts and saunters over to the stove where mama's stirring the fried squash. "Tell you one thing, Gussie. If we don't eat pretty soon, my stomach's gonna cave in."

I shuck the corn and slice the tomatoes while mama finishes warming up the pork chops and field peas that she's brought over from home. She's made cornbread, too. Grandpa Jess says a meal ain't a meal without cornbread. He sits at the table with his mouth still open, which makes him look like a half-wit.

Before we dive in, mama insists on clasping hands and saying the blessing in spite of Grandpa Jess's protests. "A-men, eat up now," she says at the end, just like Grandma Eller used to.

We eat in silence. Well, not silence exactly. When Grandpa Jess isn't tearing the pork chop apart, he's sucking at the bone; when he isn't pushing peas onto the side of his fork with a slab of cornbread, he's slurping buttermilk. At the end, he belches, gets up from the table, and sprawls back out on the porch. His snores travel all the way inside where I'm washing the dishes. Mama and me pass the time by singing hymns. She loves the sad ones like "Does Jesus Care" and "The Long Way Home." My favorite is "Dwelling in Beulahland" 'cause it's real fast.

Mama's still juning around the kitchen when I finish, so I go into the living room and plop down in the platform rocker, the one good chair in the whole house. On top of the old Philco radio is a picture of mama and daddy taken on their wedding day. The two of them look so young, even mama, who was older than most when she married, at least according to Grandpa Jess since mama don't tell her age. He's also dropped hints about it being a shotgun wedding, but I don't believe that. They met at Hoke Treadaway's barbeque place north of Goody, where mama worked as a waitress. "It was the short skirt that did it," she said once. "Your daddy claimed I had the prettiest legs." Funny. I always thought her legs were real bony-looking. When she's in a good mood, she excuses daddy's shenanigans by saying the devil put too much temptation in his path. When she's in a rotten mood, she calls *him* the devil.

Uh-oh. This is a bad thought. When you start thinking bad thoughts, Preacher Crow says, switch over to Jesus. I try Jesus, but don't get very far with Him, so then I switch over to Elvis.

Chapter Three

BY THE TIME WE GET HOME, I'VE PLANNED OUT a whole campaign for the fan club, including handing out membership blanks in the canteen. Later I might do something even fancier like holding an Elvis Presley Night over at Tanner's Skating Rink. Thinking about this makes me so excited that I have trouble sleeping.

I figure Dot and Tessie and Reba will snap at the idea when I tell them about it the next day. But it doesn't exactly go that way.

"Who's Elvis Presley?" Tessie asks, her eyes blinking fast.

"I've heard of him," Dot says. "He sings them raunchy songs."

"Is he a hillbilly?" Reba always has to put people down.

I tell them everything I know, which isn't much so I have to make up a little. I tell them he ran away from his rich family who hadn't known where he was until he got famous. I tell them girls follow him everywhere so sometimes he has to wear disguises. I tell them he loves french fries and pinto beans with homemade ketchup and hates green peas. (I hate green peas, too.) I describe, as best I can, the way he looks.

"He's hillbilly, alright," Reba says. "Anybody with a ducktail's hillbilly."

I especially try to draw Dot in. She promises to drop by the house and listen to my new record but a whole week goes by and she doesn't show up. Then on Thursday, there's a knock at the door. Mama's in the kitchen fooling with the bird. I'm in my bedroom reading *Photoplay*. Thinking it's Miz Cowan from across the street who's always coming over to borrow sugar, I make no move to answer.

"You gonna sit there all day and let them bang?" mama yells.

When I peek through the curtains and see who it is, I run to the door and fling it open.

"Troy dropped me off," Dot explains, though she doesn't have to, seeing how smeared her lipstick is. I suggest that she wipe around her mouth a little before stepping inside. She also runs a hand over her skirt to smooth the wrinkles out.

Praying that mama won't be rude, I lead her through the kitchen as fast as possible.

Dot hesitates a second, then throws up a hand. "Hidee, Miz Grubbs." Mama grunts. "How's the parakeet doing?" I can tell that Dot's making a big effort to be friendly. The way she peers into the cage, you'd think a nugget of gold was lying there. "You named it yet?"

"Nope. Just keep calling it 'Pretty Boy.' Too lazy to come up with anything original."

"Well, it fits." Bending closer, Dot makes funny little noises with her tongue. "Look at them spools of yellow. Like tiny sunsets."

Mama folds her arms and looks proud. "He *is* cute, isn't he?"

"And I just love that tiny dimple in the middle of his breast feathers. See? Right there."

"I know."

I'm beginning to wonder if they intend carrying on like this all afternoon. "Come on, Dot." I pull her toward my room. "Mama, we're going to listen to a record."

Mama frowns. "Better not shut your bedroom door. You'll suffocate."

I do it anyway.

"Your mother said not to," Dot whispers. I can't figure out how mama has her so cowed. Normally Dot stands up to people, even Mr. Baxter.

"Sit here," I say, indicating the chair by the card table.

Dot sits primly, hands folded in her lap like a proper visitor. "You ought to move over to the Inn with me."

"I'm planning to when I get my big raise." Crossing to the phonograph, I put my hand on it. My prized possession. It's slightly warm from having been played earlier. "Heartbreak Hotel" is still on the turntable. "Now, Dot, close your eyes. Let your mind float. Let it float away, hear? Ready?" Dot nods. I lift the needle.

> *Well, since my baby left me,*
> *I've found a new place t'dwell*
> *It's down at the end of Lonely Street,*
> *It's Heartbreak Hotel. . . ."*

"He has a real deep voice," Dot says over the music. "I like deep voices. Troy's voice sounds like a foghorn sometimes."

> *. . . I'm s'lonely, babieee,*
> *I'm s'lonely. . . ."*

If Dot starts in on Troy again, I'll scream. "Hush, now," I whisper. "Don't talk. Just listen." I have my own eyes closed. *I'm sitting in the first row of the Tivoli. Elvis is on stage singing. Suddenly, he spots me and smiles. "I could swear he's looking right at me," I say to the person next to me. "Why would he be doing that?" the person says. It's mama's voice I'm hearing. All through the song, Elvis keeps staring and staring. Some people turn around, wondering who I am. After the concert, fans flock over. I start to walk away, but he calls to me. "Hey! Wait a minute!" he says. "I haveta talk to you." So I wait until he's signed all the autographs, then he grabs my arm and pulls me out to his pink Cadillac.*

That's as far as I get before the song's over.

I pick up the needle and wait for Dot's reactions. Her head's propped on her hand. "Well?" I say. "Dot?"

Her head jerks up. "What?" She stares at me for a second as if she's not sure who I am. Then she rubs her eyes. "Sorry."

"I'll play it again," I say, slightly disgruntled. Then I see that she's still droopy-eyed. "First, I'm going to get you a Coke."

"That'd be good. Reckon my veins crave sugar."

I go into the kitchen, take two Cokes out of the refrigerator, and shake them up. Sometimes they spew on the floor, which makes mama mad. She follows me back toward the bedroom. "I hope you're not playing that depressing song again."

"Well, nobody told you to listen." She starts to say something else but I shut the door before she can get the words out.

"Now, that's real ugly," Dot says. She downs half the Coke before taking another breath.

I walk over to my vanity table and pull an old snapshot out of my drawer. "Look at this picture of my daddy, Dot. If him and Elvis aren't the spittin' image of each other, I'm seeing things."

Dot sizes it up, passes it back. "Yeah, they are. Sort of."

I almost show her Gene's picture, too, but I'd have to dig too deep for it. I hide it real good so mama won't find it. This time I don't suggest that she shut her eyes. While listening, she finishes the Coke and cleans under her fingernails. When it comes to the end, I switch it off. "It may be a little sad, but I think it's sad in a nice way, don't you?"

"I guess so."

I lean toward her slightly. "You know, Dot, we could start our own Elvis Presley fan club. Each member would pay five dollars." Dot whistles. "I know it sounds like a lot, but it'd make you feel like you belonged to a great big family."

Dot snickers. "I already belong to a big family," she says. "I don't want no more."

"Or had a lot of friends."

"Have them, too."

Now I'm stumped. "It'd be real exclusive. We wouldn't let just anybody join."

"Not Reba Petit?"

"Lord, no!" Then I think of another selling point. "And you could be in charge of the social committee. We'd throw parties, put up posters. The posters come free. One day we might get to meet Elvis in the flesh, who knows?"

Dot groans. "Oh, sure, sure. That's all I need. Then Troy'd get jealous and stop speaking to me. Except I wouldn't know what was wrong till it was too late. By that time, he'd be gallivanting around with another mill girl."

"Oh come on!" We both know that Dot can twist Troy Wiggins around her little finger. "Be serious. At least give it some thought."

"Thinking's cheap." She shakes her head. "*Five* dollars! When I'm already trying to scratch up enough money for Troy's birthday present?"

"I'll give you a discount price of two-fifty."

"LaVonne, I can't spare no more than a dollar, and that's the truth."

"Okay. A dollar."

"You're sure?"

"'Course I'm sure." A club without Dot's no club at all as far as I'm concerned. Besides, if she joins, maybe Tessie will, too.

Just then the quarter-till whistle blows. We both jump up.

"What's your rush?" mama asks as we run through the kitchen. "You've got fifteen minutes."

"Oh, we like to have a few seconds to talk to the boys." Dot winks at me. "Right, LaVonne?"

"What boys?" As we head for the door, mama's hot on our tracks. "I said, what boys?"

I'm already outside, but Dot pauses a second in the doorway. "Oh. Like Grady Fay Owens. He's the new doffer from Sawmill Mountain. Real cute, too."

Holding the screen open, mama shouts after us. "Huh! If anything cute ever come off Sawmill Mountain, it'd be a *miracle.*"

By Tuesday, Tessie signs on, but only after I offer her half-price. Then Loretta Quinn, who has my same job on third shift, joins under the same conditions. If this keeps up, I'll have to work overtime to pay off the membership.

Then my Elvis poster arrives. When I find it on the living room table after work, I rush into my bedroom, tear off the wrapping, and unroll it bit by bit. First comes the pair of blue-green eyes that bore right into mine, then the straight nose, slightly flared at the sides, and full round lips, almost like a girl's, with one corner curled up into a smirk. The gash in his unbuttoned black shirt goes right down to a little tuft of brown hair that peeks out just above his belly-button. Thank God he's not hairy. Not like Marvin Cowan, who has it sticking out his nostrils.

When I open it all the way, I notice how tense he is. Hunched over. Holding onto a shotgun like he's ready to mow somebody down. But I'm sure it's just a pose. In real life he wouldn't hurt a flea.

Next afternoon, I take the poster to the spinning room and Dot helps me tape it to the wall near Number 10 frame. I draw back to see if it's hanging straight. "Hope Mr. Baxter don't say nothing."

"If he does, just call me over," Dot says. "I can handle him. He's half bluff anyhow."

Later that evening, Mr. Baxter walks by and spots it. "Who the hell put this hoodlum up?" he yells out.

I leave the machine and come over. "I did, Mr. Baxter, and he ain't no hoodlum. His name's Elvis Presley, and some people say he's gonna be a big star. As long as that picture's not doing any harm, I'd appreciate your permission to leave it." I can feel my chin beginning to tremble.

Mr. Baxter puts his hands on his hips and stares at me. I look at the way his belly hangs over his belt. Bet he never gets any exercise. "Now, take it easy, LaVonne," he says. "Just take it easy. Didn't nobody say you couldn't keep it there. If that's what it takes to make you happy, it's alright with me. Why, you can have ten pictures on the wall. Fifteen . . . twenty." He goes off muttering something about how I can have the whole goddamn place covered with hoodlums if that's how I get my kicks.

It's real interesting to see how people in the spinning room respond to that poster. Especially the men. During the five-minute break, some of them saunter over. "Stick 'em up," Shorty Toles says to it, holding out a finger as if him and Elvis are having a shootout. Boley Westbrooks suggests we use it as a dartboard. They're trying to get me riled up, but I don't take the bait. Grady Fay comes around, too, but he doesn't say what his thoughts are.

By August, things are really moving along. I've got three more members in the fan club, and two of them even pay full price. Mr. Baxter gets in on the act, too. He starts taking bets on the success of what he calls "this flash in the pan." "I'll give him six months," he says. "Who'll take a year?"

By this time, everybody knows who Elvis is. A lot of magazines have cover stories about him. The most interesting one is in *T.V. Digest*. It talks about how Colonel Parker, Elvis's manager, tries to con people.

I bet Mr. Baxter has him beat, though. I've seen Mr. Baxter annoy Mollie Sue Morton to death over at the Café by pulling dead flies out of a matchbox and putting them on his plate so he doesn't have to pay for his breakfast. (You have to understand that Mollie Sue's so finicky she even rinses off the toothpicks before putting them out for customers.) And like the Colonel, Mr. Baxter's a real showman. Whenever Mr. Fortune wants to give guests a grand tour of the mill, he asks Mr. Baxter to do it. Mr. Baxter loves pointing out the new design of the machinery, the changes in the thread as it passes through different stages, all the while going on and on about what he calls "the miracles of modern textile manufacturing." After they leave, he struts around, chomping on his cigar, saying, "Well, we did it again! We sure did it! We really showed 'em our stuff." Bet a nickel the Colonel says the same thing after one of Elvis's performances.

One day Reba Petit comes in the canteen during lunch break with a big smirk on her face. She's carrying a copy of *Life* magazine, which she slaps down on the table where I'm sitting. "Here," she says. "Read this."

In spite of a sneaking suspicion that it'll be something awful, I open it up and turn the pages till I come to a spread on the Reverend Robert Gray, pastor of the Trinity Baptist Church in Jacksonville, Florida, who's held a special service to pray for Elvis's salvation.

Reba leans over and points her finger. "Do you see here where it says that he's reached a new low in spiritual degeneracy?"

"Spiritual *what?*" asks Marvin, grinning.

"Degeneracy. You know. Trashy, low-down, good-for-nothing."

Marvin shoots a glance over at me. "Maybe that's why LaVonne likes him. I know some other people like that she's liked."

Who's he talking about? And what does he know anyway?

But Reba isn't looking to be distracted. "Just shows you the difference between him and Pat Boone. You wouldn't catch nobody holding a prayer service for Pat." She sticks her face close in to mine. "Have you ever asked *your* preacher how he feels about Elvis Presley?"

I tell her it's none of Preacher Crow's business. Or hers. And I go on to say that she'd be a lot better off if she didn't go around bad-mouthing people. She gets up in a huff, but let her. If I'd thought fast enough I would've told her that I don't see how anybody who's so loving to their mama could be low-down and trashy. It doesn't even make good sense.

That's the same day Mr. Fortune comes around. When I spy him heading my way with Mr. Baxter in tow, I'm sure he's about to order me to take down the poster. But the two of them just pass me by. Naturally I'm curious about what they're up to. So I sneak around, watching over the top of the machines.

I can never put my finger on what makes Mr. Fortune different from the rest of us. It's not just the suits he wears, which are smooth-looking without being shiny, or that they fit his body perfectly, or that his hair is silver-tipped and divided on one side by a single straight part, or that he smells of cloves and often has a tan, even in the dead of winter. Even without these things, I'd still know—from the way he comes into a room if nothing else—that here is *somebody*. Maybe it's the way he carries his shoulders—not stiff, but upright and easy—or the way he makes a speech, as though he's been doing it all his life.

'Course, partly it's the way other people treat him. Even Mr. Baxter, who's not generally given to kow-towing, greets him like visiting royalty whenever he drops by. "Ah, Mr. Fortune!" he'll say (Dot can imitate him perfectly). "What a nice surprise. Come in, come in." And if he has the occasion to introduce Mr. Fortune to someone, he always starts by mentioning how *honored* he is, or how happy he is to have the *honor*, until sometimes I wonder whether Mr. Fortune's even listening. Now, here he is, at the end of Number 10 frame with Mr. Baxter right behind him. The two of them stand in front of Grady Fay Owens, and take no notice of anybody else. Then they follow Grady Fay around the frame as he doffs, Mr. Baxter occasionally taking a small notebook out of his back pocket and scribbling something, just what I can't imagine, while Mr. Fortune whispers in his ear. They even kneel down—I can hardly believe this—and examine the quill buggy that Grady Fay uses, asking him questions about it, jiggling it back and forth to see if the wheels are turning okay. I hear Mr. Fortune say that he'd like to see larger ones put on, and Mr. Baxter makes a note of it. And all the time Grady Fay pays them no mind at all, but goes right on about his business.

Soon as they leave, I hurry over. "What was that all about?"

Grady Fay shrugs.

"Aren't you interested in finding out?"

He gives me a slight smile. For the first time, I notice how blue his eyes are. "I reckon I will in due time," he says. The way those eyes look into mine, for a second I'm afraid I might drown in them.

Chapter Four

THE NEXT THING I RECEIVE IN THE MAIL IS a box of membership buttons with the name of the club and Elvis's picture on them. Right away, I stick one on my blouse, over my heart of course, and rush to the store to show it off. In one quick sweep of the place, two girls from the glove mill stop to ask where I got it. I hand them membership blanks. I tell them that we're having our first meeting real soon, and take down their addresses so I can let them know when. I also remind them about Elvis's appearance on the "Ed Sullivan Show" on Sunday night, and they say they wouldn't miss it for anything. Dot's already invited me to see it over at the Inn. There's usually a big crowd there. Sometimes Mrs. Harris, the manager, makes popcorn and passes it around. Good time to enlist people, Dot says.

But wouldn't you know that, on Friday, mama comes down with the flu and I have to spend the whole weekend looking after her? I'm real let down. But the only thing to do is give Dot the buttons and let her take my place. Sometimes I wonder if mama doesn't invent sickness just to keep me home.

Anyway, she can't stop me from watching the show. On Sunday, I start supper early so I can get it over with. About six-thirty I bring in mama's plate—country ham, red-eye gravy, biscuits. Using last week's edition of the *Goody News* as a tray, I prop her up at the end of the sofa-bed with two pillows behind her head and set the meal on her lap. Mama looks it over like she's the county inspector. She wipes the fork off good with the paper napkin. "You forgot the butter," she says.

"I gave you gravy." I point to it in case she's missed the pool of grease.

"I still want butter."

"I'll get it."

"And some preserves."

"Alright."

"Reckon you didn't want to go to the trouble of making grits."

"I made biscuits . . ." I point to them, too.

"Ham just isn't the same without grits."

I bring them in, and even make the effort of cutting her ham in little triangles like she likes it. Then I return to the kitchen and fix my own meal: three slabs of ham between biscuits. Soon as I sit down, the parakeet starts screeching, and I throw a towel over the top to keep it quiet. I gobble down the food, barely tasting it. After the dishes are scraped clean, I put them in the sink to soak and then I stand there thinking about Elvis. He must be so nervous right now, how can he stand it? Maybe he does the same warm-up exercises that Calvin gives to choir members to calm us down.

When I go into the living room, mama's lying there, flat out. She doesn't look too good either. "Is it time?" she sighs.

"Yeah, it's time." Licking my lips, I turn on the TV just as trumpets are blasting. An announcer's voice booms. "The 'Big N' and your Lincoln-Mercury dealers all over the country—unmistakably the finest— are proud to present. . ." he pauses and flings out his hand, ". . . the 'Ed Sullivan Show.'" Another blast.

But Ed Sullivan doesn't appear. Instead it's some actor who looks like an overgrown baby. His opening remarks slide right by me. It takes the announcement of the first act—the Brothers Amin or something like that—before I catch on to what they mean to do. Save Elvis till last. Keep everybody on edge.

Then comes a blonde singer who's got a tarty look about her. While she's on, I go over to ask mama if she's alright. She grunts out an answer, as if it's a big effort. Then I return to the television and push the stool closer. Once or twice I glance around to see if everything's okay.

I think Elvis must surely be next, but he's not, it's the Vagabonds. They get my vote for the corniest act in show business. All four of 'em. Especially the tallest. "Look at him," I say to nobody in particular, which is a measure of my disgust, "tying a coat around his waist like a skirt. If I was him, I'd be embarrassed to make such a jackass out of myself." But when he starts imitating Arthur Godfrey, I turn to mama. Arthur's her favorite. She keeps praying that he and Jeanette Davis will get married. "Mama," I call out. Then louder: "Ma-ma. There's a man doing Arthur Godfrey and he's pretty good, too."

No answer.

"Mama?"

I turn around. Her eyes are still shut tight. Should I go over and shake her awake? But what good would that do? Dot would say, let sleeping dogs lie. On the screen, the baby-faced man's standing there again, grinning. "I'm sure you've been wondering," he says, "what these objects are behind me." Well, *I* haven't been. In fact, I hadn't even noticed. Moving sideways, he points to several circles hanging up on a black curtain. "These are gold records," he says.

Well, finally!

". . . This is the first time in record-making history that a singer has hit the mark in such a short time. . . ." Again, I glance over my shoulder. The lump on the bed is totally still. ". . . And now, ladies and gentlemen, away to Hollywood to meet Elvis Presley. . . ." With a wave of his hand, the screen suddenly goes blank.

"Oh, Jesus, Jesus, Jesus, Jesus," I mutter under my breath.

When Elvis steps out of the shadows and into the spotlight, the place goes wild. He waits until the screaming has stopped before he says anything. I'd swap five . . . no, ten years of my life to be in that audience.

He gives a low growl that makes the crowd scream again. Then, ducking his head in a modest way, he begins a short speech that's just awkward enough to sound completely natural. "Wow . . . uh . . . this is prob'ly the greatest honor I've ever had in my life. There's not much I can say except it really makes ya feel good. We want to thank you from the bottom of our hearts. . . ." Jerking sideways, he strikes a chord. Oooooo!

Y'know I can be found,
Sittin' home all alone,
If you can't come around. . . ."

When the applause dies down, I hear mama's voice, fainter than usual. "Would you bring me a Dr. Pepper?"

Shoot! Just when Elvis's about to make another speech. "Just a minute." Reaching over, I turn up the sound.

". . . Thank ya very much" (grinning at the audience) ". . . Thank ya, ladies." He looks so *sincere* when he talks. Just how daddy used to sound with mourners. "Now, we'd like to introduce you to a brand-new song. It's the title of our brand-new Twentieth-Century Fox movie. . . . I would like to say right now that the people over at Twentieth-Century Fox have really been wonderful. . . . All the great stars in the cast, the producer, director. This is our first picture and they really helped us along." Pausing, he curls his lips, making his nostrils flare out. "With the help of the very wonderful Jordanaires, a song called 'Love Me Tender'. . . ."

This is where everybody goes wild. Crossing my legs to keep some self-control, I shift around on the stool. But I have to put a hand on my mouth to keep from moaning out loud. If I was sitting beside Gene right now, I'd be a pushover.

Then I do hear a moan, a real one. It comes from across the room. Oh, my God! I've forgotten about mama's dopie.

Rushing into the kitchen, I take out a cold Dr. Pepper, open it, and bring it to the edge of her bed. While waiting for her to take it, I glance over at the screen. Oh, no! Elvis's wave has flopped right down. Somebody ought to run out on stage and fix it for him.

"Mama, here's your dopie."

Screwing up her face, mama braces her elbows on the bed and tries to sit up.

"Here, let me help you." I put a hand behind her neck and another on her left arm. I can feel how spongy her skin is; my fingers seem to sink right into the soft flesh.

"Ooooh. Can't do it," mama gasps.

"What is it?"

"Hurtin' here." She puts her hand over her breastbone.

"Bad?" Mama nods. "I'll getcha a couple of aspirins." But as I turn to go, she grasps my hand and holds on. She doesn't say anything but her eyes look scared.

Setting the Dr. Pepper on the floor, I sit on the side of the bed, trying to figure out what to do. Elvis is just winding up the song. Giving one last strum, he bows so low that his top hair comes streaming down. I glance at mama. Her eyes are closed.

Now some foreign-looking woman is being introduced. Her mouth sounds full of lard. I tell myself that this is a good time to fetch a cold rag. Bringing it back, I place it over mama's forehead. "Bet that feels better," I say. Wipe her face, too. She tries to tell me something, but no words come out. Wonder if I should call Dr. Henderson.

Meanwhile the woman's taking her bow. Surely Elvis'll be next.

But it's another commercial. A Mercury car driving through different parts of the country: North, South, East, West. Doesn't really look like the South, though. No sagging porches, for one thing. No shacks without screens. No flies. Daddy used to say that the best way to spot white trash was to see how many flies they could tolerate.

Before it's over, I go outside to stand on the porch and get some fresh air. But whatever I'm breathing feels heavy as syrup. From the sound blaring out, I can tell that another commercial's coming on. In the sky's a full moon. I watch it a long time, then hold up my arms as if I'm reaching for something. Then I turn back inside.

At the bed, there's a slight movement. One deformed hand clutches at the sheet. Leaning over, I pull it up around her neck.

I can tell by the applause that Elvis's on again. This time his head is cocked to one side like he's rarin' to go. He does go, too, twitching back and forth, all over the place, up and down, to "Hound Dog."

I've never seen anybody twist around as fast as that.

Then I hear mama making some kind of wheezing sound. Wish she'd be quiet. "Shhh," I say. "I'm trying to hear this!" Mama'd spoil all my fun if she could. But after a few minutes, I turn around. "Mama?" But she doesn't answer. I go over and stare down at her face. The glare of the television is reflected on her face. She looks like a ghost. For the first time, I get scared. "Mama?" She still doesn't let on. Putting a hand on her chest, I feel around for a sign of life, then squeeze her cheeks. They're cold to the touch. Letting out a scream, I run from the room, yelling all the way across the street for Miz Cowan who, thank God, is home. By the time I've reached the other side of the road, she and Marvin have both come to the porch.

"It's mama!"

Miz Cowan leans over the bannister rail. "What?"

"Gotta get her to the hospital, quick!" I don't bother wiping away the tears rolling down my cheeks.

They start down the steps. I lead the way back to the house. Mama's still lying there. Not a muscle moves anywhere, not even a twitch. "Help's coming, mama. Hang on." I'm sobbing now. "Just hang on."

As Miz Cowan and Marvin rush through the door, I'm holding mama's limp wrist the way I've seen nurses do it on television. Somewhere a pulse beats, but feebly, like a dazed moth flailing against a screen. Picking her up, Marvin hurries to the car, me and Miz Cowan following.

Under the oxygen tent, mama's head looks swollen. Her eyelids are glued down with mucus.

The nurses roll in a big black machine. Dabbing her skin with grease, they set little markers on her chest. "Don't worry," one of them says to me. "This won't hurt."

I watch the needle move up, down, sideways. I wouldn't be a bit surprised if it spun off into a series of loops like the roller coaster up at Lake Winnepesauka. *Up, around, people screaming as the car hurls down the track, sure that any second it'll fly right off. . . .* I swallow hard.

The tall, hard-faced nurse, Miss Cargle, pushes me aside so she can give mama an injection. Later, Dr. Henderson comes in, takes her pulse, looks at the chart, shakes his head. "Wish you'd brought her in earlier," he says. "We'll know better in a day or two."

Know what? That I'm trapped? That there's no way out? That now I'll never be able to leave home?

A jar of glucose the size of a hornet's nest is hung upside-down over the bed.

When the Cowans leave, the room is silent. The only sound I hear is footsteps in the hall. I try to ring Grandpa Jess from the pay phone in the lobby, but nobody answers. Probably already passed out.

All through the night, nurses come and go. Once, briefly, mama opens her eyes and tries to make a sound. I lean over close. "What? What'd you say?" But she's drifted off again.

I sit in the brown vinyl chair opposite the bed. "There's a cot under there." The young nurse points to the space below the hospital bed. "Why don't you pull it out and lie down? No need to torture yourself."

I shake my head. "Whatever is, is," I say. "No sense in trying to make it better."

After breakfast the next day, I phone Mr. Baxter at home. "Of course," he says, "of course." There's no question about staying out from work. "Just take care of your mama," he says. "Nobody can replace a mama."

Late that afternoon, a potted fern arrives from Joy's Florist in Richville. The card reads, "From the gang in second-shift spinning," and they've all signed their names. Grady Fay's is at the bottom, in small handwriting, not like Mr. Baxter's show-off scrawl.

Trying to hide my tears from Miss Cargle, who's taking mama's blood pressure, I turn and place the plant in the window, then gaze out at the tall elm trees and wide green lawn. Several children run across, laughing and shouting, part of the healthy world me and mama no longer belong to.

Leaving the young nurse to keep an eye on her, I go back home to take a bath, change clothes, and feed the parakeet. Slipping in through the back door, I see that the towel is still over the cage from the night before. Naturally, the bird starts squawking the second it's off, and keeps squawking all the time I'm there, as if it knows something's wrong. Miz Cowan swears animals have a sixth sense, and maybe she's right for once.

When I return to the hospital, Grandpa Jess's sprawled in the chair eating Oreo cookies from a big cellophane bag in his lap. Wonder how he found out. Probably Miz Cowan called him.

"Don't look so good, does she?" he nods towards the bed. "Same pasty color that Eller had before she died."

He's relaxed, as if he means to stay a long time. Holding out two dollars, I tell him to walk over to the barber shop and get himself a nice shave, knowing all the time what he'll spend it on.

For the next several nights, I doze on the small cot that squeaks and shivers under my weight. I lay there in the dark and listen to the faint sounds of breathing coming from inside the tent. If they stop even for a second, I leap up to make sure that mama's still alive.

One night I have a dream. In this dream it's *me*, not mama, who's laying there . . . but with no air in the room so I can barely get my breath.

I wake up sweating and pushing away the bedsheets until finally I can't stand it no more. Running over to the window, I throw it open and stand there gasping. I've just laid back down when Miss Cargle, who's passing in the hall and I guess hears the noise, comes rushing in and shuts it again.

"Are you trying to give your mama pneumonia?" she says, glaring at me.

During this time, I keep wondering whether or not to call Detroit. But what would daddy say? "Gussie sick? I'll fly right down." I know *that's* crazy. But maybe he'd say, "Hon, what can I do to help you?" And I'd answer, "Nothing, daddy, nothing. Just needed to hear your voice, that's all." What I really want to say is, "Daddy, I'm stuck here! Tell me what to do!" Once I even go down to the lobby and pick up the phone, meaning to call long distance, then set it down again. Probably he's forgotten all about me, and doesn't want to be reminded. And suppose his wife answers? I've only met her twice, once at Hoke Treadaway's and the other time, by accident, just before daddy left. Only then I didn't know he was leaving. Mama calls her "that Indian woman" 'cause she's said to be part Cherokee. I do know one thing. Thinking about her always gives me a headache.

One afternoon Miz Cowan comes in, bearing one thin sliver of egg custard pie. I take the opportunity to walk over to the Store to see if Mr. Hicks, who runs the newsstand, has gotten in a new issue of *True Confessions,* but he hasn't. I'm about to walk off when my eye lights on the cover of the latest *Coronet,* not my favorite magazine except that this issue features an article on Elvis so I have to buy it.

By the time I get back, Miz Cowan has already left and mama's eating the pie. I've just opened the magazine when she asks me to take the plate and rinse it off so it can be returned. Then I have to let the bed down . . . takes five minutes before I get it right. After that the sheets have to be straightened, which takes even longer. Finally . . . finally, I'm able to sit down. But no sooner have I settled myself than mama asks for a Coke.

"Can't you wait?"

"My mouth's so dry, I can barely swallow."

I shuffle out to the lobby where the Coke machine is. On the way back, I hold the cold bottle to my cheek, which gives me relief for a second.

Pouring it out, I insert a straw and hand it over. Then I sit down and pick up the magazine again. There he is. Elvis playing the guitar. Across the top of the page, it says, "A guitar-thumping whirling dervish who also sings, he sells millions of records which drive teenagers mad. . . ."

"Here. I'm finished." Mama holds out the glass.

"Just set it down."

"You better wash it so it don't draw ants."

Gritting my teeth, I get up, take the glass, walk over to the sink and turn on the water so hard that the front of my dress gets drenched.

"Maybe you'd let my bed up a little."

"Thought you wanted it down."

"I been *down*. Now I need *up*. You have to change around, otherwise you get wore out."

"Is that enough?"

"Little more. . . . That's okay."

Going out into the hall, I clutch the wall with my fingertips and beat my head against it several times, only stopping when I glance up and realize that Miss Cargle's staring at me like I'm out of my mind.

As mama begins to improve, the paraphernalia is taken away: the glucose bottle, the shots for sleeping, the oxygen tent. The more alert she becomes, the more demands she has. She asks for the bedpan, for a sip of water, of Coke; for the bed to be let up, let down; for her pillow to be fluffed, turned over; for the bedpan again; for an icepack, a kleenex, more water. . . .

Somehow she can't get comfortable, she says; her back aches, her shoulders feel cramped. But mostly she complains about having nothing to do to pass the time, nobody to talk to.

This is probably a swipe at my going back to work. But I can't stand hanging around the hospital another day.

When Dot spots me coming up the steps on Monday morning, she races down and gives me a big squeeze. Then Tessie comes up with the news that the novelty department of the Store is now stocking Elvis's records. And over in my own section, I'm surprised to see Grady Fay waiting for me. "Glad you're back," he says, not looking me in the eye. "How's your mama?"

"Kicking and screaming. Which means she's much better."

I move to the end of Number 10 frame, to be sure nobody's bothered anything. Sure enough there's Elvis, almost life-size, still holding onto the gun and scowling straight-out as if to say, "Nobody'd better mess with me!" Makes me feel like I have somebody strong protecting me. And right now I need all the strength I can get because my fingers feel stiffer than lead pipes. Strange how being off just two weeks can make that much difference. Reckon it's because what I do is so automatic that when the motion stops, it's like a thread breaking. Something like that.

"Now I got to get the hang of it all over again," I complain to Mr. Baxter when he stops by to say hello.

"Why, it won't take *that* long," he says, snapping his fingers.

He leans over and pats the frame. "See how Grady Fay kept her oiled for you?"

I sure do. Whenever I put my hands anywhere near the spindles, they come away smeared with grease.

A couple of times I spy Mr. Fortune hanging around. At first it makes me a little nervous, but soon it's obvious that it's Grady Fay he's watching, so I go on about my business.

On Friday, just before the supper break, there's a crisis on Number 8 when one of the travelers guiding the thread up and down on the quill flies off the ring.

I rush over to the office to tell Mr. Baxter, who goes to fetch Boley Westbrooks. Within five minutes Boley arrives carrying the red flannel cloth that he wraps his tools in. Spreading the cloth on the floor beside the frame, he arranges the tools so that he can pick up what's needed in a flash. There're six wrenches, a metal cutter, four sizes of pliers, four screwdrivers, three packages of nuts and bolts, a hammer, a file, two tubes of liquid soldering, a roll of electrician's tape, and any number of loose wires and screws.

Turning off the switch, he checks the bolster, the spindle blade, the whirl, the acorn. Several times he spits on the end of his fingers and runs them up and down the spindle at a fast rate. (This reminds me of something I saw Grandpa Jess do once when he didn't know I was around.) Then he moves on to a ring where the traveler is still working right and twists it as though testing its strength. Throwing the switch back on, he stands there for a minute. "Just as I thought," he mumbles. "It's going too fast for this size traveler."

"What?" I'm peering over his shoulder trying to see what he's talking about.

"I said, these travelers are too light to take this kind of spindle-speed, so they get over-heated and fly right off the ring. I'll turn down the machine and put on heavier ones." Picking up a huge wrench, he walks to the end of the frame. I follow him. "Same system as in outer space," he tells me as he adjusts the gears. "Small planet goes round and round till it builds up so much momentum, it flies right out of the universe."

"Is that true?"

"Would I lie to you?"

Grabbing a pair of pliers and a cutter, he returns to the middle of the row and begins splicing through the old travelers, replacing them with new ones. After a few minutes, he straightens up. "There," he says, "that ought to do it."

Mr. Baxter appears at his elbow. "Did you get her all fixed up?"

"Yep," Boley says, wrapping his tools back up in the flannel cloth.

"She'll be okay now. Turned down the speed a notch to take off some of the pressure."

"Well, as long as she's not too slow. It's important that we have all the machines working full-tilt. Especially now when something big's about to happen."

"What's that?" Boley asks.

"You'll find out in due time." Mr. Baxter blows out his cigar smoke and gives him a mysterious wink. "In due time."

A few days pass before Mr. Fortune pays another visit to the spinning room, and when he does, it's to address the whole department. Even the sweepers such as Marvin are on hand, gathered at one end of the big room by Mr. Baxter, who sent Dot around with a summons.

I'm sitting on one side of Shorty Toles and Boley. Grady Fay's on the other side.

"What do you suppose this is all about?" Shorty asks, glancing around.

"Unions," Boley replies, without a second's hesitation.

"Unions?"

"Believe me, nothing else could bring the big boss around."

"Unions," Grady Fay repeats under his breath and crawls over to where I am. "This is about unions," he whispers.

"Really?" 'Course, I've overheard their whole conversation.

"That's what Boley says."

Before he steps through the crowd, Mr. Baxter stops and lets Mr. Fortune go ahead of him. Before starting, Mr. Fortune gives Marvin a dime and asks him to get a Seven-Up out of the vending machine in the canteen. Marvin doesn't look too happy about it, but he does it anyway.

"Okay, okay." Walking to the front of the crowd, Mr. Baxter throws up his hand for silence. "We are honored this evening to have our general manager, Mr. Fortune, with us. He has something to tell you, and when he's finished, I'm sure you'll be just as excited about it as I am." Everybody looks at each other, wondering what he's talking about. "And now, without further ado, it's my honor to introduce Mr. A. S. Fortune. . . ." What on earth could the A. S. stand for? Arthur Stowe? Albert Steven? Allen Stewart?

"Folks," Mr. Fortune says after taking a long sip of the Seven-Up that Marvin has just handed him, "we are starting something that I hope will eventually become an annual event. The success or failure of it largely depends on you. Before I explain what it is, I'd like to mention some of the history behind it." Pausing a second, he looks up at the ceiling as though gathering his thoughts. "It began several years ago when a mill in Alabama claimed in a textile magazine that one of its doffers was the fastest in the world. Now, as you know, that's a tall order, and it wasn't long before a South Carolina mill challenged the statement, even going so far as to fly their own doffer down to Alabama to have a contest with this so-called champion. Well, as it turned out, he wasn't much of a champ at all, because the fellow from South Carolina beat him, hands down. Pretty soon, the South Carolina mill began making its own claim. 'We have the *real* superdoffer,' they boasted. So in turn they were challenged by other mills in the Southeast, until now it's developed into a Superdoffing Bowl, with prizes and trophies and chances to travel to other mills." He takes a big swig of Seven-Up, then sets it down.

"There are two reasons that Goody Mills is joining the competition this year. First, as members in good standing with the Southeastern Textile Association, we want to do our part in focusing the spotlight on a much-neglected industry. Second, the success of the winning doffer will be reflected in prestige for the company he represents. So if we have a winner here in Goody, all of us will benefit from it. What I'm asking for is your support. I want you to stand behind the doffer representing your shift as he competes with doffers from the first and third shift. This will be our local competition. The winner will go to Augusta, Georgia, where he will challenge doffers from other mills in Georgia. If successful, he will then be flown in our company plane to Avondale, Louisiana, where he will participate in the semifinals. The winner of that match will have the pleasure of hosting the finals at his own mill." He picks up the bottle and takes another swallow. I wait for him to belch, but he doesn't. "Well, I guess that about covers what I have to say at the moment. Except that in the next few weeks, I plan to spend a good deal of time in this department, so if you see me wandering around, don't pay any attention." He gives a salute, nods toward Mr. Baxter, and walks out.

As everybody shuffles back to their own sections, Marvin says, within Mr. Baxter's hearing, that he hopes, even though he's a sweeper and only doffs when someone's out sick, to have the chance to show how fast he is because he feels he's never been fully appreciated.

"When's all this happening," Boley asks Mr. Baxter as he passes by.

"Read about it in the *News,*" Mr. Baxter says, tapping the end of his cigar. "It'll be announced soon."

Boley says it doesn't seem to amount to much. But at least I'll have some news to tell mama when I go to the hospital.

My habit for the past week has been to spend mornings and part of the afternoons with mama, and walk directly from there to work. After work, I go home and sit at the kitchen table with the light off and the back door open, and listen—when the wind's right and carries away the roar of machinery from the finishing plant out back—to the sound of birds. They sure make a nicer noise than parakeets.

Every morning I set my alarm at seven-thirty so by eight-thirty, I'm already at the hospital door.

One day, when I'm walking through the hall, I hear shouts and moans coming from mama's room, and think, "Oh, my Lord, it's all over!" Turns out, the shouting comes from Preacher Crow and the moaning comes from mama, who keeps saying, "A-men, a-men," over and over.

Another time, Calvin has tagged along, and while Preacher Crow's praying, Calvin's hand slips up from behind, rubbing and pinching me the way mama does melons when she's testing for ripeness. I feel like taking that hand and bending the little finger back far enough to teach him a lesson. But Dr. Henderson warned me about not exposing mama to any undue excitement and I'm afraid that breaking a finger might qualify.

As the days go on, I find myself waking up later and later. Sometimes it's eleven by the time I've fed Pretty Boy, toasted a cheese sandwich for myself, and raced across the plaza, over the bridge, along Broad Street, past the Inn, finally reaching the hospital in a sweat.

On Saturday, I decide to give myself a treat. Instead of dashing off right away, I make up my mind to relax a little. Don't know whether it's mama's absence or the bright sunny morning, but I've not felt so light-headed in a long time. Then the phone rings. At first I don't recognize the voice. It sounds a whole lot deeper. But when he calls me "baby," I know who it is. Nobody does that but Gene. I'm surprised because I haven't heard from him in a long time. Not since he got a job way north of Chattanooga.

"Heard your mama's real sick." He sounds cheerful about it.

"She's better now."

"Oh." There's such a long pause that I wonder if he's hung up. "I was hoping to see you while she's laid up."

"She's coming home on Monday."

"What about Sunday night?"

I let a few seconds pass before I answer, but I have to admit my heart's racing. "Okay."

His voice goes real soft. "I been thinking about you, baby. Night and day. It's all I do. And you're gonna make ol' Gene happy, aren't you?" His voice is dripping with insinuations. "Aren't you?"

"We'll see." I finally get the words out.

"I know you are. Because you and me love each other." Then his tone changes. "I'll be in front of your house by eight. Listen for my horn." He hangs up before I have the chance to ask how he knew about mama.

I put on "Love Me Tender," Elvis's latest record, and turn up the volume so I can sing along. I waltz around my bedroom, then into the kitchen where I whirl between the refrigerator and the stove. But I'm feeling so good, a narrow room can't hold me. I run out the door into the yard and fling myself around as Elvis's voice drifts through the open window. Then I go back and sit on the steps. Reminds me of a morning long, long ago when daddy returned from North Carolina where he'd been on an ambulance call.

He comes over to my bed and tickles me under the chin to wake me up. Finally he can't wait another minute and plops a big sack down on my legs. Inside is a red pail and a shovel and a sifter. Sneaking outside in my gown, I sit on the bottom step, digging up dirt and sifting it onto my feet. The dirt, already warm from the sun, makes my toes tingle.

Don't know why, but that minute or two sticks in my mind as the happiest of my whole life. Maybe that's the reason I fling off my mules now, and scrunch my feet around. But the ground feels cold, and as much as I try to recapture the old feeling, I can't.

Chapter Five

WHILE MAMA'S IN THE HOSPITAL SEEMS a good time to throw a fan club party. I've been wanting to do that for weeks, and besides it'll keep my mind off Gene. So I make it for Saturday night. I now have seven members. Six say they'll attend, and two are bringing along extra people who might also want to join. Dot's a little wary about my having it at the house without getting mama's permission, but I remind her that what people don't know don't hurt 'em, especially when it comes to heart attack patients. So she helps me shop for the refreshments, mostly finger foods, like pimento cheese sandwiches cut into the shape of musical notes (this is her idea, she's real good at thinking up things that are different), carameled popcorn, Rice Krispie squares, and cheese balls made of cream cheese rolled in nuts. Since Elvis's favorite food is peanut butter and banana sandwiches, we also make a few of them for diehard fans like myself.

Dot likes R.C.s, so we get a whole case, and four big bags of potato chips, and two of pork rinds, which are Tessie's favorites.

"Well, we're all set," I tell Dot as we tote the stuff home from the Store, making two trips back and forth. "Except figuring out some party games."

"We could play pin the tail on the donkey, using one of the Elvis posters for the donkey," Dot says.

This shocks me. "Dot, how could you be so disrespectful!"

"Don't get riled up. I was only kidding."

"What about some kind of guessing game? You know, like an Elvis quiz?"

"That's good. But what do we give as a prize? We have to have a prize. You could donate Pretty Boy, except nobody'd want him."

"Seriously, Dot." I frown when I say this.

"Okay, okay. I'm thinking."

We finally decide to make a grab-bag of as many Elvis items as we can put together (including going back to the Store and buying two records): buttons, magazines, and one photograph, which we stick in a frame that had one of my old baby pictures in it.

Everybody arrives either at seven or a few minutes after. We have a quiz first, then a little floor show with Dot giving bad imitations of different singers that the rest of us have to guess. While she's on the final number, I put the refreshments on the table. I'm just passing around more potato chips when the phone rings. I'm thinking it might be Gene calling again about tomorrow night, but it's mama.

"LaVonne, Dr. Henderson was just in here, and said I could come home tomorrow. Thank the Lord! Anyway, you have to . . . " Suddenly she stops. "Who's there?"

"What?"

"I hear voices. Who is it?"

"Oh . . . I've got the television on."

"Well, turn it down so I can hear myself talk."

I put my finger up to my mouth, but nobody pays much attention. "Go ahead, mama."

"You have to call Bub and be over here by ten o'clock. You hear me? Ten o'clock."

"Okay."

"Are you sure nobody's there?"

"Who would it be? 'Bye." I hang up.

When I put the phone down, everybody asks me what's wrong, I guess because I'm looking real down in the mouth. Dot's sure something's happened to mama, and she comes over and puts her arm around me. I tell her mama's alright. It's Gene I'm thinking of. What will I do now?!

The fun has gone out of it for me, so I listen to the others talking and don't say much. Dot keeps looking at me, as though she's wondering what's wrong. I do tell them before they leave that I hope to hold more social gatherings in the near future. One girl asks if boys can come along next time, and I say, "Why not? I might invite somebody, too." By the time everybody leaves, it's nine, and I have to scurry around cleaning up. Dot hangs around to help, but since she doesn't want to be too late getting home, she doesn't stay long. I don't get in bed till one o'clock, and then I have to be up at eight to call Bub.

Bringing mama home from the hospital turns out to be more of an ordeal than I'd expected, and I expected it to be an ordeal. In the first place Bub hems and haws that he's not sure whether or not he'll be available, so

I take the hint and offer him a dollar extra. To make things worse, it's pouring rain. When he picks me up in front of the house, I say, "Shoot!" and grab an umbrella and run.

At the hospital, mama's all packed and ready to go. "Thought you were never going to get here," she says.

"Bub was late," I say by way of excuse. My shoes are dripping water on the tile floor and I stand with my feet halfway under the bed so Miss Cargle won't notice while she's changing sheets. "It's raining outside." I'm trying to be pleasant.

"I know. I got eyes." She gazes out the window. "Just my luck," she says, "to go home on a day like this."

I take the small suitcase and shopping bag while mama—complaining that she doesn't trust me not to chip off the gold paint—carries the artificial flower arrangement that Pearlie B. Bramlett sent on behalf of the women of the church. I think it's pretty ugly anyway, but don't say so.

We stand at the main door to see if it lets up. "If we stay here much longer, Bub's gonna charge extry," she says, waiting for me to go on ahead of her.

By the time we've walked from the hospital to the car, from the car to the house, we're both soaking wet. I settle mama in the platform rocker, and pull out the faded brown slippers she always wears. Reminds me of some rotten animal. Then I kneel to help her remove her wet shoes and stockings, peeling them down, exposing the network of veins that shine like tiny threads of purple neon just beneath the skin. Pray to God I don't inherit them.

Mama complains about the room being chilly even though it's August, but to stave off an argument, I hurry out to the coal shed (used as a garage when daddy was here), gather up a scuttleful, bring it back, and pour half of it into the heater. But it takes a long time to fire up, and longer than that to get the room as warm as she likes it. She goes into the kitchen with her arms drawn together inside her sleeves. From underneath the towel that hangs over the top of the cage, there's a fluttering noise. Jerking it off, she bends down. "Hi there, Pretty Boy, hi there! Mama's back. Yes, I am. Are you glad to see me?" She lets out a tuneless little whistle. The bird nods its head and raises its wings slightly. "Now that's the first welcome home sign I've had." She turns to me. "Have you been talking to him?"

"When've I had time?"

"Well, now I'm home, I'm gonna start teaching him." She puts her lips up close to the cage. "Yes, I am. Yes, I am. Hi, Pretty Boy, hi. . . ."

If she lays down, maybe she'll stop that cheeping business. "Shouldn't you rest now?"

Suddenly her body seems to sag. "I *am* wore out." Saying

goodbye to the parakeet, she goes into the living room and lays back on the rocker.

I look at my watch. It's quarter of eight. "Why don't we exchange rooms for awhile, mama? I hate you sleeping in the living room when you're sick."

"Good a place as any."

"Wanna see television then?"

"Might as well."

I turn the knob as loud as I can without her complaining. "How's this?" It's "The Virginia Graham Show."

She lays her head on the pillow and closes her eyes.

Sneaking outside, I sit in the porch swing. Finally a black Ford drives up. I race out waving my arms.

"What's wrong?" Gene asks. I can see he's got all dolled up, and slicked his hair back.

"Mama came home early."

"You mean to say, you're not going?" He's glaring at me. Even in the half-dark I can tell that.

"I can't leave her alone. She might have another attack."

"Best thing that could happen," he mutters, screeching off like he's real mad.

When I go back in the house, mama's got her eyes closed. I should be mad, too, but instead I feel kinda sorry for her, lying there like a bag of old bones. "Want me to get another program?"

"One thing's the same as another. Might get a few laughs out of it anyway."

When I go to bed, it's a long time before I get to sleep. Instead of counting sheep, I count missed opportunities. One right after another.

Mama likes getting laughs, but she also likes crying, which is why "This Is Your Life" is one of her favorites. Sometimes when she's in a really bad mood, she'll imitate Ralph Edwards and say, "Gussie Wooten Grubbs, this is your life, and it's all over." I'm feeling the same way now that Gene's gone. The only time the sound's turned down is when visitors come, and there aren't too many of them—mostly Miz Cowan, who barges in bringing one of her Coca-Cola cakes that always sag in the middle. 'Course, mama pretends not to notice 'cause she doesn't want to hurt her feelings, especially since Miz Cowan's offered to keep her company while I'm at work. Naturally we'll pay her for it—fifteen dollars a week, which isn't bad for just sitting.

Sometimes, though, I have to say, she gets to talking about her sister-in-law up at Delphi and overstays her welcome. I can tell mama doesn't feel like listening to other people's troubles, and I don't blame her. "Got my own," she says to me afterwards. Once, just to get rid of her, she tells Miz Cowan that she has so much gas on her stomach she can hardly straighten out, and if the chance comes she'll just have to let it pass no matter who's here, so she's apologizing in advance. Both of us laugh to see how quick Miz Cowan hightails it out the door.

Dr. Henderson warns me that heart attack patients often suffer from depression. When I ask him what that means, he says they get real sad. But I don't believe him till it starts happening right before my eyes.

First of all, mama has Cootie Bledsoe draw up a will leaving all of her worldly goods to me, except fifty dollars that she wants Grandpa Jess to use to buy himself a new suit of clothes for her funeral.

"Oh, mama!" I make a face. "Don't be so morbid. You're not going to die."

"Never know. Here one second, gone the next. Have to live with that, like it or not."

She even plans her funeral, dictating the instructions, making me write them down on a clean sheet of paper so there'll be no questions about it.

"Remember Mr. Cowan?" she says when I balk at this.

"Just barely."

"They had him cremated though I'm certain as can be that he didn't want it that way."

"But his head was bashed in, wasn't it?"

"Never mind the reason. It happened because he hadn't made out a will. I want everything down in black and white. Then there'll be no mistake."

As she goes on, a tiny bubble of spit forms at the edge of her lips. I can see that she's really relishing being the center of attention, even if she's dead when it happens. "I want Pearlie B. Bramlett to play 'Rock of Ages,'" she says, "so that everybody who has a mind to can cry. And I want my head to rest on one of my own little pillows." Holding up her deformed hand she studies it as though it's a book she's reading. "But the two things I hope for with all my heart," she tells me, still looking at her hand, "are for Marvin Cowan to have the courtesy to wear a white shirt to my funeral instead of those loud-colored things with flamingos and palm trees that he's so fond of . . . and the second request is for your Grandpa Jess to be sober for once."

"Mama, this is the craziest thing I ever heard of!" I bear down so hard on the pencil I'm writing with that the point breaks.

"And I'm telling you this." I see tears forming in her eyes, which is a bad sign. "I know I haven't been a perfect mother, but nobody can say I didn't try, *nobody* can say that. Wasn't easy either. Working my head off in the glove mill, then rushing home to fix supper, not just cornbread crumbled in sweet milk either, like some folks had, but Cream of Wheat and eggs and bacon, and then at night fried chicken with gravied mashed potatoes. Like to broke my back, but I did it."

"Wish you'd hush. Nothing's going to happen to you." But the words sound more feeble the second time around.

Wiping her nose, mama continues. "The thing I feel most awful about is that first Christmas after your daddy left, when he sent you that teddy bear and a letter, and I got so mad about the letter that I had to throw something, and the bear was the closest thing. But I did promise to glue on another eye, remember?" I nod halfheartedly. I'll never forget how scared I was. "Only you wouldn't let me."

"It was already done."

"And when the stuffing come out, I did seam it up for you, didn't I?" She sniffs again. "Sometimes that Wooten temper gets the best of me."

"Mama, it's over and done with." Dear God, just let her stop. To distract her, I ask her to roll over on her side so I can straighten out her sheets. Then I turn off the television. Without it blaring, the room is so quiet. For the first time in a long while, I can actually hear the clock ticking. I start to leave and go to my own room, but something— maybe the sight of her back all humped up—stops me. I bend over and kiss her cheek, and whisper. "I love you, mama." Can't remember when I last said that.

That night I dream that daddy is pulling me on a sled through high snow drifts. He goes faster and faster, and I start screaming. The next thing I know, daddy has disappeared and I'm heading down a steep hill all by myself. Over to one side, I see Gene waving.

Several weeks go by before mama starts feeling better. Then she launches into big dinners again: roast beef, turnip greens, cole slaw, candied yams, apple butter, cornbread. When I'm really deep in a Grace Livingston Hill book—they're my favorite—I can hardly bear to drag myself up, and I keep saying, "Just a minute. Be there in a minute." Then five minutes pass and she's banging again. She can't stand for food to get cold. If it gets cold, she throws it out.

So I come in, and see the whole table covered with dishes. I'm worried that all this cooking might be too much, but she insists on doing it. "Got to try and get my appetite back," she says, as if it's some pet that's wandered off. Whenever she puts a hand to her chest, I get scared. "Should I get the nitroglycerin?" I ask, rising out of my chair.

"I'm sure it's just indigestion."

"Isn't that what they all say?"

"All who?"

"Heart attack patients."

"Have no idea what *they* say, I'm only interested in what I say, and I say, sit down."

Oh well, if she's going to be *that* way.

"Eat up now," mama says, waving her hand over the table. For the life of me, I can't recall a single meal that didn't start this way: "Eat up now." The "now" business was a running argument between her and daddy, who never cared what he ate, or when, and was prone to come walking into the kitchen just as mama and me were finishing.

"Didn't you hear me calling you?" mama'd ask.

"I was out back working on the car."

"You must have heard. I was screaming my head off. Food's cold."

"It's alright," he'd say, washing his greasy hands in the kitchen sink, which was another thing that irritated mama.

"I go to a lot of trouble fixing a hot meal and then you never come when it's ready." He'd watch her remove the bowls of vegetables, the meat platter, the skillet of cornbread. "I'll fix myself a sandwich." Then he'd take out a jar of peanut butter and two slices of Holsum bread, pour himself a big glass of milk, and sit at the table, one finger tracing an invisible pattern on the worn oilcloth.

Sometimes in summer he'd carry his sandwich outside and sit on the bottom step where I'd join him, bouncing a ball off the side of the house while he ate. I barely remember mama and daddy and me sharing a meal together. If we did, there was probably an argument.

"Eat up now," mama says again, but I don't pay much attention. By now it's automatic.

After finishing, though, I'm careful to wipe my greasy chin with the paper napkin folded by my plate. Mama's real proud of the fact that we don't use the backs of our hands like the Cowans, who she says come away from the table with their knuckles shining.

Eating at the mill's different. I love sharing food with Dot and Tessie. While we eat, Dot and I take turns reading aloud the latest bulletins from the national fan club. Sometimes we have a competition with Marvin Cowan, who likes to read from his accident diary. The story that gives us the biggest shivers is the one about J. D. Price. Don't know whether it's true or not, although I'm pretty certain J. D. was a real person 'cause daddy helped bury him. He claimed it was like burying a legend.

Anyhow, as Marvin tells it, when J. D. worked in the Weave Room, he had a hard time with noise, and would use heavy ear plugs to shut everything out. One evening he forgot to take the plugs out and went moseying across the railroad tracks, whistling to himself and staring at the ground as usual. All of a sudden, the Central of Georgia whizzed round the bend by the warehouse and struck him down. According to Marvin, it cut off both his legs, and they had to haul him to the hospital. Later the ambulance attendants were sent back to the tracks to pick up what was left of him. When they got there, they found lots of blood around but no sign of the legs. Marvin claims they just up and walked off by themselves. He says, whenever somebody hears footsteps or any strange clomping noise, we can be sure it's J. D. Price's legs trying to catch up with the rest of him.

I'm hard put to match Marvin's tales, but I try. I tell about the old maid who sent Elvis her dead birds, wrapped up in shoeboxes, through the mail, asking him to bury them in his backyard. Or the mother who named her twins—male and female—both Elvis. Or the jealous husband who followed Elvis around on a motorcycle, threatening to cut out his tonsils with a butcher knife. Even Reba stops to listen on her way to the ladies' room, and for once, doesn't say one word by way of criticism.

I've been so distracted by mama's illness and by the fan club that I almost forget about the contest, except when Shorty Toles mentions it.

"So what's the Big Boss up to now, LaVonne?" he asks on our lunch break. "I seen him over in your section."

"Keeping an eye on Grady Fay."

"He the main contender?" When I say I don't know, he waylays Boley Westbrooks, who's walking by with his tool bag. "What d'you think, Boley?"

"My motto is, 'Don't count your chickens. . . .'"

"Yeah?" Shorty looks around to see if anybody's watching, then spits on the floor. "That's a pretty good motto, but I don't see how it fits."

"Think about it, Shorty." Boley puts a finger to his temple. "Think!"

But I say nobody wants to spend time mulling over something that seems so far away. We all have more pressing things on our minds. Least I do. *Love Me Tender* opens Saturday at the Tivoli Theater, and I'm trying my best to persuade Dot to convince Troy to drive us up to Chattanooga to see it. "Didn't you read about it in the *Chattanooga Free Press?*" I ask. She shakes her head. "Well, it starts out with Elvis and Debra Paget being married. . . . Dot! Are you listening?" I wave a hand in front of her eyes.

"Yeah, I am. Go on."

"But she doesn't really love him."

"Why not?"

For dramatic effect, I take a long pause like Preacher Crow does in his sermons. "Because she's in love with his older brother."

"Who plays that part?" Dot asks, tilting her chair back against the wall.

"Uh . . . Richard . . . oh, I know his name as well as I know my own. Egan. Richard Egan."

"Richard Egan is gooood-looking!" Tessie says.

"He's okay, but the point is, Elvis is younger. He's younger and less experienced."

"In what?" Marvin drawls, sticking his head between us. He has a terrible habit of butting in on other people's conversations.

I have to think a minute before answering. "In getting what he wants."

"So what happens then?" Tessie asks. She seems more interested than Dot.

"Debra thinks he's been killed in the war." I say this in a real sad voice to prepare them for what's coming.

"Who?" Tessie asks. "I don't understand."

"Richard Egan. The oldest brother."

"Oh."

"So him and Debra get together. Then Richard Egan comes back, and Elvis dies."

"He *dies?*"

"Uh-huh."

Tessie is silent.

"But I think they bring him back," I add quickly. "Sort of. Long enough to sing 'Love Me Tender' anyway."

"LaVonne." Dot's face is stern. "That doesn't sound like a picture that would interest Troy. Now if it was me, I'd be off like a shot. But Troy hates mushy movies. Besides, he's got his heart set on going to Lake Winnepesauka."

"Oh."

"I could tell you stories about *that* place." Marvin is ready to start in when Dot shushes him.

"Troy wants to get a crowd together for Saturday," she says. "It's the last night of the season."

"Count me in." Marvin raises his hand. "And I can take three others. Two besides Shorty. He'll come."

"I will, too," Tessie says.

"Then it's settled." Dot claps her hands. "How about you, LaVonne?"

But I don't plan on saying yes so quickly. "I don't think so."

"Oh, come on," Dot says. "Don't be a spoil sport. You can see that movie another time."

"No telling who you might run into," Marvin says out of the corner of his mouth.

Tessie catches my arm. "We'll ride the roller coaster together."

I say I'll think about it.

"Bet she just wants us to beg her," Dot says. "Maybe Grady Fay'll come."

"Naw." Marvin waves Dot's suggestion away. "That boy don't go nowhere."

"We'll see," Dot says.

The next morning, I tiptoe into the kitchen where mama's busy trying to coax the parakeet onto her finger.

"Mama."

"Shhh."

"I have to ask . . . "

"Shhh, I said. I'm trying to train Pretty Boy. Here, Pretty Boy, here, come on, Pretty Boy, come on, come on now, come on, Pretty Boy."

"Dumb bird," I mutter under my breath before escaping into the living room where the latest copy of the *News* is spread over one end of the sofa. I pick it up, curious to see if there's a mention of the contest.

In a minute, mama comes in, drying her hands against the sides of her apron. "What is it?"

"Nothing."

"You'd better spit it out."

"I was just thinking . . . you haven't invited Miz Cowan over to play Rook in a long time. Why don't you ask her for Saturday night."

Knowing how I feel about Miz Cowan, mama's immediately suspicious. "Why?"

"Well, a group of spinning room people are going up to the lake on Saturday night and I thought I might join them. I don't want to leave you here by yourself, that's all."

"Who's driving?"

"Marvin."

"I don't understand why you have to go that far for fun. Young people used to be able to have fun at home. Now they have to be doing something all the time." She gives me a look. "Just don't be midnight getting back."

"I'm not thirteen, you know, mama."

"You could've fooled me."

She always has to have the last word.

Chapter Six

LATE SATURDAY AFTERNOON, MARVIN HONKS for me. Shutting my ears to mama's last-minute instructions, I run out. I'm expecting some comments from Marvin and Shorty about wearing my fan club pin, but so what?

Tessie and Shorty are already in the back seat, along with Marvin's spare tire. I climb in front and look around for a place to set the big thermos of coffee I'm holding. "Mama sent this," I say, "in case anybody needs caffeine to stay alert."

"She means me." Marvin shifts gears and pulls away.

"Are Dot and Troy ahead or behind us?"

"Don't know. We're supposed to meet by the entrance gate."

"Hope we can find each other. You know there'll be a big crowd."

"Yep. Including pickpockets. Fellow used to work in the spinning room makes a good living up there. Bet y'all didn't know that."

Tessie leans forward. "At Lake Winnepesauka?"

"See him every time I go. His fingers got so nimble from piecing up that he can do just about anything with them."

"Is that true?" Tessie asks.

"Would I lie to you?" Marvin says, imitating Boley. "No need for you to worry though. You're with me."

I'd know the Lake Winnepesauka road even if I was blind, which I'm not, knock on wood. Ruts big enough for Grandpa Jess's hogs to root around in. "You'd think we was on one of those rides already." I'm holding on to the dashboard with my right hand. As we round the curve leading to the lake, I lower my window all the way so I can hear the music.

We have to drive around a good ten minutes to find a vacant space, but finally a car pulls out at one end of the parking lot. I don't understand why Marvin's so particular about locking up since there's nothing inside that anybody could steal except a frayed piece of rope and an old battered copy of *Field and Stream.*

Shorty climbs out, hitches up his pants, and smooths down his hair. "Well, here we are. . . ."

It's a real pretty sight, even if I would've preferred going to the Tivoli. Lights blink on the ferris wheel, the swings, the high, winding track of roller coaster that's supposed to be the scariest in the whole state. As the cars come hurtling down, the screams of the passengers give me the heebie-jeebies. I keep looking around but there's no sign of the Holsum Bread truck. When we step up to buy tickets, though, I hear a familiar voice.

"Hey! Y'all! Wait for us!"

Turning, I see Dot running toward us. Behind her walks Troy and what looks to be Grady Fay Owens. I'm surprised she was able to talk him into coming, though if anybody can, it's Dot.

There's the usual back-slapping and hugging, as if we haven't seen each other in weeks. "See you're advertising," Dot says, pointing to my Elvis button.

We make our way through the crowd. Looks like Snuffy a hundred times over. A pale, thin woman with a screaming tow-headed baby pulls along four tow-headed kids. Seems to be searching for somebody. Husband probably. In front of the fun house, a big plaster turbaned head sways from side to side.

"Wanna start there?" Dot asks.

"Why not?" answers Tessie.

I don't say nothing, neither does Grady Fay. He keeps giving me sidewise glances though. The tow-headed family are in front of us in the ticket line.

First we have to squirm through a jungle of long cowbells that set up enough racket to make my head swim. Then comes a moving platform that carries us into a pitch-black room where we all grope around to find each other. Suddenly a calloused hand grabs mine. "That you, Lois?" I pull away real quick.

The next room's filled with mirrors that make you look tall and pencil-thin or squat like a fat little pumpkin. Marvin's peeking over my shoulder. When his crewcut gets lifted up to a cone-like peak, it makes me giggle.

Outside we buy big puffs of cotton candy. I show Grady Fay how I like to swoop off a strip and wind it around the tip of my tongue.

"The bumper cars are over there," Troy says. "We have to try them."

"Sure, sure," Dot says, smiling. "The last time I almost lost a tooth, remember?"

Troy puts an arm around her. "I'll protect you, hon."

"Protect me! You were the one doing the damage!"

But she lets him lead us over to a huge wooden building with chicken wire around the sides and a long ramp where a line of customers are waiting for the next set to begin. I stand watching all the cars smashing into each other. Each time a big blow comes, Marvin cackles. "I seen a woman get her neck broke here," he says.

"How?"

"Somebody hit her hard and it snapped her neck back. She tried to get some insurance out of it, but I don't think she ever did."

The operator reaches up to turn off the power. Three seconds later, the cars stop dead in their tracks and people haul themselves out. The others rush to the empty cars, but I stand back, unsure whether or not I want to try it. Just watching's enough to give me a headache.

"Come on, LaVonne! Come on!" they all shout.

"If I can, you can," Tessie calls out, while Shorty makes those pluck-pluck-plucking noises of his that're supposed to mean I'm a chicken. Grady Fay's the only one who doesn't say anything. He just looks at me.

But it's this look more than anything that makes me walk slowly across the metal floor and choose a green car, not on account of its color, but because it's off to one side and nobody's likely to hit me for at least five seconds.

The operator waits for me to adjust the safety strap. While I'm doing this, out of the corner of my eye I notice a group of latecomers come rushing in and take the last few empty cars. When he pulls the switch, every car, except mine, shoots ahead. "Oh Lord!" I gasp.

I finally get the thing moving, but it goes around in circles. "Steer it!" Dot yells at me. "Steer it!"

My steering is mostly dodging. The second anybody gets close, I veer off in another direction. That's when I notice a redhead with a lot of makeup putting herself right in Troy's path so he can't help but plow into her, at which point she throws back her head and laughs. Then I see Dot do a U-turn, though it's against the rules, and slam her around.

Then Marvin's coming at me, but luckily Tessie hits him from behind and he gets sidetracked. I'm still trying to keep out of everyone's way. If this is all there is to driving, I ought to save up for a used car and not have to depend on Bub all the time.

Up ahead, I see Grady Fay trying to restart his car. Passing him with a grin, I'm just about to round the far turn when I notice a red car heading straight for me from the other direction. I start to scream, but it sticks in my throat. Instead I sit there with my mouth hanging open. When the blow comes, I barely feel it, I'm too busy staring. I don't believe it! He moves alongside me until we're eyeball to eyeball. "Hi, baby," Gene says, looking me up and down. For a second, his eyes light on my Elvis button, then he smiles and moves on.

I'm so dumbfounded to see him that I can't do anything but be a sitting duck to every car that passes. I must get knocked around fourteen or fifteen times before the power finally shuts off. Then I sit fumbling with the safety strap until Grady Fay comes over to help. As I'm climbing out, I see Gene looking in my direction. Then I see him motion to his two buddies and saunter off. He's still got the sassiest walk around.

Shorty and Troy want to ride the cars again but Dot manages to steer everybody out and over to the food stand where we buy hot dogs and french fries and eat them while we walk around—me secretly looking for Gene all the time—then come back for R.C.s. Hoping to get them away from the roller coaster where Troy wants to go next, I point to the glass house next door.

"Nothing to that," Shorty sneers.

"You don't think so?" Marvin pulls a dollar bill out of his pocket. "A buck says you can't find your way out of there in five minutes."

Shorty juts out his chin. "You playing Mr. Baxter today, Marvin? Well, I'll just take you up on it. Troy, you hold the money. Let's go, LaVonne." He grabs my arm.

Dot, Troy, Grady Fay, Tessie, and Marvin stand outside watching while I let myself be pulled in. When Shorty goes to the left, I accidentally turn to the right, then I can't get back, though I can wave to Shorty through the glass and he can wave at me. I'm wandering in and out, paying no never-mind where I'm going. Pretty soon I see Shorty outside. He's signaling me to hurry up, and I try to, but I'm really stuck. I go this way, a dead end, *that* way, a dead end. In fact, I'm beginning to feel a little desperate when all at once I turn a corner and I'm out, just like that, one-two-three, easy as pie. Everybody cheers as if I've just made a homerun.

"Thought I was gonna have to go in and haul you out," Shorty says.

While Marvin and Tessie and Shorty head for the swings—which make me nauseous—the rest of us walk over to the edge of the lake to watch people rowing boats. Is Gene in one of them? I crane my neck, but don't see him. It's growing dark, and all the colored lights seem to float on the water.

"Wanna rent one?" Troy asks.

"That'd take ages," Dot says. "We'd probably have time to ride the boat chute, though, if we rush over."

"Let's go," Troy says, pulling her in that direction.

I don't know whether to follow or not, and Grady Fay doesn't help much. He just stands there as if waiting for somebody to tell him what to do.

"Y'all come on," Dot turns and shouts.

The man who sells tickets has the bushiest beard I've ever seen. As he puts a hand down to steady the boat, the tattoo across his knuckles catches Grady Fay's eye. A M A, looks like.

"What's that mean?" Grady Fay asks.

At first the man acts like he has no intention of answering. Then without looking up, he says, "Love, it means love." Laughing soundlessly, he tugs at his beard. "Least, it used to. Letters kinda faded by now. See, I was young then. Back during the war." Clasping Dot's elbow, he guides her into the back seat, then holds the boat as Troy climbs in beside her. He reaches out to help me into the front seat. After Grady Fay gets in, the man gives the boat a shove with his foot. "Y'all have yourselves a real good time now." He grins.

"Looks like a cave, doesn't it?" I say as we drift toward the entrance.

"Are you afraid, LaVonne?" Troy pipes up from behind.

"Wish you'd stop making me out to be a scaredy-cat," I say. But to tell the truth, I don't feel so good about this long tunnel. And when we turn a curve, it's completely dark. I hear giggling from behind. It's not hard to figure out what's going on. Troy said they wanted to sit in the back so they wouldn't get sprayed with water, but I know the real reason.

The slightest noise seems ten times louder: the lap of water, the boat bumping the sides of the tunnel, crickets chirping, the sounds of bodies shifting. Bet Troy has his hand inside Dot's dress by now, because I also hear a moan or two. Wonder where Grady Fay's hands are.

Troy leans forward. "Did you know a girl was bit by a snake in here once?" he says.

I let out a squeal. What a time to tell a thing like that! "When?" I ask.

"When did it happen? Ohhh, 'bout twenty-five years ago." I can hear him chuckling. "You better protect her, Grady Fay." He takes Grady Fay's arm and puts it around me. Now all I can think about are snakes crawling over me. Suddenly I shiver.

"What's the matter?" Grady Fay says.

"Nothing." *I feel Gene's arm around me, then him gradually sliding it down. . . .* "I was just thinking about what Troy said."

"About the snake? Aw. . . ."

. . . unbuttoning my blouse and slithering inside, making my skin crawl. . . !

"Just relax," he says a second later.

. . . touching my nipples till they stand out. . . .

"Relax," he says again.

. . . taking my hand, pulling it over to his lap. . . .

"You're safe with me."

. . . rubbing it back and forth over his bulge. He unzips his fly, and his wingding pops out. . . . I shiver again, this time a big shudder, as if I've been just given an electric shock.

"I wouldn't let anything happen to you."

. . . taking my hand, he moves it up and down, up and down.

"Careful! You're rocking the boat," Grady Fay says.

Gradually the darkness gives way to outside light, and I can see Grady Fay's face again. Out of the corner of my eye, I also see Dot and Troy kissing.

When we're completely out of the tunnel, the boat stops for a second to hook onto the chain that carries us up the incline, then slowly we start to rise. On the other side, I hear squeals as people hit the water.

When we get to the top, Grady Fay reaches over and takes my hand. He must think I'm still scared. It feels sweaty and I want to pull away, but don't. I can't bring myself to move closer, though, and when the front of the boat goes up in the air and comes flying down, we're both sitting stiff as dummies, not like Dot and Troy, who are all huddled together. We hit the water with a loud wallop that shoots waves over the side, spraying our faces and clothes. I scream and a few drops of dirty water go right in my mouth.

Marvin and Tessie and Shorty are at the food stand having another hot dog as we come walking up.

"What y'all want to do now?" Dot says. Like she's our entertainment director.

Marvin waves a mustard-streaked hand toward the track of lights that follow the roller coaster. "We can't leave without riding the Cannonball."

Immediately I begin shaking my head. "Uh-uh, you're not getting me on that thing!"

"We'll put you on the merry-go-round," Shorty says.

"Hey, hey!" Dot claps her hands. "Everybody ready? Let's go."

I clasp my arms together. "I told you, I'm staying put."

"Killjoy," Tessie says, cleaning off her glasses so she can see what she's screaming about.

"I'll wait with you," Grady Fay says.

"I can't let you do that," I say, pushing him ahead. While they're gone, I intend to look around for Gene.

I watch them climb into the cars and the cars slowly disappear into a twinkling darkness that rises up as close to heaven as some of them— namely Marvin Cowan—are ever likely to get.

I stand watching for a few minutes until I realize that I'm being jabbed and shoved from all sides. Pretty soon, I stop resisting and let myself be pushed along with the crowd, further and further away from the roller coaster until the plink-plonking music of the merry-go-round grows fainter and I find myself near the arcade. I creep through the hordes of men, boys, and even a few hard-faced women who are sinking submarines, crashing cars, shooting at airplanes that explode and fall through the sky. But Gene's not among them. Then I spy a fortune machine and, pushing the nickel through the slot, take the card that drops out. DON'T DO ANYTHING DRASTIC, it advises me. Do I ever?

The exit lets me out in an unfamiliar area, and I have to get my bearings. The air is thick with voices and music.

How long it takes me to reach the roller coaster again, I have no idea, but by the time I get there, everybody's disappeared. That is, I see plenty of faces but not a single one I recognize. Surely, they haven't gone off and left me. If Marvin did that, mama'd kill him.

For awhile I lean against the ticket stand waiting for them to return. When they don't, I wander around (mostly in circles I decide when I see the ferris wheel rising before me for the sixth time. Gene always said I had no sense of direction).

Then I hear someone calling my name, although it's faint, like an underwater gargle. A few seconds later, a hand grabs my arm. Certain that I recognize the grip, I think, Well, finally! and spin around expecting to see Gene.

"Are you alright?" Grady Fay asks, releasing my arm.

"Where the hell have you been, girl?" Troy says.

Dot comes up behind him. "We were beginning to worry."

As if my disappointment wasn't enough, Marvin has to lecture me about keeping them waiting.

It's odd when we drive up to my house because the porch light's not on. Probably mama has dozed off and forgotten about it. But as I walk up the steps, a figure steps out of the shadows.

"Mama, what're you doing still up?"

"Didn't I say, be back before midnight? I been half out of my mind with worry! You never give a second's thought to anybody else."

"That's not true."

"I'll tell you one thing, you better not stay out this late again."

I can only stare at her. "What do you mean?"

"As long as you're living here, you live by my rules."

Now *I'm* getting mad. "Then I'll move. I hate it here anyway."

"You better think twice. . . "

"I've always hated it!" I say, my voice rising as I pull open the screen. "Hate it, hate it, hate it." I let it slam behind me. Though I regret the words as soon as they're out of my mouth, there's no taking them back. The naked truth catches me off-balance. I stagger into the bathroom.

My reflection in the mirror looks like something wild; my hair blown apart, my lipstick rubbed off, a little dab of ketchup in the middle of my chin. Tossing my hair, I march to my bedroom and pull the sheet up over my face in an effort to shut out the whole world.

Next morning, when the knock comes at my door, I don't answer.

"Get up," mama yells. "Bub'll be here soon."

Still, I don't let on I'm awake. I lay there, daydreaming about Gene. Finally I hear Bub honking, the screen door open and shut, a car motor rev up and fade away. Turning over, I try to go back to sleep, but can't. I wonder vaguely if Calvin'll be disappointed when I don't show up. Probably he'll just start in on Jeanette . . . already there've been signs.

I do love the quiet—not quiet exactly, because I can still hear the parakeet yapping in the kitchen, but calm.

After a while, I get out of bed and go over to the vanity table where I sit for a long time, just staring at myself, every now and then picking up the brush to see how my hair might look in a different style. I decide to try using a barrette like Jeanette does, and remembering that there's one in my jewelry box, I open the first drawer and pull out the tiny cedar chest. Inside is my entire collection: an angel pin (presented to each member of the Sunshine Choir after the big revival); a birthstone ring (now missing the stone) that I got for my birthday; a tarnished stretch bracelet that daddy brought from Detroit when he came down to Granddaddy Grubbs's funeral; a few odd ear screws; and last of all, the barrette. But it's the bracelet I take out. I sit there running my finger over the engraved initials. When daddy gave it to me, I was so tongue-tied that I couldn't think of a thing to say, not because of the gift but because he seemed to come from a different world. Then he started teasing me, asking if I still made those delicious mud pies, and I began laughing and forgot my shyness, at least enough to ask what Detroit was like. I told him I couldn't imagine living in a building with a hundred and forty other people. He mentioned my two stepbrothers and said he hoped I'd come up for a visit.

That summer he sent me a train ticket, and Grandpa Jess drove me up to the station in Chattanooga, but mama cried so much that I backed out at the last minute. To tell the truth, I was too scared anyway, without really knowing what or who I was scared of.

Sticking the jewelry back inside, I close the lid and put the chest away. But the smell of cedar remains.

By the time mama gets back, it's turned chilly and I'm huddled in front of the heater trying to keep warm. Spread out on the kitchen table is a round circle of soiled mimeograph sheets.

"Mama, how could you do this?" I ask, pointing my finger.

"Do what?"

"Use one of my fan club newsletters to line the cage."

"You were finished with it."

"No, I wasn't. I promised Dot I'd bring it in and let her read it. From now on, I'm going to keep my things in my locker over at the mill . . . "

"Go ahead."

". . . so nobody'll fool with them . . ."

"Go ahead."

". . . without my permission."

"I *said* go ahead. Just don't make a fuss about it." She takes a deep breath. "People with heart trouble . . ."

"I know what you're about to say." I put my hands over my ears.

". . . can't tolerate . . ."

"I *know.*"

". . . fuss."

Chapter Seven

SUPERDOFFER COMPETITION UNDERWAY

Competition to find Goody's Superdoffer will begin right after Christmas. Competition is being held on each shift to determine shift winners. The shift winners will then compete for the title of Goody's Superdoffer. Rules for plant competition are as follows:

1. All entrants will doff three (3) frames. Each frame will be timed separately. The winning score will be determined by the highest number of bobbins or quills per minute.
2. In the event of a tie, the doffers shall doff additional frames on a "sudden death" basis until a winner can be determined.
3. At the start, each frame will be beared down with all ends up.
4. The doff box should be pre-positioned.
5. Bobbins or quills may be pre-positioned in the doff buggy, if the doffer desires.
6. Time will begin when the doffer grasps the thread guide, to raise it.
7. Time will stop when the doffer completes a cycle of piecing up ends after starting the frame. The doffer shall signal completion by putting both hands in the air.
8. The doffer may not run.

9. Shift winners will be decided on each shift.
10. Plant winner competition will be held on the first
shift. The plant winner will receive a trophy and one
hundred dollars ($100) in cash.

Even after the announcement appears in the *News*, nobody except Mr.
Baxter seems to take it very seriously. But it does give the fellas something
to joke about.

"Better eat all that sandwich, Shorty," Boley says with a big leer.
"Gotta keep up your strength, stoke the boiler, get the fires going."

"Oh, pipe down," Shorty drawls, opening a pack of Camels.

"My God, you're not smoking!" Grabbing the pack out of his hand,
Boley tosses it to Marvin. "Don't you know it cuts down on your speed?"

"Hey, gimme that!" But Marvin holds the cigarettes out of reach.
"Cut it out, you guys!"

"We're just trying to help you win," Boley grins.

"Sure, sure. Now give it back."

But because he's far and away the favorite, Grady Fay's the butt of most
of the teasing.

"My Lord," Boley says, leaning over his shoulder at the table. "Look
at that."

"What?" Grady Fay turns around.

"Them fingers. They're a disgrace."

And in fact they are, with dirt caked around the cuticle and under
each nail. Maybe it comes from not having a mama around. Or, as mama
says, maybe it's just trashy.

"You better get yourself a manicure before this competition starts,"
Boley says with a stern look.

"But I'm a farmer . . ." Grady Fay protests.

"No, you ain't, boy, you're a doffer, and a doffer's got to have clean
fingernails. You look like you been making mud pies."

"I been putting up a fence around my pasture."

"Same difference."

Of course, whenever Mr. Baxter walks by, everybody sobers up and
speaks real serious.

"What about first shift, Boss?" Boley asks. "Think they got somebody who can beat us?"

"Let you know next week," Mr. Baxter says, taking the cigar out of
his mouth. "I got my scouts out."

"Scouts!" Boley comments later to Shorty. "Did you hear what he said?
Scouts! As if he's talking about some goddamned football league!"

64

"Yeah, and here comes Zeke Bratowski," Shorty says just as Grady Fay walks up. He's puzzled why they break out laughing.

For some reason I've been more or less avoiding Grady Fay since that trip to Lake Winnepesauka—that is, as much as two people who work on the same set of machines *can* avoid each other. There's one awkward minute when I drop a whole handful of quills and he helps me pick them up. Otherwise I move around the frame at my own pace, spotting him over here, over there. Sometimes he glances my way, but I have too many other things on my mind to take much notice. I expected Gene to call, and keep wondering why he hasn't. He sure looked pleased to see me. Like all his anger had disappeared. I think about us meeting again and going out together. Like a story from *True Confessions.* I've read some of them so many times I know 'em by heart. *Love? What had it ever meant to me? I learned its meaning that night when Gene's arms held me close and his lips found mine, whispering their need and their hunger. And I answered yes.*

When I daydream like this, though, I have to be extra careful about keeping my attention focused on the thread, and I'm actually pretty good at it. The only thing I stop for is to pick the lint out of my eyes and nose. The lint seems worse lately, don't know why. A big vacuum that we call a "suck" goes around the frame sucking in loose threads but, far as I can tell, it's not doing much good. I try to ignore the bad things, though, and not complain the way mama does. She complains about everything. I especially have to be careful now that Mr. Baxter and Mr. Fortune are coming around all the time, mostly watching Grady Fay of course, but once in a while they might just glance my way, and when they do, I'll be *ready.* When they see how steady I am—not running to the bathroom all the time the way Reba Petit does—then they'll surely give me a raise. Then finally, finally, finally, *finally,* I'll be able to move over to the Inn. When that day comes, I'm gonna sing and shout like Ettie Mae Tucker does over at the church. Hallelujah! Hallelujah!

But first there're the holidays to get through. Don't know which is worse, Thanksgiving or Christmas.

At Thanksgiving, I have the bone to contend with—the turkey breastbone that mama dries and hangs on the rim of a big jelly jar above the kitchen sink with all the other bones. Some still have dates inked on them. Isn't that weird? She started saving the bones after daddy left, probably to give the occasion some importance and to make up for the two of us staring at each other across the table. If Grandpa Jess's sober enough, he'll join us, although, in actual fact, it's better without him. Every Thanksgiving, mama vows that she's never going through the trouble of cooking a turkey again, that next year we'll eat out.

Then next year comes and we do the same thing, till now we've got twelve years full of next years, and nothing to show for it except bones. Isn't that always the way?

So on Thanksgiving, guess what? Here I am, at the same kitchen sink, washing the same two plates, two glasses, two knives and forks that I've washed before, while mama strips the breastbone of all its meat so she can clean it and put on the date.

I'm trying hard not to feel sorry for myself, though. I'm thinking of something good. I'm thinking of going down to the Coochee Theater where *Love Me Tender* is playing. I know that Dot and Troy are with her family, and Marvin is driving Miz Cowan up to Delphi, so the only choice is to call Bub, even though he charges double on holidays, and sometimes triple, depending on his mood. Mama overhears me talking to him.

"Where're you planning on going?" she asks, soon as I've hung up.

"To the picture show in Richville."

"On *Thanksgiving?*"

"It's the best time. There won't be a crowd."

"I'll be left here by myself."

I knew it would come to this, I knew it! I have to bite my tongue from saying anything other than, "You can come, too." "You might have to hold your feet up, though," I continue. "Marvin says the place has big rats running around." I figure this will do the trick, but I'm wrong.

"Oh, that's just another of Marvin's stories. Where you go, I go," she says. "Like in the Bible."

If the Bible's involved, I'm not likely to change her mind, so I just nod my head.

I try to time it so the picture's just starting as we arrive. Sure enough, when we walk in, there're the titles up on the screen. Mama wants to sit in the back so we can get out easy, and, see, I'm making a big effort to go along with everything.

I was right about the theater being pretty empty, although there're a few people scattered here and there. Down front a row of boys are chain-smoking what smells like Bull Durhams. Really stink up the place. Mama holds her nose and says that she intends to complain to the manager, but I talk her out of it.

In the middle of the picture—one of the really good parts, too, so I'm surprised that I even look around—I see a familiar figure shuffling up the aisle. It's Gene Hankins. I think he spots me, only I'm sure he won't let on with mama here. Hope she doesn't notice, or she'll get suspicious right away and think it's a set-up job.

I never would have believed that I'd have a hard time concentrating on Elvis, but the truth is, I can't keep my eyes off the back of Gene's head and that ducktail haircut he's got now. Also, mama keeps fidgeting, which doesn't help. Just before the end, she stands up.

"Come on, LaVonne, let's go."

"It's not over yet."

"Everything that's gonna be *is*. Betcha Bub's waiting."

"Just let me hear the rest of the song."

But mama starts walking out. Following her blindly, I keep turning around to see Elvis's face up in the sky, and the clouds drifting by. Also— I can't deny it—to see if Gene looks my way.

"Wasn't that sad?" I say to mama once we're outside.

But she's intent on going straight to the taxi, and nothing else. I'm trailing behind. "Come *on!*" she shouts from the front seat where Bub's already revving up the motor. "Let's go."

I crawl in the back. As Bub pulls away, I twist around, first one way, then the other, trying to spot Gene.

"What's the matter with you?" mama says. "You got worms?"

By this time, the Bull Durham boys are standing on the sidewalk. As I look out the rear window, I think I see Gene staring.

After Thanksgiving, everybody's thoughts move on to Christmas. Except mine. Somehow the Christmas spirit just passes right by me. I know it's time to be shopping, but somehow I can't make myself. Every time I go in the Store, I end up at the magazine counter instead of the other departments where I should be looking around and figuring out what to buy people. One of my biggest problems is Grady Fay, whose name I've drawn for a "Secret Santa" present. I have no idea what to get him.

One Saturday I wake up realizing that there're only a few more shopping days left. I rush through breakfast, then put on my jacket and gloves.

"Where you off to in such a hurry?" mama says. She's cleaning out Pretty Boy's cage. While she changes the paper, he sits on her shoulder pecking at her hair.

"Over to the Inn to ask Dot's advice about something."

She grunts like she does whenever Dot's name's mentioned. I think she thinks Dot's a bad influence, and if she means Dot's urging me to move out of here, she's right. "And when will you be back?"

"In time for supper."

"Wear a scarf, then. It's turned raw outside."

I'm almost through the door when her voice stops me. "By the way, somebody's been calling here and hanging up. Next time they try it, I'm going report it to the police."

"The police can't do nothing 'bout that, mama. Probably a wrong number," I say, which is like throwing a false scent before a bloodhound because I think I know who it is. Or who I *hope* it is.

The large windows at the Store are decorated with the usual empty Christmas packages and fake snow. I stop for a few minutes to look at the hardware display. There're fly rods and 22-gauge shotguns, hunting knives and tool boxes, tackle boxes and kerosene lanterns, camp stools and fishing nets, all sprinkled with glitter. Even so, they don't give me a single clue about Grady Fay.

I walk past the mill, across the foot bridge, along Broad Street, and then down the whole length of sidewalk that leads to the Inn. I pass by it all the time, but when I pause long enough to really take it in, I realize all over again what a beautiful place it is, with the red-bricked porch and big white columns. Inside, the huge lobby is filled with leather chairs and smells of the fires that burn all winter long in the big stone fireplace. Off in one corner is a seven-foot Christmas tree, its blue and green lights spaced so even that it looks like somebody measured them (maybe the high school math teacher who lives on the second floor). That person has also brushed the tip of every branch with Lux soap, and strung popcorn across one side, and hung silvery icicles all over. When I look at it, the Christmas spirit comes flowing back.

I go upstairs to find Dot, passing the first floor, which is for temporary guests, and the second, for teachers and second-hands, up to the third, for ordinary mill folks. Here the rooms are small, the paint on the walls chipped, and the floor bare of rugs. But I love what Dot has done to hers. To add to the standard bed and chest of drawers, she's bought two small shag rugs, a big money plant to go in the corner, and a desk with one of those green-shaded lamps on top. And of course there're umpteen pictures of Troy around. Best of all, she can have visitors anytime she wants, night or day, as long as they don't make too much noise.

When I knock on the door, there's no answer. Shoot! I wait a few minutes, then walk back down to the lobby where Mrs. Harris (who Dot has introduced me to several times so she ought to know my name by now) is showing one of the maids how to wax the bannister.

"Excuse me . . . have you seen Dot Ledbetter?"

Mrs. Harris glances over briefly. "She left with that boyfriend of hers . . . Roy, Foy . . . whatever his name is. Have no idea where she went except that she was dressed up for a change. That's all I know," she says, and flicks her hand as though dismissing me, the way my teachers used to when they felt they'd explained enough.

"Well, thank you."

On the way out, I pause by the tree to let the aroma of pine needles seep in. Wish I could bottle up that smell and take it home with me.

"Mama," I say later when I'm back home. "Let's get a real Christmas tree this year."

"You mean one that sheds and makes a big mess for me to clean up?"

"I'll clean."

"Hah! There's a big space between saying and doing."

On Monday I come up behind Dot as she's taking a Coca-Cola bottle out of the machine. "Where were you Saturday? I stopped by the Inn."

"Troy drove me down to Richville to have my picture taken." She giggles. "That's what he wants for Christmas. When we got to Lamb's Studio, I made him walk around the block till I was finished, otherwise there'd be no surprise to it at all."

She's not looking for agreement, but I nod anyway. Then I lower my voice to a whisper. "Dot? Don't tell anybody but I drew Grady Fay's name. What can I give him?"

I'll say one thing about Dot. When she sets her mind to thinking, nothing stops her. "My feeling is," she says after a minute or two, "it should be something but not much."

"Something but not much," I repeat out loud, then silently. *Something but not much.*

As Dot leaves, I follow her out the door. She takes my hand and we walk along together, swinging our arms. "That's the prettiest tree you have in the lobby. I'd give anything for one like it."

As usual, I put off shopping for Grady Fay's present until the day before the spinning room Christmas party. Then I spend the whole morning wandering around the Store, picking up an item here, an item there, turning it over, putting it back. "Something but not much," I keep saying to myself. I examine the sport shirts in the men's ready-to-wear, the dark ties with tiny bug-like patterns (which I can't imagine Grady Fay wearing), the felt hats that somebody's already creased; and in the drugstore, bottles of shaving creams and cologne with smells that mama says remind her of roach spray. 'Course I could always buy him a box of chocolate creams, but somehow it doesn't seem right for a girl to give a man candy.

I end up in hardware among the rubber worms, the axes and hatchets, the different-sized knives, the glue and putty and rodent killer and insecticides and fertilizers and lawn mowers, and then, at a tiny side counter containing key chains and keys, I find something small that's still *something:* a rabbit's foot. The hardware manager lets me rub it over my cheeks, and it tickles slightly. "This is it," I say, and pay for it.

The spinning room's annual Christmas spread is put together, as usual, by Mollie Sue Morton at the Café, so nobody's surprised to walk in the canteen and find on the table the same thing we had last year (and probably the year before that, although I wasn't here then). Picking up a chicken leg, Marvin bites into it and asks if it's left over from last

Christmas, a joke Mollie Sue doesn't seem to appreciate.

After we've eaten and the gifts have been handed out by Mr. Baxter, who loves playing Santa Claus, and I've done a solo of "White Christmas" (Dot says I sound better than Rosemary Clooney), and we've all sung three verses of "Silent Night," then everybody files back into work, except me and Dot, who're the clean-up committee. I've just finished washing off the tabletops when Grady Fay sticks his head in.

"LaVonne, thank you for the present."

"It was nothing. I drew your name."

"I know, but it was real thoughtful. A good luck piece for the contest."

For a moment, I'm speechless because the contest hadn't been on my mind at all, in fact I'd forgotten all about it. "You're welcome, Grady Fay. And I hope it does bring you luck."

"It will. I know it will." He looks embarrassed. "Uh . . . will you be home tomorrow before work?"

"I reckon . . ."

"Because I'm bringing you something."

"What?"

"It's a secret. Dot said you wanted one."

What do I want? To see daddy again, to see Elvis one time at least, to go out with Gene, to move over to the Inn, but outside of these, my mind's a complete blank.

So imagine my astonishment when I hear his old truck chugging up the next day, and go outside in time to see him unloading a huge Christmas tree from the back. Instead of being thrilled, though, my first thought is, Oh, my Lord, what will mama say?

But mama doesn't say anything because when Grady Fay walks in with it, she's too stricken to speak. In fact, I'm afraid she might have an attack.

"Hidee, Miz Grubbs," he says, taking off his plaid wool cap with the ear flaps when I introduce him. "Dot told me LaVonne was wishing for a real Christmas tree so I brought her one. Cut it down myself. Woods are full of 'em back of my house."

He doesn't seem to notice the stunned expression on mama's face, and while he goes back to his truck to get a saw, I reassure her that I'll clean up every bit of the mess, starting with all the needles scattered across the floor. 'Course the tree's too tall for our ceiling, so Grady Fay has to cut two feet off, and when he's finished, there's a pile of sawdust besides.

"Jesus Christ!"

The minute I hear mama taking the Lord's name in vain, I know it's serious. "It's okay, mama, do you hear me, I'll take care of everything

70

now, don't worry." I keep whispering this while Grady Fay's nailing a flat wooden stand on the bottom.

"Do you have any lights?" he asks, hoisting it upright.

The ornaments are kept in two big shopping bags in the back of the closet. The string of lights hasn't been brought out in years—maybe since daddy left—and I doubt they'll work. But a few of them do, and he winds them around the tree. Meanwhile mama disappears. I find her on the back porch fanning herself even though it's thirty degrees.

"He's ruined my Christmas," she says, her chin quivering. "Just ruined it."

What's to ruin? I almost say. "I told you, I'll clean up the mess."

But at that moment, the quarter-to-four whistle blows, and I run back into the house to warn Grady Fay in case he's too busy to listen. In the middle of a big pile of trash, the tree stands, lights blazing. He stands beside it grinning. "Looks pretty good, doesn't she?"

"Beautiful. Just beautiful." I'm grabbing my coat from the closet. Then I rush into the kitchen where mama's just come in from the back porch. "Mama, I got to go now, but leave everything . . . I'll clean it all up when I get back." My words trail off as Grady Fay pushes me out the door.

But when I return from work, the room's already been dusted, swept, and the trash put away. Next morning, mama tells me that she had to stick two nitroglycerin tablets under her tongue, she was that upset.

Hardly an hour goes by that she doesn't complain about it, until even I begin to see it as an eyesore. At first I loved the smell, but after a while this begins to grate, too—maybe because it grates on mama—and the needles that fall off are a constant nuisance, I agree, watching mama stalk it with a broom and dustpan.

How do other people manage, I wonder.

In the last few weeks, Calvin's called several rehearsals of the Sunshine Choir's special Christmas program, which I'm not able to attend because of work. I know he's given my solo to Jeanette, which seems only fair, although I do wonder if she's been putting out some special favors for him. Anyway, when I go over with mama on Christmas Eve, it's without much enthusiasm, and I feel even less after Jeanette gets up and sings "O Come All Ye Faithful" in such a rousing way that Ettie Mae starts shouting *during* the song without even waiting for Preacher Crow's sermon. This time, his words are short and sweet. He keeps repeating, "Happy birthday, Baby Jesus, happy birthday, Baby Jesus," over and over, and ends up by asking everybody to sing the happy birthday song instead of a regular carol.

On Christmas morning, mama and me sit on the sofa—as far away from the tree as possible—opening presents.

"That's for Pretty Boy," I say as mama flings aside the last piece of tissue on the package she's unwrapping. "It's a little guitar."

"Where on earth did you find it?" She holds it in front of the cage, but the bird is too busy pecking at seeds to take much notice. "Cutest thing I ever saw. Listen, Pretty Boy." Touching one of the strings, she makes it ping.

Mama gives me a new dress that she's made herself for me to wear during revival, and a set of Revlon Fire and Ice nail polish and lipstick. I give her new bedroom slippers and a tiny bottle of Tigress cologne.

Then Grandpa Jess arrives, carrying two brown paper bags that must be his idea of Christmas wrapping. "Any of them gifts for me?" he says.

When he sees the bottle-shaped package that I hold out, a grin breaks over his face. "I sure thankee. Yessir, I can sure use that."

Making a face, mama stands up. "It was LaVonne's idea, not mine. I thought it offered too much temptation."

"Why, Gussie," he says, crossing to the kitchen to fetch a glass. "Don't you know you can't tempt the devil?" Cackling to himself, he leaves us to ponder that.

By the time the last of the pine needles have been swept out—mama says they're as hard to get rid of as ticks—and the tree has finally been thrown away, the first round of the contest is announced.

"On January 29th," the *News* says, "competition will take place between members of the same shift."

"Lessie Cowan claims everybody's in for a big awakening," mama says one day while we're having dinner.

"What awakening?"

"The day of the contest."

"What're you talking about?"

"She says Marvin's been practicing."

"Practicing *what?*"

"Doffing."

"How in the world can you *practice* doffing?"

"Beats me, but apparently he's doing it." She covers her mouth with her bad hand to keep from snickering. "She says . . . he's gonna win!"

I can't help laughing, too. "Not even Mr. Baxter would take odds on Marvin."

Then I rush around, getting ready for work, and just when I'm about to dash out the door, the phone rings. I beat mama to it. "LaVonne," a voice says. Right away I know who it is. "It's me, Gene. Didn't I see you at the Coochee a while back?"

"Yeah, you did."

"Thought so. You sure took off."

"I didn't see you," I lie.

"I was there. Did you like it?"

"What do you think?"

"Bet you like anything with Elvis in it. Am I right?"

"You're not wrong," I say, giggling.

"What are you doing now?"

"Right this minute?"

"Yeah."

"I'm about to go to work."

There's some noise in the background as if somebody's scufflng. "Maybe I can figure out a way for us to see each other soon."

"Do you still have that same job up in Tennessee?"

"Naw, I quit that a while ago. Was working in McMinnville for a few months, but that didn't pan out either. I'll be in touch." Then I hear a click and he's gone.

"Who in the world was that?" mama says, all ears.

"An old friend," I say, and grab my coat before she can ask me any more questions.

The best thing about the contest is that we get to stand around drinking R.C.s and eating potato chips. 'Course we're supposed to be watching what's going on, and sometimes we do, but not like Mr. Fortune and Mr. Baxter, who act as coaches, cheering squads, and time-keepers. Mr. Fortune takes a position near the head of the frame where he holds a stop watch in one hand while the other hand waves away floating lint.

"Okay," he says, throwing down an arm after Shorty finishes his round. "Thirty-eight." Turning to Mr. Baxter, who's standing there with a pad and pencil, he says, "Did you get that down? Thirty-eight."

When it's Marvin's turn, Dot gets up to go to the bathroom.

"Aren't you going be here?" Marvin says. "To see me win?"

"If you win," she calls back, "I'll give you a fifty dollar bill."

"You ain't got no fifty dollar bill."

"No, but I'd get one up."

Marvin always works in an undershirt and as he moves along the aisle, I can see mounds of hair sticking out in back, leading clear up to his neck. Makes him look like one of those werewolves you see in movies. When he finishes the frame, Mr. Baxter frowns. "Five minutes and thirty-one seconds."

"Five minutes! That can't be right!" Marvin goes over.

Mr. Baxter shoots him a sharp look. "Are you accusing Mr. Fortune here of not timing correctly?"

"No, but maybe he lifted his finger off too soon. Nobody's perfect," Marvin mumbles.

But the next time, his score is even worse, and the last round, forget it!

"My ol' lady could do better than that," Boley says.

"Okay, Grady Fay," Mr. Baxter says. "You're up next."

Setting his Coke down on the windowsill, Grady Fay strides over to the frame as casually as if he's on his way to the drinking fountain. The only sign of nervousness is the way he rubs his palms on his pants legs, but even this is something I've seen him do dozens of times.

While he doffs, I finish my potato chips and start in on a package of Cheezits. Mr. Baxter asks for quiet during the doffing, so there's practically no conversation. Though I sit there, trying my best to look interested, it does occur to me that the whole thing's a lot of fuss over nothing. If I had a wall to lean my head against, I'd probably doze right off.

"Two minutes and forty-five seconds," Mr. Baxter announces when Grady Fay holds up his hands. "Good going, son," he says, slapping him on the back. "But you'll have to do even better against the big boys." He turns to the rest of us. "Okay, everybody, that's it. The winner . . . no surprise, I reckon . . . is Grady Fay Owens!" There's a small and scattered applause. "I thank y'all for your cooperation, and we'll keep you posted about the next round."

"Yeah, you do that," Boley mutters, yawning and rising off the floor. "Can't wait, can you?" When he nudges me, I smile and shake my head.

Chapter Eight

BUT BY THE MIDDLE OF FEBRUARY, the contest begins to get serious. It starts with Mr. Baxter tacking up a big notice on the bulletin board just outside the canteen. At the top, in black lettering, is the word "SUPERDOFFER," and under it is a picture of Superman—all bulging muscles and a big "D" on his chest—zooming into the sky holding a quill in one hand and a bobbin in the other.

"Now don't that look exactly like Grady Fay?" Marvin says, as a group of us gather round to read it.

> The first round of the world's most unusual athletic event will take place Friday morning, March 2nd, in the spinning department of the Grey Mill, as the leading doffers from each shift compete with one another for the title of SUPERDOFFER. The winner will be honored by a banquet at the Goody Café. In addition, he will receive a hundred dollars, a trophy, and the chance to compete in the regional finals.

"A hundred bucks!" Marvin says. "If I'd knowed that, I woulda tried harder."

"Oh sure," Dot says, crossing her arms and giving him one of her significant looks.

"Do we get to see the contest, Mr. Baxter?" Shorty asks.

"See it! You're the supporters. You can't have a contest without supporters. Which reminds me. I want a note sent around urging every shift to turn out."

"Hear that?" Boley says as Grady Fay walks up. "We're all your supporters. Better be nice to us."

Grady Fay squints at the sign and moans. "Ten o'clock! I miss a whole day of farming."

"But think about the prize money. You can buy a new calf for that."

"If I win."

"Of course you're gonna win." Mr. Baxter clasps his shoulder. "I'll see to that."

"I've just about had it with Mr. Baxter," I remark to mama at the dinner table a few days later. "He hangs around our section all the time now. Stands there with a stop watch checking on Grady Fay's time. And when he's busy somewhere else, he has me doing it. Then I have to catch up on my production work. It's like having two jobs."

"That's not a bit fair." Mama draws herself up the way she always does when she's indignant about something. "I think you oughta complain."

"Who would I complain *to?*"

"Well, I said all along that Grady Fay Owens was getting blowed up way past his britches."

One evening coming out of the mill, I notice a strange car parked in front, but figuring it belongs to someone on third shift, I forget about it and walk on . . . until I hear somebody calling my name. "Pssst! LaVonne! Over here!"

It's a dark night, and although the lights from the mill and the streetlamps both glare, it takes a second to recognize who the deep voice belongs to.

"Gene!"

"Yeah, it's me, baby." He leans against the car and motions for me to come closer. "Are you glad to see me?" He looks different. His hair's longer, and pompadoured on top. He's grown sideburns, too.

"It's been a long time. Thought you'd forgotten about me."

"Me, forget? Never, not if I live to be a hundred. You're my girl. I just been up in Knoxville. Working. But me and the boss had a run-in, so I quit." Taking my hand, he holds it up to his lips. "Listen, the fellows and me," he points to two other men, who I can't see too good because their faces are shadowed, "thought we might go over to Tanner's a week from Saturday night. Think you could meet us there?"

Right away my mind starts racing. "I'll . . . try."

"You gotta do better than that, baby. You gotta be there." He pulls me closer until I can feel his hot breath on my forehead. "I've missed you, baby. I've missed you real bad. I keep telling the fellas about you. I say, I got the prettiest little gal you ever saw, and I want you to meet her." He stares into my eyes, making his nostrils flare like Elvis does. In fact, either I'm crazy or he's beginning to resemble Elvis. His lips touch mine. He gives me a kiss that leaves me limp. Then he lets go. "I'm counting on it." He gets back in the car and takes off with a screech.

On the way home, I'm wondering how in the world I can get over to the skating rink without being too obvious about it. Then I remember my idea about a fan club party. All I have to do is get Dot and Tessie excited about it. Surely that won't be hard.

Next day I go up to Dot on the steps. Handing her a stick of Juicy Fruit, I unwrap another for myself. "Don't you think it's about time for the club to throw a little shindig over at the skating rink? And invite boyfriends?"

Dot chews the questions over along with the gum. "When?" she says finally.

"A week from Saturday night. Then we have time to call everybody."

"I'll see how Troy feels about it."

"If you go, he'll go."

"I said I'd see."

I have to confess, I'm a little worried about the outcome. But Dot reports to me on Monday that Troy turned thumbs up. So right away we get on the phone. Two members will be out of town, but the others accept. One person asks if it'll be okay to bring a girlfriend and I say, "You betcha. Better'n staying home by yourself." I feel good about Gene being somewhere in the background even though Dot has asked me to ride over with her and Troy.

It comes as no suprise that mama doesn't exactly approve of the idea. "Knowing that Troy Wiggins, he probably drives like a bat outta hell," she says.

"You can hardly drive like a bat outta hell in a Holsum Bread van," I tell her.

"You haven't been skating for a long time. What makes you think you can?"

I'm in no mood for mama's put-downs. "I'll get the hang of it in no time."

"You can be some kind of side-show attraction, too."

"Skating's not that hard to pick up."

"If you don't break a leg, first."

Actually the thought of breaking a leg doesn't bother me. I just pray not to make a fool of myself in front of Gene.

Tanner's Skating Rink is situated in the part of Goody known locally as Rotten Hollow. For years—that is, until the new processing plant was built over by the river—the Hollow had been used as the town dump;

but when the modernized garbage system was installed, the mayor ordered Rotten Hollow to be covered over with a thick layer of top-soil; then it was sold to Brice Tanner with the understanding that he would build some sort of recreational facility on it. Yet certain habits have a way of dying hard, and for the first few years, Brice was plagued by people continuing to throw garbage onto his property. They'd bring it in paper bags, croker sacks, lard cans, bushel baskets and toss the whole thing overboard, container and all, sending the empty cans rolling down the hill, scattering the coffee grounds, the egg shells catching on the branches of the tiny shrubs he'd planted. In exasperation, he erected an expensive metal fence running the entire length of his footage. Whenever anybody complains about the high admission charge for skating, his stock answer is that it's paying for the fence. To hear him tell it, it'll be a couple more years before he sees any profit at all.

The only way you'd know I'm nervous is to notice how I lean forward when Troy's van comes to a halt in front of the rough-boarded building covered over with tar paper. Under the TANNER'S ROLLER RINK sign is scribbled, "Kilroy Was Here." I look around for Gene, and it doesn't take me long to spot him.

Near the entrance three guys are chug-a-lugging beers. Besides Gene, there's a huge, burly fellow and a little short twerp. I go past, smiling but not daring to speak to him with all the others around. Anyway, I'm sure he'll follow me inside.

The first set has just finished, which means that the chairs and benches lining the sides are all filled up and we have to wait for a place to put on our skates. Dot's lucky. She has her own pair—shiny white with pink pom-poms at the end of the laces. I have to rent mine, but that's okay as long as I don't get athlete's foot. Dot finishes before I'm halfway done, and drifts off into Troy's outstretched arms.

I've called Brice beforehand and arranged for him to reserve a section for the fan club. I see the sign at the far end. There're already some people. He said if we had over ten, he'd also give us a discount on refreshments.

The minute I stand up, my legs threaten to shoot out from under me. I hang onto a nearby seat to get my balance, all the time waiting for Gene to appear, but he doesn't.

"Aren't you coming?" Dot yells.

"Be there in a second."

I stand watching the girls in blouses and long ballerina skirts and men in blue jeans (a few in overalls) gliding around the floor to the tune of Pat Boone singing, "Ain't That a Shame." They look so sweet together. If Gene drinks too many beers, he won't be any better at skating than I am.

"Come on," Dot yells again as she and Troy glide by. "The only way to improve is by doing."

But I'm too embarrassed.

Splitting from Troy—which must have been hard—Dot comes over. "Want some help?"

"I wouldn't mind a tiny hand. Just to get to where the club members are." Before we start off, I take one more look around.

"You expecting someone?"

"Not especially."

"Well, I am."

I stare at her. "Who?"

She gives me a sly smile. "A mystery guest."

Probably Marvin Cowan, who'll blab to mama.

"Here. Take my hand. Ease yourself up, real slow. That's it. Not so bad, is it?"

I stick out my right foot, wait for a second, then my left, right, left, right, left. "It's beginning to come back to me."

"You're doing fine . . . take it easy now . . . don't try to go too fast. . . . " Dot's using the same sing-song voice that taught me how to piece up.

When I finally get to the far end, some of the members start cheering. I thank them for coming and tell them about the discount. Lorena's brought a friend from Richville who's interested in joining, and I take down her name and address and promise to send her a membership form.

"Okay, okay, that's enough jawing," Dot says. "Everybody on their feet. The best skater gets a prize."

"That's news to me," I say.

"Don't you think I deserve something for hauling you around this rink?"

I let myself be led onto the rink again. This time I don't take my eyes off my feet. "Hunch forward," Dot says. "Pull your shoulders together." It does seem to work better.

"Try it on your own now." Just as I'm about to protest, Dot falls behind.

Approaching the curve at the end, I try to angle my skates to the left, and almost fall over. Luckily though, I'm able to catch hold of the side railing in time. I feel Dot's hand on my shoulder. "Are you alright?"

I nod, trying hard to stay upright.

"Guess who's here?" Dot says. But instead of telling me, she glides away.

Does she know about Gene? How could she, unless she's a mind reader? Carefully I push off again. Left, right, left, right. I go slowly, trying to keep time with the music.

How much is that doggie in the window?
The one with the waggly tail . . .

But then I turn too quick and lose my balance—enough to cause me to tip slightly and, waving my arms, wobble backwards, one leg swinging out. I land with a loud whack.

"LaVonne!" a voice calls. "LaVonne!" Way on the other side of the floor it sounds, but near enough to see me in the most mortifying position. And it would be just like Gene to tease me about it.

But when I glance up, the person skating toward me isn't Gene Hankins at all, but Grady Fay Owens. What's *he* doing here?

Coming closer, he puts out a hand. "Here. I'll help you up."

How can he help when he seems as awkward as me? Still, he takes my hand and manages to pull me upright. Then, with an arm around my waist, he guides me . . . or am I guiding him? It's hard to tell by the way the two of us teeter from side to side, sometimes lurching over, but always managing to right our balance at the last second. As we approach the front where the benches are, I see Gene—dressed in black as before, but with his hair and sideburns darkened and a new sultry look to his face—standing there with his two friends, watching. If a hole suddenly opened up in the floor, I'd be happy to drop through. As it is, I duck my head and skate right by him.

"Wanna rest?" Grady Fay asks.

"No! Keep going!" Maybe there's a tiny chance that Gene hasn't seen us.

We continue around the bend and start up the other side. Without realizing it, I'm skating faster and faster.

"Hey! You're doing pretty good," Grady Fay says.

I remove his arm. "Maybe I should try it on my own now."

I *am* getting better. Pretty soon, I might be able to do some fancy steps like Dot, who's over at the benches entertaining some of the fan club members by twirling around.

Then vaguely I'm aware of something else going on, some kind of disturbance near the front of the rink. But it's only when I hear Dot screaming at me from the sidelines that I realize what's happening. "LaVonne!" she shrieks. "Get off! Quick! They're playing Crack the Whip!"

Glancing toward the part of the room where Dot's pointing, I feel the same kind of panic that I've experienced only once in my life, on my first (and only) trip to Panama City, Florida, when I waded out too far and a huge wave came toward me, and daddy had to run in and pull me out! Now there's no one to help, unless I count Grady Fay, who's calling to me from behind. I barely reach the railing before the line of three skaters—with Gene leading, his pompadour leveled out and threatening to cover his eyes—speed past. But Grady Fay's not so lucky, and when the line skates by, the one on the end grabs his arm.

"No . . . no . . . !" I see him stagger as he's yanked around. "No!" he yells again, and tries to push the hand away, but the person holding him has a fierce grip.

Not wanting to be caught in a brawl, the other skaters have left the rink, giving Gene and his gang a clear field to go faster and faster. Every time Gene rounds the bend, he shoots me a sulky look. Grady Fay is all hunched over, barely moving his legs, letting himself be pulled along. Since he's on the end, I can imagine him being slammed into the wall, or into the rows of chairs with the fold-out seats that Brice purchased from the Goody Movie Theater when it went out of business a few years ago.

Feeling a hand touch mine, I turn. "Dot, I'm scared!"

"Me, too. Troy's gone to get Mr. Tanner. They're not supposed to do this. It's too dangerous."

"I wish he'd hurry." The words are barely out of my mouth before the line whizzes by again and I get a quick look at Grady Fay's face. It's deathly pale. Whenever they come to a turn, he holds his right arm over his eyes as if he's afraid to see where he might be headed. I notice that once or twice he just misses, by a couple of inches, smashing into something. Still, the line of skaters drives on. "Faster, men, faster!" I hear Gene cry. What's he trying to do?

"Sit down on your skates, Grady Fay!" Dot yells when he comes around again. And then, in a lower voice, "Why is Mr. Tanner taking so long?"

"They must be going twenty-five miles an hour," I whisper.

The people on the sidelines, including the fan club members, are now staring open-mouthed. There's no longer any talking, only the sound of wheels rumbling over the wooden floor. I see Grady Fay struggle to crouch lower, but the man next to him—who must weigh about 250 pounds—keeps pulling him back up. "No, you don't, bud," he laughs. "No, you don't!" With his free hand, Grady Fay clutches his stomach.

Suddenly I see him fall over, but the man jerks him upright. "Come on, you!" he shouts in a furious voice. "You're slowing us down!"

From his position at the head of the line, Gene glances back, smiles, and picks up speed. I'm standing there watching, unable to believe what I'm seeing. After three more turns, each one faster than the other, he yells, "Let him go now! Let him go!"

The big guy gives a shove that sends Grady Fay hurtling under the railing into a whole row of chairs. Even from that distance, I can hear the crack. "Oh my God!" I have to turn my face away. The next time I look, he's sprawled, face down. There's a gasp in the crowd, and several people rush over.

The first one to reach him is Troy, who comes running out of the office with Mr. Tanner right behind him. He turns Grady Fay over. By the time me and Dot get there, Troy has a handkerchief out, trying to stop the flow of blood that spurts from Grady Fay's forehead.

"Here's a clean kleenex," Dot says, holding it out, but Troy shakes his head.

"Need more than that," he says.

"I'll get bandages," Mr. Tanner says, and disappears.

In a few seconds, he's back carrying a first-aid box that he passes on to Troy. Then, with a determined look on his face, he walks toward the other end of the rink where the line of skaters is still speeding.

"Hey!" Mr. Tanner calls, waving his arms. "Get off there!" But they keep going around as if they haven't heard one word. "If you're not off in one minute," he yells louder, cupping his hand to his mouth, "I'm gonna call the police!"

That does it. The line begins to slow down, then break up.

"Me and the boys were just having a little fun, Mr. Tanner," Gene says, grinning at me. He skates toward him and wheels to a stop.

"Fun, hell! Not on my floor, you ain't!" he points to the spot where Grady Fay is sprawled out. "Look what you done!"

Gene glances over. "Aw." Putting his hands on his hips, he toes the floor. "We didn't mean nothing by it." He catches my eye in a blazing stare. Mr. Tanner turns around to see who he's looking at. I bend over and fiddle with my skates.

"We were just providing a little extra entertainment."

"If I'd wanted them to have *extra,* I'da provided it myself. Now you all," he glares at each of them in turn, "get your skates off in a hurry and vamoose outta here. I don't wanna see none of your ugly mugs for at least a month. Try, and you'll be stopped at the door. Is that clear?"

I see Gene nod, and go off mumbling to the others. I can tell his pride's been hurt, just like it was in high school. He takes things real hard. I'm torn between running after him, and going over to Grady Fay. But Dot's looking at me, so I walk over.

Troy's daubing at the gash with cotton soaked in alcohol, and Grady Fay winces. Then Troy stops and lifts Grady Fay's head while he vomits into one of the folding chairs. (Some of the fan club members, who'd been so interested in seeing the blood gush, now turn away in disgust.) Afterwards Grady Fay accidentally tips the seat up so that everything drips right onto the floor. Me and Dot run into the office for towels, which Mr. Tanner hands us, probably hoping that we'll clean it up.

Actually it's Dot who does most of it because, after wiping a little bit, I'm afraid I might be sick myself. "Oh, this is *nothing,"* Dot says, casually swabbing down the arms and legs of the chair as well as the seat. "Once I had two of my older brothers puking at the same time in different corners of the house. *That* was really a mess." Nodding toward the refreshment counter, she says to me, "Why don't you go get him a Co'-Cola, maybe it'll help settle his stomach."

I should've taken time to take off my skates, so that I wouldn't lose half the Coke on the way back. But Grady Fay seems to be thankful for what he gets, and while he sips it, Troy finishes putting on the bandage.

"That's good," Grady Fay says, as the last piece of tape is stuck on. "I feel better." But when he starts to lift himself up, he cries out and clutches his arm.

"What is it?" Troy asks.

"Feels like my shoulder." His face is all scrunched up. He must surely be in a lot of pain to look that bad.

Mr. Tanner catches hold of his waist. "Steady, son. We're going to get you to the hospital and let them x-ray you."

"Don't need no x-ray," Grady Fay mutters through clenched teeth. "Just wanna go home."

"Well, we have to check it out first. I don't want no lawsuit on my hands." He turns to Troy. "I'll drive him over, and you follow. You'll have to take him home. He can't drive himself."

"Tell you what." Sticking his hand in his back pocket, Troy turns. "I'll drive his truck and, Dot . . . " he holds out the keys, " . . . you take the van. I'll pick it up in the morning."

"Okay. Come on," Mr. Tanner orders, barely giving us a chance to put on our shoes before he's hustling us all out. Some of the club members have already left and I say goodbye to the rest. I'd like to tell them that we're having another meeting soon, but somehow it doesn't seem appropriate. By the time I've finished, Grady Fay, looking pale and like he's about to faint, is being helped into the car, and as soon as he's settled, Mr. Tanner backs out. I look the other way while Dot and Troy have their goodnight kiss—more like a peck from the sound of it—then Troy climbs into Grady Fay's old truck and takes off.

"Well," Dot sighs, "that leaves you and me. You ready?"

"I reckon. Sure don't want to do any more skating."

"Tell you the truth, I never seen nothing like tonight. By the way," she glances over, "did you know those boys? One of 'em kept giving you the eye."

"No." I'm glad it's dark so Dot can't see my face.

We drive along in silence, not speaking until we reach Chimney Road and pull up in front of the house. "Hope Grady Fay'll be alright," she says.

I let a few seconds pass before I answer. "I'm sure he will be. Let's look on the bright side. It coulda been worse." There's a long silence. "Also, he coulda resisted a little more."

"*Resisted!*" Dot looks at me like I'm crazy. "With that hulk holding onto him? It was three against one!" Again, there's silence. Finally Dot says, "Well, keep your fingers crossed."

That seems my cue to get out, and I do.

But Grady Fay's *not* alright. At eight o'clock the next morning, the phone rings. It's Dot. She tells me the whole story, most of it second-hand from Troy. Turns out, Grady Fay's shoulder was broke bad in several places. At the hospital, he was taken upstairs and a cast was put on that covers him from neck to fingertips. He also had a tiny fracture of the skull. "Hairline," Dr. Henderson called it, and made him stay there overnight, until he stopped feeling dizzy. Dot says Mr. Baxter's beside himself.

"He went to the hospital, too?"

"Yeah, and so did Mr. Fortune, soon as he heard about it. Mr. Baxter says that does it for the contest." There's a pause. "He asked me what happened."

"What did you answer?"

"I told him all I know. Not much." Another pause. This one feels like a long finger poking me. "Why did those guys pick on Grady Fay?"

I draw in a breath and hold it. "Have no idea," I say, but so soft my lips barely move.

"Mr. Baxter says he might investigate."

"Investigate what?"

"He says some other mill might've been trying to sabotage our chances."

"That's crazy."

"You know Mr. Baxter."

Maybe I do, and maybe I don't, but I know one thing. When the phone rings a little later, I wait a while about answering. When I finally do, whoever it is has already hung up. I'm pretty sure it must have been Gene. I feel like a whole bundle of confusions.

Though I don't see a way of getting out of going over to Snuffy with mama, my mind's not on singing, and certainly not on the sermon.

"What's the matter with you?" Calvin keeps asking. He wants me and Jeanette and Bobby Echols to hang around after church for quartet practice. We're calling ourselves the Sunshine Quartet, from the Sunshine Choir. "We haven't got much time to get in shape," he says. "Revival's only three weeks off. . . . LaVonne, are you listening?"

"LaVonne must be in love," Jeanette laughs.

Calvin gives me a quick glance. I wish she'd quit teasing me. "Oh, y'all hush!"

"Okay, let's get down to business," Calvin says.

He's so serious that I feel like I must have dreamed what'd happened before. Only when I'm leaving does he sneak in a tiny pinch. That brings me back. Black is black, white is white, and Calvin is Calvin. I'm sure he does the same thing to Jeanette, because all of a sudden she starts giggling for no reason.

In the mill on Monday, the mood is doom and gloom. Everybody seems to be affected by it, from Mr. Baxter on down. Even the lint's worse than usual. I keep glancing over at the Elvis poster. Usually it makes me feel better, but now it's the other way around. I'm worried that somebody might find out the connection between me and Gene, tell Mr. Baxter, and then he'll fire me. Dot is the only one who could possibly suspect. If she keeps her mouth shut, everything's alright. When she comes around collecting money to send Grady Fay a potted plant, I stick in three dollars.

"Overdoing it, ain'tcha?" she says sarcastically.

I don't answer. Figure the best thing to do is mind my own business, keep an eye on the thread as it comes off the rollers like water trickling down.

Marvin's the only one smiling, because he's been taken off sweeping and put on Grady Fay's job. He's much slower, and sometimes I have to give him a hand, just so I won't fall behind in piecing up. Every time Mr. Baxter comes my way, I think, "Uh oh! This is it!" I'm living on borrowed time.

Shorty's picked to take Grady Fay's place in the doffing contest, though everybody knows he doesn't stand a chance. Ray Shoals from first shift is pretty good, so nobody's surprised when he wins. Hardly anybody from second shift attends the match, except a few of us out of sheer loyalty. Mr. Baxter says he doesn't blame them. He says that when Grady Fay's shoulder got smashed, his own enthusiasm just went right out the window.

"There's always next year," I say, trying to add an upbeat note to all the sourness.

"Next year! Huh!" Mr. Baxter frowns. "We don't know whether that boy will *ever* be able to doff again, much less win a contest."

The thought of this turns us all speechless, including me. Heads down, we walk back to our machines like people at a funeral. On the way, I glance over at Dot, but she won't look at me.

Chapter Nine

DURING THE BIG WINTER REVIVAL MEETING, preached by the Reverend Buddy Shields of the Delphi Church of God, mama goes to Snuffy every evening. On Saturday, the final night, the Sunshine Quartet's scheduled to sing. I'm a little nervous about it. It's like a premiere, I tell her, remembering how the *Elvis Presley Newsletter* described the opening of his second film, *Lovin' You*. There'd been spotlights and long Cadillac limousines and hundreds of fans all crowding in on him so he had to have a police guard. I don't crave that part, but I sure wouldn't mind being escorted over to the church in something besides Bub's taxi. Bub lets us out at Grandpa Jess's so mama can make sure we have a ride home.

But we have to hunt Grandpa Jess down. I finally spy him out back by the pig pen slopping the hogs. The second he walks in the back door, still carrying the dirty old bucket scummed with suet, we can smell the liquor on his breath.

"Papa, you promised!" mama says, her face tightening.

"What?" he mumbles, shifting his eyes away. "Now what's wrong?"

"I asked you to go easy on that stuff so you could drive us back. Remember I told you that Bub has to take somebody to Chattanooga tonight. And here you are, reeking of it already."

"*Reeking!*" Grandpa Jess sets the bucket down with a bang. "Don't know how I could be *reeking* when I had just enough to keep my blood from freezing up, and that's all." He blows on his hands. "Mighty cold out there." Picking up the bucket again, he moves past her to the sink, fills it with warm water, swishes it around, takes it to the back door, and pours it out. Clouds of steam rise from the ground. "When d'ya wanna be picked up?"

"Ten-thirty," mama says. "And don't be late."

At the church, lights are blazing. Preacher Crow stands outside in a light tan jacket welcoming everybody. When mama asks if he's not cold, he replies that he trusts in the Lord to keep him warm, and so far the Lord hasn't let him down.

When I enter the side door, I find Calvin Toombs pacing up and down with Jeanette and Pearlie B. both doing their level best to calm him.

"What's happened, for heaven's sakes?"

It's Pearlie B. who answers. "Bobby Echols has the flu . . . so it'll be the Sunshine *Trio*."

"What're we gonna *do?*" Calvin stops pacing long enough to hold his head and groan.

"Why don't you carry the bass part?" Pearlie B. says.

"Me? I'm the lead."

"Let LaVonne sing lead."

"No, uh-huh," I protest. "I'd be too nervous."

"She would." Calvin nods. "You know how she gets, singing a solo with the choir. It'd be worse with the trio."

"Well, it's the only choice I see," Pearlie B. says. "Unless of course you cancel the whole thing."

"We can't do that. It's in the church bulletin." Calvin thinks a minute. "Well . . . maybe LaVonne leading *is* the answer. Just this once. Think you can manage it, LaVonne?"

It's the *manage* it that does it. Of course I can *manage* it! Haven't I always *managed* it? It's only later I confess to Pearlie B. in an undertone that I'm afraid of forgetting the words.

"We can do something about that," she says.

"What?"

Instead of answering, she claps her hands as if she's making an announcement. "Okay, everybody! We're going to work out some motions to the song, like they do on television. Won't take long . . . "

"We got ten minutes," Calvin says, looking at his watch.

"Ten minutes is enough. Now, watch me." She holds an imaginary phone to her ear. "Telephone to glory . . . " When she lifts her arms to the ceiling, she signals for the rest of us to do the same. "O, what joy divine! . . . " Then she cups her ear as if listening hard to something. "I can hear Central . . . " She stops, perplexed. "I don't know what to do with the next line."

"I got it!" Calvin cries, inclining his head and sticking out his tongue like a man hanging from the end of a rope.

"Uh-uh." Pearlie B. shakes her head. "We're talking about a *phone* hanging . . . maybe we should just repeat the first motion."

I tell her I hope these won't distract people from the song itself because it's one of my favorites. Makes me think of Willie Ruth Teems sitting in front of the switchboard at the telephone office, plugging everybody in Goody up to God.

"If you get stuck," Pearlie B. turns to me, "just look around and see what the others are doing."

After a prayer and a suitable introduction by Preacher Crow—which is to say, he claims we need no introduction ("True, true," mutters Calvin under his breath)—Pearlie B. sits down at the piano and starts the lead-in while the three of us take our places in front of the altar. Pearlie B.'s fondness for extra trills *almost* causes me to jump in at the wrong place, in fact I've already opened my mouth when Pearlie B., realizing what she's done, saves the situation by jumping to a higher key, trilling around some more, and then coming back once again to the lower key, this time nodding.

I can barely manage to keep my voice from trembling. Behind me, I hear Calvin striving for the bass notes that Bobby Echols has no trouble at all grabbing hold of. I have to say that the motions and the words seem a *little* at odds with each other, though by the way the Reverend Buddy Shields smiles at us afterwards, I assume it's gone okay. Only later, during the sermon, do I realize that he *always* smiles, probably due to the false teeth bracing out his lips on each side. He'd been a pilot in World War II, he says, which accounts for the title of his sermon, "Let God Be Your Radar." He talks about how radar saved his life and compares it to love. But not the kind found in *True Confessions*. This is the "do unto others as you'd have them do unto you" variety. As I listen, the knot that's been in my stomach ever since the accident begins to tighten up again. It doesn't help that, only yesterday, I received an unsigned note from Gene saying that "after the ruckus dies down, we'll get together. When I want something bad enough, I can be real patient." And there was a P.S. "I may be going to Cincinnati next week. But don't worry. I'll be back."

Following the sermon, I grab Preacher Crow's sleeve. "Can I talk to you alone?"

Nodding, he follows me over to a corner. "What if, without meaning to, you'd caused somebody to get hurt?"

"Then I'd make amends."

"How?"

He looks thoughtful. "By showing I cared."

"It'd be okay then?"

"It'd help."

89

The first thing I do at work on Monday is walk up to Dot with a suggestion. "Why don't we visit Grady Fay sometime soon? Take him something."

"That's a good idea. I could make fudge."

"And I'd make a pineapple pudding."

"Troy says my fudge is out of this world."

"Would he drive us over?"

"Bet he would."

"Tell him we want to do some cheering up."

"Troy thinks it should be sooner rather than later," Dot says the next day. "He says Grady Fay's spirits are real low."

"How about this Saturday?"

"That's what Troy suggested. This Saturday."

"You're gonna make fudge?"

"Yep."

"Then I'll make a banana pudding."

"Thought you said pineapple."

"Or maybe a cobbler pie. Mama's got some canned peaches."

"I bet Grady Fay's the kind who would love a good apple pie."

"I don't know how to make apple."

"Oh, well," Dot says, throwing up her hands. "Then make a pudding."

I squat beside mama, who's coaxing the parakeet onto her finger. "Will you show me how to make an apple pie?"

"Shhh. This is Pretty Boy's training hour."

"You're wasting your time. That bird's never going to talk."

"Oh, ess he will, won't he, sweetie?" Then, in a clearer tone, she says, "Hello there, hello there, hello there," and stops and waits. But the bird merely stares at her. Then she tries, "I'm a Pretty Boy, I'm a Pretty Boy, I'm a Pretty Boy," repeating it until I think I might be sick.

Turning away, I open the drawer near the sink and take out the old cookbooks and recipes—some yellowed with age—that mama's cut from newspapers over the years. "Don't you have one for apple pie?" I ask, interrupting the sing-song.

"I'm sure I do," mama says, holding the parakeet in one hand and rubbing its head with the other. "What do you want it for?"

"Dot and Troy and me are going over to Sawmill Mountain to visit Grady Fay Owens, who's been laid up. Wanna take him a pie."

"What about lemon icebox?" mama says. "It's easier." At first I make a face, then think it over. True. It *is* easier. "Besides," mama continues. "I wouldn't waste good cooking apples."

Since Saturday afternoon threatens rain, Troy suggests we get an early start. By nine-thirty we're already pulling onto the highway. It's at least an hour's drive, the last part of it over a dirt road packed hard with frost and filled with icy ruts. In several places, the van skids over to the shoulder so that Troy has to grasp the steering wheel with both hands and hold on tight. Once we've crossed Armuchee Pass, the road changes to a tar surface and we're able to make better time. At the top of the ridge, we come to a crossroads where several signs point in different directions.

"It's not far now," Troy says.

I stare out the window at fields that look as bleak and gray as the sky above, and wonder how Grady Fay can stand to live in such a place. There're very few houses, only now and then a barn stuck off the side of the road with a few bony cows wandering around.

Further on, Troy puts on his signal and swerves right into a narrow lane that winds down to a tiny house and, off in the distance, a broken-down barn.

"Well, here we are," Troy says, turning off the motor.

"*This?*"

"Yep."

Holding on to the pie plate, I climb out, Dot behind me.

Troy leads the way to the house. "Watch it," he says. "Couple of these steps are rotten." There's not room enough for all three of us on the small porch, so while Troy knocks at the door, I wait in the yard.

"Come on," Troy gestures.

"Is he there?" Dot says.

"Where else would he be?"

Troy opens the door and we troop in, one behind the other.

The inside of the house is so dark that it takes a minute to make out Grady Fay lying on the sofa, his feet hanging over the edge, reading a newspaper. He's wearing an old flannel bathrobe, brown shorts, and gray socks. The cast shines in the half-light and looks enormous.

"Oh." Lowering the paper, he blinks at us. "If I'da known y'all were coming, I woulda got dressed. I better change." He starts to get up, but Troy pushes him back down.

"No, no, buddy. Stay right where you are."

"We don't plan to be long," Dot explains.

I nod, unable to bring myself to say anything. There's a musty odor in the room that I can't quite identify.

"Sit down." Grady Fay points to two straight chairs on either side of the heater. Dot and me sit, balancing plates on our laps. Troy leans against the wall.

"We just wanted to see how you're feeling," Dot says.

"I'm okay. Be glad to get back to work, though." There's a silence. "Get fed up with doing nothing." We all nod. When he turns toward the light, I can see the bandage on his forehead. Putting a hand in his bathrobe pocket, he scrunches around. "See what I got here?" He holds the rabbit's foot in my direction. "The good luck piece. Keep it with me all the time." When I look closer, I can see the trace of his blood on the fur and for a second, I'm afraid I might be sick. It's Dot that picks up the slack in conversation.

"Me and LaVonne . . . brought you a little something. Didn't we, LaVonne?"

"Uh-huh."

"That's real nice. My daddy's been doing all the cooking. I'm ready for a change." He smiles and I try to smile back.

"Where is your dad?" Troy asks.

"He went to Delphi to buy feed." With his free hand, Grady Fay twirls the sash on his robe.

Dot shifts in her chair. "Do you think you'll be back to work soon?"

"Well. I'm supposed to see Dr. Henderson on Tuesday. Hoping he'll take this off," he says, thumping the cast. There's a long silence. For the first time he looks at me directly. "How's everything going in filling?"

"Okay." I don't know whether to mention the contest or not.

"Ray Shoals is going down to Augusta in two weeks," Dot pipes up. "You know he won't win."

"He might," Grady Fay says. "Never can tell."

Again, silence. I twist around trying to make myself more comfortable, and catch the pie just before it falls off my knees.

"You can take that in the kitchen," Grady Fay says. "Uh . . . don't know what kinda shape it's in. My dad's not much of a housekeeper."

Dot and me step into a mess that makes Grandpa Jess's kitchen seem spotless by comparison. Beside the door is a slop bucket that looks like it hasn't been emptied in days. Shoving over some dirty cups, we set the plates down on the table.

"Sure could use a woman's touch, couldn't it?" Dot murmurs.

Soon as I see Dot jiggling her knees up and down in the chair, I know that she's ready to go. I've been ready ever since I got here.

"Well," I say, rising.

Grady Fay looks at me. "What's your hurry?"

"It's Saturday," Dot reminds him. "We got chores to do. Now you stay right there. We'll let ourselves out."

The three of us start toward the door.

"Say hello to everybody," he calls out.

"We'll do that," Dot says.

"Tell Mr. Baxter I'll be back in top form."

"Sure."

"And when you get outside," he directs this toward me, "take a good look around. It's all my land."

"See ya, buddy." Troy waves.

Once inside the van, nobody says anything, not until we're starting down the mountain, and Dot sighs. "Glad we come, aren't you?"

I nod, though without much enthusiasm. I've got a splitting headache, which bumping around in the van doesn't help.

By the time I get home, it's worse. So, without stopping to talk to mama, I go straight back to the kitchen, swallow a whole package of B.C. powders with part of a Coke, then go into my bedroom where I lie down and shut my eyes.

A newsletter from the National Elvis Presley Fan Club arrived this morning, but I haven't had time to look at it. After awhile, when the throbbing eases up, I pick it up and begin to scan it. On the front page is a photograph of the two-story mansion that Elvis just bought. He calls it Graceland. With the white columns, it looks like something Scarlett O'Hara might step out of. Or into.

Stepping into is what I see myself doing. *Shaking hands with Miz Presley. Who's so natural. A homebody in every way. Pointing out all the things for me to see. Statues and cabinets filled with stuffed animals, playing cards, gum, ornaments. So much glitter and shine. A hundred mirrors reflecting other mirrors reflecting . . . makes me dizzy to think of it.*

"Call me Gladys," Miz Presley says, opening closet doors so I can peer inside at Elvis's things: monogrammed shirts, suits shimmering with gold threads, silk scarves in red, black, green, purple; pants with creases sharp as knife blades. And the jewelry boxes stacked on the dresser with huge diamond and gold rings spilling out, the stones as shiny as the wings of green flies.

It's a temptation to touch something, to run my hand over the soft suede, the shiny gold, the grainy leather. And I do brush my fingers—as if by accident—across the front of his black motorcycle jacket with the stars and red stones and zipper like a long silver scar.

Then mama sticks her head in the door . . . without knocking as usual. "You must be feeling better," she says.

"Why?"

"You're smiling. Which you sure weren't doing when you walked in here."

"I had a headache."

"How's it now?"

"Gone mostly."

Then her eye catches the newsletter. "What's that picture?" She picks it up.

"The fancy place Elvis just moved into." She holds it out from her eyes so she can see it better. "Doesn't it remind you of the Inn?"

"Can't say it does."

"With the fancy columns and all?"

"Nope."

"Anyway. . . . " Buttoning my lip to further talk, I snatch it from her and lay it aside.

Chapter Ten

I'M CERTAIN THAT WHEN GRADY FAY RETURNS, everything'll be okay. Yessir, when I see him lift his arms and pull off quills with those big hands of his, my secret guilt will vanish away.

Shoulda known better. Shoulda known that things don't spin up and down without sometimes breaking, that once a thread drops, it's hard to pick up again. And Grady Fay shoulda known it, too. His arm will only go so high, as if the bone's stuck in that position. He has to doff with one hand, which cuts his production in half.

Seeing the trouble he's in and remembering Preacher Crow's words, I try to console him. "It'll just take a little time," I say.

Sometimes he gets so impatient that, unlike his usual calm self, he beats his good fist on the side of the frame.

"Where's Grady Fay?" Boley asks one evening in the canteen.

"Working," I tell him. "Trying to catch up."

"Maybe I'll be back doffing before long," Marvin grins.

I give him a hard look.

"Hope that accident didn't do nothing to him," Boley murmurs.

I put down my ham sandwich. "Whatta you mean?"

"They say when there's any kind of split in the skull, the brain's liable to ooze out."

"Is that true?"

"Would I lie to you?"

Mr. Baxter's concerned, too, and so's Mr. Fortune. I know because I hear them talking about it one afternoon in Mr. Baxter's office. I've gone over to ask about Boley or somebody examining one of the rollers on Number 6 frame, but when I see the two of them involved in what looks to be a serious conversation, I stop at the door and stand to one side.

"I spoke to Doc Henderson," Mr. Baxter's saying. "He gave me the name of a bone specialist in Chattanooga."

"Can you make an appointment and take him up there?" Mr. Fortune asks. "I'll foot the bill."

"Sure, sure." Mr. Baxter pulls out two cigars and offers one to Mr. Fortune, who shakes his head. "What if he says there's nothing to be done?"

"Then we've just lost the best chance we ever had," Mr. Fortune says and walks out. If he notices me standing there listening, he doesn't let on.

I wait a minute before going in . . . maybe more than a minute because by the time I do, the room's already filled with smoke. One of these days, Mr. Baxter'll asphyxiate himself, and maybe the rest of us along with him.

He stands with his back to me, looking out the window, which, dirty as it is, offers a good view of the Store, the plaza, and the glove mill. Something tells me not to interrupt whatever it is he's thinking about, so I tiptoe back out and for the rest of the evening, put up with rollers that are slightly wobbly.

Nobody tells me, or anybody else for that matter, why both Grady Fay and Mr. Baxter should both be absent two days in a row. Of course I know, but don't let on. It also comes as no surprise that Marvin takes Grady Fay's place, Spud Bankey comes in to act as supervisor, and Shorty's temporarily promoted to second-hand to assist Spud.

"Hey!" Boley calls out once the announcement's been posted. "Shorty's gonna shut down the machines and give us a holiday. Right, Shorty?"

"Wrong," Shorty shouts back. "I'm padlocking the door to the canteen and putting up a no smoking sign in the hallways."

"Hell, Shorty, I thought you was one of us."

"I am. That's how come I know what you're up to."

During these two evenings, Marvin keeps asking me if I think he's getting faster. "I mean in comparison with you know who," he adds.

"Who?" I have no intention of giving him an inch.

"The Superdoffer. Who ain't so *super* anymore." He tries to put an arm around me, but I jerk away. "Maybe you better get used to working with me. I know somebody who'd be real pleased about that." And he winks.

I don't know whether he *does* know something, or whether it's more Marvin Cowan hooey.

When Grady Fay returns, it's like he's brought a swarm of bees with him, because a lot of activity gets stirred up. It starts with Mr. Baxter announcing that Grady Fay has to take therapy. I don't know what that is, but he explains it's an exercise routine to get broken bones back in good running order.

Then he pulls Boley Westbrooks off the floor, and sets him up over in the corner near Number 10 with all his tools and a weird collection of parts, including a metal rowboat that Boley takes apart with a blowtorch.

Instead of flying off to the canteen at every opportunity, folks get into the habit of strolling over to see what shape "The Machine" is taking. Mr. Baxter drops by, too, to blow out great clouds of smoke and declare Boley a "mechanical genius."

The only one who doesn't pay much attention to it all is Grady Fay. He goes on about his business of one-handed doffing. I try to help him as much as I can by pushing the quill buggy closer to his side, and picking up a quill when he drops it. Every once in awhile, he turns away from the frames for a few minutes, picks up a long steel ruler and, using both hands, tries to hoist it up as high as possible. Right now, he can't get much further than his waist, and he makes a tiny pencil mark on the wall at exactly that level.

"What's that for?" I ask. This is after Mr. Baxter's handed me a stop watch, and asked me to see that Grady Fay stays at it for at least five minutes.

"That's the bottom line," Grady Fay answers, gritting his teeth and trying to push his arm higher. I hate watching because I can tell how much it hurts.

"You look like *you're* the one in pain," Reba Petit says when she saunters by. And for once, Reba's right. I have the odd feeling that I've taken on some of Grady Fay's injury because when he talks about pins shooting through his arm, I can actually feel them.

"It's called sympathetic response," Dot says when I tell her about it. "I get the same thing with Troy."

When Boley's finished with "The Machine," Mr. Baxter invites everybody in the department to come over for a free Coke or R.C. and see it in action.

"We have to give it a proper launching," he says, grabbing a bottle that hasn't been opened and holding it up.

"Thought that was a gal's job," Shorty says, and immediately Mr. Baxter passes the bottle on to me, and asks me to do the honors.

"What honors?"

"Smash it over the end of the machine. Don't you go to movies?"

Of course I do, but any resemblance between this weird contraption and a real ship is purely coincidental. Anyway, covering my eyes with my free arm so I don't get any flying glass in them, I let 'er rip. When the neck finally breaks, everybody claps, except Marvin, who has to do the sweeping and mopping up.

Mr. Baxter rubs his hands together. "Let's have Grady Fay try it out now."

After Grady Fay settles himself down in it, he takes hold of the poles on each side and strains to pull them back. Back and forth he goes. Dot starts singing, "Row, row, row your boat . . . " and pretty soon, everybody joins in.

"Aw," Grady Fay stops suddenly, hanging his head in embarrassment.

"Boley put on an instrument gauge," Mr. Baxter points out, "to total up mileage."

"Go ahead," Dot calls out. "Let's see how far you can go in that thing. Pretend you're on the Coochee River rowing from town to town. Six miles to Richville, twelve miles to Delphi."

"Shorty, I want you to tack a mileage sheet on the wall," Mr. Baxter says. "Then we can keep track. And LaVonne, I'm putting you in charge of the operation."

"Me?" I'm having mixed feelings about all this.

"Yep. It's your job to see that Grady Fay does these exercises at least three times a day. I'm borrowing some weights for him, too. You'll keep a weekly chart and give it to me on Friday, okay?"

"But what about production?"

"This *is* production," he says, and walks off with Shorty right behind him.

Grady Fay climbs out of the machine and shakes himself while Boley kneels to adjust one of the "oars."

"You gonna patent this?" Dot asks Boley.

Boley says he might. Which causes Marvin to mumble that "you can't patent a piece of shit."

During the next few weeks, I begin to feel like Grady Fay's trainer. I even throw him a towel when the sweat starts rolling into his eyes. It's like doing two jobs, and if I didn't feel so bad about the accident, I'd complain long and hard to Mr. Baxter. As it is, I keep my mouth shut (even to mama because I know what *she'll* say) and go on badgering Grady Fay to work harder, making him stick to it as long as possible, afterwards toting up the numbers. They're climbing higher and higher. The main test is Grady Fay's arm, which, thank God, is climbing too. His progress excites Mr. Baxter, and he pats me on the shoulder.

By mid-April, Grady Fay can lift his arm level with the spindles, which means he can start doffing with it, although at first it's slow going. Every evening, I follow the same routine: checking on his speed with a stop watch, then timing him while he raises Marvin's broom about twenty times in the air. Last comes the rowing.

"You got a good regimen going, LaVonne," Mr. Baxter says when he drops by.

By the end of May, Grady Fay's doffing has improved so much, Mr. Fortune comes over to witness it. Amazed, he follows Grady Fay around the frame three times, then stops to shake his hand.

"You should shake LaVonne's, too," Mr. Baxter interrupts. "She played a big part in it."

Mr. Fortune squeezes my palm so hard that his gratitude seems to seep through my skin. "If Grady Fay wins this contest, there'll be a big bonus in it for you," he whispers. "Just keep that in mind."

A big bonus! Spurred on to work harder, I push Gene out of my thoughts entirely. Not Elvis though. His songs set the rhythm of my piecing up.

"Is it going to be 'Don't Be Cruel' or 'Teddy Bear' today?" Grady Fay teases.

Three Elvis songs are at the very top of the chart. His star is getting so big that it's in danger of flying right out of my orbit. Pretty soon I won't even be able to daydream about him anymore.

Both newspapers and almanacs are predicting that the summer of '57 will be one of the hottest on record. From the way it feels already—and it not even June—I'm thinking they may be right. My whole upper body has a tickling sensation from perspiration drops rolling down and bunching at my waist in one big sweat band. For this reason, I stop wearing a belt and choose my loosest dresses to work in. Folks seem unable to talk about anything but the heat.

"'Nother scorcher today, ain't it?" Marvin says in the canteen, wiping his brow.

"Yep," Tessie says. "They say tomorrow's gonna be worse."

"No!"

"What they say."

Or, "Hey, Boley, is it hot enough for ya?"

"It's drying me out. My insides are rattling around like butterbeans."

"That's just your brain y'hear."

Or—this from Dot—"If I sweat much more, ain't gonna be nothing left of me but a pinch of salt."

As always in hot weather, my appetite goes, and when I sit down at the table, I'm only able to eat a few small bites.

"Eat up now," mama says, laying out piles of meatloaf, mashed potatoes, fried okra, tomatoes, and cantaloupe.

And I do try, really *try,* taking a bite of this, a bite of that, before setting down my fork. "Mama, it's too *warm* for hot food!" I complain when she urges me on to more helpings.

"That's exactly when you need it most."

"What? *Why?*"

"Because it gets the boiler going so you can perspire. Keeping all the sweat inside is what causes the trouble. Same as wearing a black cloth over your head."

"I don't understand."

"It's not a question of *understanding.* Just take my word for it."

After dinner, she moves the parakeet out to the porch where it's cooler. Then she hauls out a chair for herself from the living room and sits there trying to teach it to talk. If I drag out a chair, too, or make any noise at all, mama hushes me. Sometimes I get up in a huff and go over to the Inn to visit Dot. Other times I just sit, wondering how mama can be so stupid.

Then one day toward the end of the summer, it happens. By mama's reaction, you'd think the heavens'd opened up and fourteen angels had floated through.

Mama's just called me into the kitchen. "Everything's on the table," she says. "Sit down and start buttering your cornbread." She pulls out a chair herself. "Nothing in this world worse than lukewarm cornbread." Then she passes the pinto beans, straight from the stove and bubbling still, and the potatoes, barely browned and shaped like tiny bridges with scads of grease dripping off the ends.

"Eat up now," mama says.

But I can only pick around, dabbing my fork in and spearing a bean or two, then sticking it into my mouth and going back for two more, and all the while mama getting more and more impatient.

"Eat up," she says again, this time frowning.

But I can't. I just can't. I sit there, piling the food into a mound and stabbing it in the middle in order to watch the beans scoot across the plate.

And next to me, on the cabinet, the parakeet crackles away, though I don't pay much attention, thinking instead about how I'm going to get Grady Fay to take me to see *Lovin' You.* Without looking directly at her, I sense mama stiffen.

"Shhhh," she hisses, putting a hand up.

"I didn't say anything."

"I *said* shhhhhh!"

For a second everything's quiet. I look at mama, who's staring at Pretty Boy. I turn. The dumb bird's sitting on its perch the same as always. "Is something wrong?"

"Shhhh!" This time her shush is sharp and quick. Her head's tilted back and her hand raised, as if it's frozen in midair. "Did you hear that, or am I going crazy?"

"Hear what?"

"Shhh. . . . "

The parakeet's squawking again, and this time I sit up because anybody listening hard can pick out a definite sound. Poor imitation of a human voice, maybe, but a sound all the same. Saying . . . what is it? "Eat . . . eat up now." And again, "Eat up now." Like mama speaking over a radio that's lost one of its tubes.

Letting out a yelp, she runs over and kneels in front of the cage.

"My God!" she says, pressing her mouth against the bars. "My Pretty Boy can talk good as anybody, yetz he can." Opening the door, she pours half a box of millet seeds into the feed dish until it overflows. "There. That's for him being so smart." She whistles and purses her lips.

"Can't eat no more." I march my full plate over to the garbage pail and rake it out.

"Mmmmmm," mama murmurs, listening only to the bird.

"Going to work now." At the door I turn and say real loud, "Don't worry about my not taking any supper. I'll share Dot's and Tessie's."

Normally mama would've thrown a fit at this news. Now she merely nods.

Reaching the Grey Mill early, I wait on the steps for the others to arrive. Grady Fay comes over by way of the Grey Mill sign and the little group that's always gathered around it. I can hear them exchanging a joke or two about the fall harvest on Sawmill Mountain.

"Hear y'got enough corn to feed the whole state."

"Hear y'got watermelons big around as the moon."

He takes it all in good humor, answering, "Yeah, yeah," to each one until he reaches the steps. "So." he flings himself down. "What's new?"

My usual answer to this question is, "Nothing much." But now, two things are on my mind. "Mama's bird talked today. For the first time. She thinks it's a miracle." Pausing, I sit there wiggling my toes inside my white sandals. "Reckon you know that *Lovin' You* is coming to the Coochee Theater next week?"

"*Lovin' You?*" Grady Fay crooks his bad arm and rotates the elbow round and round. I'm so used to counting for him that I can hardly stop myself from doing it now.

"The new Elvis movie."

"Oh yeah." Reversing his motions, he circles backwards. "You going?"

I smile. "You have to ask?"

"Wanna go with me?"

This is exactly what I'd hoped to hear. "I don't mind."

"What time does it start?"

"Seven-thirty, I think. But we oughta get there early. Sure to be a big crowd."

"Pick you up at seven."

"Quarter till. And I'll be at the Inn." This is so I don't catch any flack from mama.

So, quarter till it is.

Or is it?

I'm sitting in the lobby of the Inn, glancing up at the clock. It's now almost seven. Doesn't he understand how important it is to be early? Dot and Troy—promising to save us seats if they can—left fifteen minutes ago.

Struggling out of the deep leather armchair, I pace back and forth, only stopping to pick up a *T.V. Digest* from the magazine rack in the corner and thumb through it, skipping the story on Gizelle MacKenzie's bachelor apartment to glance at the latest Arthur Godfrey gossip so I can tell mama. Finally I throw it down. Maybe Grady Fay's forgotten and gone to my house by mistake.

I walk over to the pay phone to call, but think better of it. How can someone be so unreliable? A horn sounds. Racing to the window, I see his truck.

"Where you been?" I ask as I climb in. "We'll be lucky to get a ticket."

He nods toward the door. "Be sure you slam it good."

Isn't it just like him not to apologize for turning me into a bundle of nerves! Wish he'd drive faster. "Oh, please help us get a seat, Lord," I pray silently.

In the long run, though, it's more Dot's doing than the Lord's. In spite of people making all kinds of nasty comments, she's held on to two empty seats in a middle row. Me and Grady Fay slip in just as the picture's starting.

The story line is close to Elvis's own life, at least the rise-to-fame bit. He's such a natural singer that after he wins the talent contest, Tex asks him to join the band. Every time Elvis opens his mouth, the girls go wild. He makes everything look so easy. My daddy made things look easy, too. Wonder if Grady Fay can feel—through the spot where our legs touch—the nerve ends crawling beneath my skin.

Out the corner of my eye, I see Dot all scrunched up next to Troy. Every now and then, he turns her face in his direction and gives her a kiss that sometimes lasts so long people behind yell, "Down in front, down in front!"

Glenda, Tex's ex-wife, is always making up to Elvis, even though she's old enough to be his mama. Anyway, I'm rooting for Susan, the girl singer.

And all the time I keep waiting for Grady Fay to take my hand or something. But he doesn't. It stays on my lap, prim as a paper napkin.

The white convertible gives Elvis extra dash. Susan sits beside him, her hair blowing in the wind. Wish I looked like Susan. From the way they gaze into each other's eyes, you can tell they're dying to kiss.

Once in a while I glance over in Dot's direction to see how she and Troy're making out. Actually they're pretty quiet now. Troy's big knuckles rest right over Dot's crotch. Mama was shocked once to see them sitting like that on a bench in front of the Store. "His hand ... right *there*," she said. "In front of everybody. That's what I call cheap!"

Then things get a little tangled up. Poor Susan pining away, and Elvis driving like a demon. I cover my eyes so I won't see the car crash. It's Grady Fay who leans over and whispers, "He's okay." First words he's spoken since the picture started.

Then a turn for the better. A winning streak. Elvis looks Susan in the eye and tells her in that deep voice of his how much he loves her. It clinches everything. Elvis and Susan, Tex and Glenda. No loose ends.

When the house lights come on, I blink. After the bright technicolor, everything seems so drab.

"Wanna go to Hookey's for a hamburger?" Dot asks.

Grady Fay shrugs as if he's leaving the answer up to me. I shake my head. "Didn't you love it?" I whisper to Dot.

She looks at Troy and grins. "Sure did."

Dot and Troy go off arm in arm. Grady Fay and me stand there a few minutes, then he leads the way to the Western Auto store where his truck's parked.

Driving back, I roll down the window to let in some air. The second it hits my face, I feel weightless. I glance over at Grady Fay. He's even quieter than usual. "If we were in a convertible right now, we could look up at the sky. Imagine."

"Then you'd complain about being cold."

The wind sweeps my hair away from my face. Raising my arms, I take a deep breath and lean back against the seat. Wish this road would stretch on forever. Wish we could drive straight to Memphis.

Instead, we drive straight to Chimney Road.

Surely, *surely* he doesn't intend to simply pull up in front of my house and let me out. Doesn't he have *any* imagination? The truck begins to slow down.

"I'd . . . like to ride around a little bit. Would you?"

"Where do you want to go? Not far, I hope. I don't have that much gas."

"How about up to the golf course?"

"The golf course! Nobody's there now." But I notice he puts his foot back on the accelerator.

"We can sit and talk. And if we want some music, we can always turn on the radio."

"Radio doesn't work."

"Well, then, I can sing." I begin humming, then singing, the tune from the movie. After a second or two, he joins in.

I will spend my whole life through
Loving you, loving you
Winter, summer, springtime, too,
Loving you, loving you. . . .

I listen to his voice, surprised at how deep it goes, at the way it slides up and down the scale. At the end, I'm silent for a second. "That was wonderful! You should join our church choir."

"Aw. . . . " He turns into the dead-end road that leads to the golf course and, beyond that, to the river.

"I mean it."

"Better be careful."

"Why?"

"You'll turn my head." He turns and grins at me, but keeps both hands fastened on the wheel. If it was Elvis sitting there, he'd reach out and pull me over next to him, close enough for me to feel the thud of his heartbeat through his shirt. And if I made the slightest move to draw away, he'd hold me real tight, and then, first chance he got, he'd turn my face around and graze my lips with his.

At the clubhouse, Grady Fay slows down. "Wanna stop here and walk around?"

Walk around? I shudder. "No. Let's go on."

The road down to the water's so narrow that branches whip the sides of the truck, making me roll my window up.

"Hope none of the paint's getting scratched off," Grady Fay says.

We twist along the narrow ruts until the road abruptly opens up into a clearing by the river's edge. Grady Fay stops the truck and turns off the motor. "Hope I can get back outta here," he mutters, glancing behind him.

But I'm looking straight ahead. "This used to be the place where they'd bring in cotton bales by boat. My daddy told me. That was before they built the big dam."

"Really?"

"And before that, it was a Cherokee campground."

"You know a lot," he says.

"Well, I've lived here all my life. And my daddy lived here, and *his* daddy. My granddaddy Grubbs, he's dead now, but he used to drive one of the Goody wagons down to the Rome depot and back. That's where they shipped the cloth from. He told me a story about him getting home late one Christmas because one of his old mules took sick and he had to walk to the nearest farm for a replacement. He didn't reach Goody till after midnight. Sang Christmas carols to himself to keep up his spirits. Granddaddy had a wonderful voice. He was songleader and main soloist at the Baptist church for over forty years. Mama said some folks wouldn't know they's dead without him singing 'Asleep in Jesus' over their caskets. My daddy had a good voice, too."

Then I stop. Don't know what's got into me. Never, in all my life, have I talked so much about myself at one time.

"Wanna get out of the truck?" Grady Fay asks.

"Okay. Wish we had a blanket. Then we could spread it out and sit down."

We walk to the water's edge. Except for the silvery curls made by the tiny ripples, it's completely black. I stand very still.

He comes toward me. I'm prepared for him to kiss me the way he kissed Susan in the movie, mouth puckered against mouth. But this is different. Tracing the outlines of my lips with his tongue, he digs the tip inside. And what that tongue does cannot be described in the pages of True Confessions. *It swims in like a fish into a tank, wiggling through my teeth, squirming against my own tongue.*

Suddenly I get goosebumps and rub my arms up and down.

"You're not cold, are you?" Grady Fay asks.

"No."

Picking up a stone, he throws it into the distance. Then he tries it with his bad arm. A second later, we hear a distinct plunk. "Wish I could get it all the way across," he says.

I bend down and grope around for a stone, too. "When I was little, some of us girls had a game we used to play."

"What's that?" Grunting, he throws again, this time harder.

"We'd get different-shaped sticks and toss them into the river. Then we'd watch them float all the way downstream. The one whose stick went the fartherest without getting stuck would be the one who'd get married first."

"Did your stick float all the way?"

"Sometimes."

A hand pushes up my skirt, fingers brushing against my panties, groping inside.

"Did you hear anything?" Grady Fay asks.

"What?"

"Did you hear my stone hit the water?"

"No."

"Then maybe I did it. I'm gonna try again."

I hear him take a deep breath. And all the time I'm staring at the water. It's so dark. *So* dark. "Something real sad happened here once. It just came to my mind."

"What?"

"A little boy—well, he was older than me, but then I hadn't started to school yet—was drowned here. In this very spot. I still remember his name. . . . Frankie . . . Frankie Teems. He was swimming across with some friends and the current got too much for him and he couldn't make it. It took them the longest time to find his body and pull him out. Because of the dyes. My daddy was the one who embalmed him. Said his lips were still green, and there wasn't a thing in this world he could do about it. I sure would hate to die with green lips, wouldn't you?"

"Yeah."

"Hope I didn't depress you. Don't know what got me started on that."

"You didn't."

"I'm glad because I didn't mean to."

"No," I whisper. *"No, don't do that."*

"I have to, sugar, I have to. Watching you, I just itch to be there, right *there. Does it feel good to you?" I hesitate. "Tell me. I wanna hear you say it. Say it, baby."*

"It feels . . . oh, I can't!"

"Tell me, baby. Tell me."

"I can't. . . . *"*

"Want me to do it more?" I nod. "Then say it, baby, say you never want me to stop. Say it."

"I don't. . . . "

"Say it."

"I never want you to stop. Oh, God," I moan.

Grady Fay turns to me. "Are you about ready to get back in the truck?"

"Guess so." I trip over a rock and almost stumble, but he catches my arm.

. . . and all the time me thinking that I'll be punished for letting myself go in a second of weakness, a fallen woman, like Eve, like Mary Magdalene, like the young girls in True Confessions. *"One false step and that's it," mama's always saying. A slip as good as a mile. The devil on the mountaintop. The snake in the grass. How can the Lord have made it plainer?*

106

We climb back in the truck. "This is going to be really hard," Grady Fay says, starting the motor.

I see him struggling with his pants, taking them off, flinging them aside. . . .

"What?"

Grady Fay has opened his door and is peering out. "I said, would you help me look on that side, so we don't hit so many branches?"

"You're okay. Just go on back."

"Relax now. Relax." As he bends over me, I try to speak. He puts a finger to my lips. "Shhh, baby, shhh. I won't hurt you." His face comes closer. In the half-dark his eyes are enormous. His nose flares in and out. Raising my body slightly, he begins pushing into me.

"I'll never drive in here again, tell you that," Grady Fay says. "Too hard to get out of." He passes the clubhouse, then we're back on the main road.

At first I shut my eyes, but then as he keeps thrusting, I open them wide and look into his. When I scream, my voice seems to soar right out the window.

"You're awfully quiet," Grady Fay says, turning to me.

"Just thinking."

. . . and he answers with a final plunge.

"Anything the matter?" he asks as I take a deep breath and lean my head against the seat.

"Just tired, I guess."

"Hope I didn't keep you out too late."

"No."

Pulling up to the curb in front of my house, he starts to get out but I hold up a hand like a traffic cop. "You don't have to do that. Anyway, we might wake up mama."

"Oh. Right."

"Thank you." I press down the handle. "I really enjoyed the movie."

"LaVonne . . . I have something I been meaning to tell you." He stares down at his fingers gripping the wheel.

"What?" I step out of the truck and wait. Maybe he'll ask me to go steady. Maybe he'll say that I look just like a movie star.

"You're . . . a . . . real nice girl."

Before I have the chance to answer, he's already shifted gears, and I barely have time to shut the door before he's chugging off. Both taillights on the truck have holes in the middle as if somebody shot a B-B gun at them. Remind me of two bloodshot eyes disappearing into the night.

Chapter Eleven

BETTER THIS WAY. BETTER I DON'T get too wrapped up in Grady Fay. Better I don't get involved with a lot of romantic stuff and blow my big raise. Like I say to Dot, "Grady Fay and me keep moving onward and upward." But the onward means nothing more than the mileage numbers, and the upward is Grady Fay's shoulder.

I don't tell mama *nothing*—not about the accident, not about the Machine, not about the training, certainly not about Mr. Fortune's promise because she'd be sure to put two and two together. "You planning on moving to the Inn?" she'd say. "Leaving *me?*" Then I'd have the choice of lying or telling the truth, and either way'd be awful. When the time comes, I mean to simply pack up my things and walk out. Make a clean break. Just like daddy.

When daddy left, it was the Church of God of the Prophecy that saved mama. That's why if she can do something for the church, she will. So when Calvin Toombs calls and asks her to make identical dresses for me and Jeanette to wear in the quartet, she not only says yes, but promises to have them ready by October third, our premiere singing engagement over at the Sandy Creek church. The dresses are panels of navy blue and white with full skirts and necks that she describes as "lower than necessary but the way Calvin wants them." Jeanette drives up from Richville, where she works as a receptionist in an insurance office, to try on hers during lunch. I've never seen her outside church before, so I had no idea until now that she dolls up *every* day the same way she does on Sunday: nails manicured, hair so perfectly styled she must wear a hairnet to bed at night (and of course she never has to worry about pieces of cotton getting stuck in it). I'd envy her to the bone if I hadn't also found out how old she is: twenty-six and still unmarried!

She has a peculiar way of talking about Calvin—Calvin says this, Calvin does that. From the things that slip from her mouth, it's obvious that her and Calvin have been doing some rehearsing on the side, and I suspect it involves more than singing. At Sunday practice, I'm sure my suspicions are right. When Calvin tries to position us, Jeanette keeps sidling forward or sideways so he's always having to put his hands on her waist and move her back until it begins to look like the two of them are doing some kind of slow dance together. And is it my imagination that Jeanette's given more solos than is normal for an alto?

Sure seems that way the night we sing at Sandy Creek. I might just as well phone in my performance for all the difference it makes. Afterward, people crowd around Jeanette, and only as an afterthought turn to me and say, "You did well, too." The lowest blow comes with mama saying in her driest voice, "Were you up there? I didn't notice."

But on the whole, the quartet does pretty well. We already have several dates for the holidays, the most important being a Festival of Praise to be held up at the Delphi Church of God on Thanksgiving night. Singing groups from all over north Georgia'll be there, and some from as far away as Gadsden, Alabama.

At one time or another, I've heard the Travelers, the Crusaders, and the True Apostles, but others, like the Ark of Lights and the Triumphant Return, are brand-new to me.

"Why don't we change our name?" I suggest to Calvin one Sunday during our practice session. "Make it more interesting."

"What's more interesting than sunshine? That can be mentioned in public, that is." He snickers. Sometimes his one-track mind can be so annoying. Especially with him and Jeanette mooning all over each other.

"Too bad if Mrs. Toombs gets wind of it," I whisper to Pearlie B. "She'll send Jeanette packing."

On Monday I mention the Festival to Dot. Several of her brothers live in Delphi, and might want to attend.

"I'll come myself," Dot says. "If I can manage to drag along my fiancé, that is."

"Fiancé!"

"Troy's giving me an engagement ring for Christmas." She puts a finger to her lips. "Don't tell anybody, it's supposed to be a surprise . . . even to me."

"Then how'd you find out?"

"I opened the glove compartment in the van, and inside was this tiny velvet box with a ring in it. The diamond must be at least three carats."

"Dot! I'm so happy for you!" I manage to give her a genuine squeeze even though I'm so jealous I could die. Will *I* ever find the right man?

Will the right man ever find *me?* And where is Gene Hankins, anyway?

In the meantime, we're getting all revved up again for the contest. And Mr. Fortune's back, stepping through the lint as though it's confetti in a parade. He pauses long enough to watch Grady Fay go through his exercising paces. Once in a while he even makes a suggestion, but most of the time he just nods and clasps me on the shoulder as if to say I'm doing a wonderful job. That raise is on its way!

According to the mileage meter, Grady Fay has now rowed 541 miles. One day Shorty comes over carrying an atlas under his arm and sticks it under Grady Fay's nose. "Wanna know where y'all could've gone if this contraption was the real McCoy?" Without waiting for Grady Fay's reply, he opens it and thumbs through the pages. "From New Or-leens all the way up the Mississippi to Memphis. Think what you mighta seen!"

Not what, but *who,* I almost say, meaning Elvis, of course. Instead I nod. "Or you could have gone to Nashville and back twice over." That'd mean attending the Grand Ole Opry, which I've always longed to do.

"Instead," Shorty says, "you are getting nowhere fast." He slams the atlas shut. "Don't that strike you as odd?"

"Dunno, Shorty." Grady Fay climbs out of the boat. "Maybe yes, maybe no."

"I'd give my eye teeth to see Graceland," I put in.

"Niagara Falls gets my vote." Dot holds up her ring finger as though there's already something shining there.

"I'll take Vegas myself," Shorty grins.

"Not me." Grady Fay shakes his head.

"What's your choice?"

"Don't have one."

I give a snort as if I don't really believe him. "You kidding?"

"I'm satisfied right on my farm."

I think, Well, you can have it! Then I gather up the two towels he's been using and stick them in a laundry bag, which I sling over my shoulder and carry into Mr. Baxter's office where it'll be picked up by the cleaning people. Marvin's constantly complaining about Grady Fay causing him to do extra work. He doesn't know what *extra* means.

Before the Festival of Lights, there's Thanksgiving dinner to get through—turkey, cornbread dressing, giblet gravy, cranberry salad, candied sweet potatoes, green beans. I stare at all of it piled on my plate and look away. "I'm too nervous to eat, mama," I say, laying my napkin aside and returning to my room before I have to witness, once more, the scraping and washing of that breastbone. The blue and white dress, just ironed, lays across a chair, ready to be put on. I close my eyes. Wish daddy could hear me sing.

The Festival officially starts at four; at seven, they'll adjourn for an hour to give people the chance to sample everybody's Thanksgiving leftovers. (Mama's taking a plate of turkey, stuffing, and a small bowl of gravy.) Calvin's notified quartet members that we're to perform in the second half. He plans to pick me up around six so we can have a practice session beforehand. Mama'll come later with Marvin and Miz Cowan.

But as I walk toward Calvin's car, I can tell right away that something's wrong. For one thing, everybody's stiff-looking, and for another, there's barely a word of greeting as I climb in the back seat between Bobby Echols and Jeanette. Jeanette looks like she's been crying. Calvin and his wife are in the front seat. Calvin's face is stony. When he jerks the gear down, we fly off with a screech.

He drives up to Delphi and into the church yard the same way: with a grind of brakes that pitches us all forward, followed by a pause while we collect ourselves. Then he gets out, slams the door, and goes on into the church, leaving Mrs. Toombs to her own devices, which I suspect don't amount to much.

Not long after, Pearlie B. arrives in her beat-up Chevy, and we start rehearsing—if you can call it that. Jeanette's on the verge of tears, and Calvin's words come through clenched teeth.

"This is going to be awful," I whisper to Bobby, and catching Pearlie B.'s eye, realize that she's thinking the same thing.

The place is beginning to fill up with singers. Names are bandied about—the Carter Family, the Blackwood Brothers, Curly King and the Tennessee Hilltoppers—names I've heard all my life, especially the Carter Family, who sang "Careless Love," which, for some reason, I always thought had something to do with daddy. A beefy man from the Ark of Lights remarks that "Elvis Presley got a lot of his style from the Blackwood Brothers." Don't know how he's come by this information since it hasn't even appeared in the *Newsletter* yet. By the time I slip closer, he's already on to Ola Belle DeBusk, whoever that is.

When a chair comes vacant, Bobby Echols points to it, and I sit down while he stands beside me. Over at a long table against the wall, women are arranging the dishes, setting out paper plates and cups. Somebody walks through ringing a dinner bell and then the audience files in, talking and laughing; after the Delphi preacher says a prayer, people line up for food: men first, then children, and finally the ladies. I see Calvin take a heaping plate over to Jeanette before he goes back to fill his own.

Preacher Crow's the guest speaker for the evening, and I have to admit that he outdoes himself. He preaches a short sermon, about music being "inspired by angels," that gives me goose bumps. Maybe this is one reason the singers in the second half sound so different. The Ark of Lights leads the way with a rousing rendition of "Keep on Moving," followed by a familiar LeRoy Abernathy song, "Over in the Gloryland," which they give an extra twist to by speeding up the rhythm and adding a guitar in the background.

The Holy Rollers are next, and they live up to their name . . . as do the Triumphant Return, who not only have a guitar but an *electric* guitar—which I've never heard before with a gospel group—and a fiddler backup who moves in for a few turns after each chorus. The other two members hold tambourines, and they're not shy about using them, especially on their last number, "O, What a Day!" Everybody in the church starts tapping and swaying.

When I hear the emcee announce the Sunshine Quartet, my stomach turns over. Bobby Echols pulls me up and we manage to walk down to the altar beside Pearlie B. We stand there while a deacon runs to fetch Calvin and Jeanette. In a few minutes he returns, holding out his empty hands. "Maybe they took a walk," he says, hopefully. In freezing cold? I almost ask aloud.

Meantime the Holy Rollers come back to sing an encore so me and Bobby can comb the Sunday School rooms. But all we see are curtainless windows, cane chairs, and pictures of Jesus. In desperation, we run outside, our breath ballooning into the air. When we see that Calvin's car's missing, we know there's no point in looking further.

"Run off together!" Pearlie B.'s mouth hangs open. "What'll I tell Mrs. Toombs?"

"The truth, I reckon," Bobby mumbles. We're all feeling gloomy. This spells the end of the Sunshine Quartet.

Slipping in beside Mrs. Toombs, Pearlie B. coaxes her up from the pew. "Something's happened, hon. Come on. We'll see that you get home." Looking at her face, Mrs. Toombs immediately guesses what the "something" is and her face folds up like an accordion.

I help Pearlie B. settle her into the front seat of the Chevy, then climb into Marvin's car, along with Marvin, Bobby, Miz Cowan, and mama. They go on and on about how awful Calvin and Jeanette are to do such a thing, but to tell the truth, I half envy them. Wish I had the guts to run off with somebody.

At the mill on Monday, Dot apologizes for not coming. "Had to go with Troy to visit my future in-laws."

When I hear the word "in-laws," I look away and don't say anything. Just hope she doesn't get so carried away with married life that she cuts off all her old friends like some people do.

"Are you planning on a church wedding?"

"I don't care *what* it is," Dot says, "as long as it's me and Troy and the preacher."

Jealousy comes walloping right up from my stomach. It's hard to choke down my ham sandwich, and I have to buy an extra R.C. to wash down all the stale crusts.

"Well, you're in the home stretch now," Dot comments as we're leaving the canteen.

"What?"

"The contest."

"Oh, that. Yeah."

"Is Grady Fay ready?"

"Think so."

"He better be. You and him got a lot riding on it."

I'm not sure whether this statement pulls me out of my slump or puts me into a deeper one.

Singing at the Christmas church service normally lifts my spirits, but since Calvin and Jeanette are still gone, and no one knows their whereabouts—although it's rumored that Mrs. Toombs has gotten a crumpled postcard from Waco, Texas—the choir has disbanded until we find a new leader.

The Secret Santa I draw this year is Reba Petit, of all people. I give her a big box of chocolate-covered cherries in hopes she'll eat them all at one time and make herself sick. Dot gets candy, too (from Marvin Cowan). As she opens the package, she winks at me. "Whatever this is, I'll love it. Because I already know that this is going to be my best Christmas *ever.*"

I give mama a subscription to *McCall's Patterns,* and a large square of beautiful silk material from the remnant department. To run my hands over it is such a blessed relief from touching cotton!

Mama gives *me* twenty dollars, which is to be used for an Elvis concert "if he ever comes close enough." Although twenty dollars is a small fortune, I have a suspicion that mama plans to go along, too, and this spoils it.

The one surprise gift comes from Grady Fay . . . and it's not a Christmas tree. (I informed him, as casually as possible, that mama's allergic to resin, which I suppose in some ways is true.) He doesn't give it to me the night of the mill party, either, but waits until Christmas day and leaves it for me to find when I open the door to see who the horn-blowing belongs to. (To Gene, I'm hoping, until I glimpse Grady Fay's truck going round the bend.) The square package—wrapped in tin-foil with a white ribbon around it—has been placed just inside the screen. At that instant, mama sticks her head out. "Who's that from?"

"Grady Fay Owens."

She makes a face that'd be off-putting at any time, but especially at Christmas. "Why?"

I shrug. "Don't know. The card just says 'thanks.'"

Beneath the cotton is a silver chain attached to a tiny disc with my name engraved on it. I hold it up to the light. "It's an anklet. Isn't it pretty?" And it *is* . . . only . . . I feel so ungrateful for thinking this . . . ankle chains are out of style. They aren't even advertised in *True Confessions* anymore.

"Always considered them things vulgar," mama mutters, returning to the living room.

"Aren't you the one who's fond of saying 'it's the thought that counts'?"

"Yeah, but in this case it don't count for much."

I don't know why Pretty Boy—who's been brought into the living room to witness the opening of presents—picks this second to start squawking, but I toss the square of silk over his cage.

"What're you doing?"

"Telling him to *shut up.*"

'Course, mama takes it off again, and that's the way Christmas goes: mama and me ya-yaing back and forth. By the time "Your Hit Parade" comes on that night, I'm so bored that I lie back and watch it in spite of the music being as out-of-date as the ankle chain. Especially Snookie Lanson's version of "All Shook Up." When I comment that he's ruining Elvis's song, mama nods and makes a face at the screen.

Hurray! At last we've found *something* to agree about!

Chapter Twelve

ON THE DAY AFTER CHRISTMAS, Dot comes in looking like something warmed-over. Turns out, the diamond ring hadn't been meant for her at all. Turns out, it belonged to Troy's cousin, who'd asked him to keep it for him. Now it's *my* turn to boost *her.*

I hadn't realized how much her high spirits infect the whole department until they're not here anymore. And Mr. Baxter doesn't help because all of his thoughts are on the contest. He boasts that it's putting second-shift spinning "on the map." He also advises Grady Fay to start getting serious about it, and soon Grady Fay's coming in early to do the exercises before work. Sometimes I join him, just to let Mr. Baxter know that I'm keeping up my part.

Of course he wins the first round hands down because no one on second shift can come near him, not even Shorty. But Mr. Baxter predicts the second round'll be harder. "Understand there's a new boy on third shift who's a lot faster than Ray Shoals," he says. "Just want you to be aware of the competition." He puts an arm around each of us. "This is no time to slack off, children."

And we stay at it, the mileage climbing to an unheard-of 728. No one jokes about the Machine anymore, not even Marvin. In fact, I begin to notice a change in people's attitudes toward Grady Fay. They treat him with a new respect.

The first time I'm aware of this is just before the second round's due to start. Everybody's gathered in the canteen, drinking coffee and eating doughnuts. When Grady Fay walks in, they all shift slightly to let him pass, the same way they do for Mr. Fortune. Several of the men reach over to pat him on the back. He looks all done in, though. Immediately Mr. Baxter's at his side.

"You alright?"

Grady Fay nods and leans against the wall. Is he sleepwalking?

"You *sure?*" Mr. Baxter frowns and motions for Boley to bring over a cup of black coffee.

"Yessir. Little tired, that's all. One of my mules got loose this morning and I had to chase it down."

Several people come up to Mr. Baxter with dollar bills in their hands. Chomping on his cigar, he brings out his pad and pencil to jot down their bets. He says the odds are split 20-45-35 in favor of Grady Fay, but I don't understand what this means. When Boley returns with the coffee, Mr. Baxter hands it to him as he would to a child. "Now drink this down. If it don't work, we'll get you something stronger. Right, Boley?" But as soon as Mr. Fortune appears, he quiets down and sticks the pad back in his pocket.

Hoyt Teems, the third-shift doffer, stands over by the Coke machine, a matchstick working itself around and around his mouth. Soon as Ray Shoals walks in—his hair sticking up as if he's just come straight from bed—everybody moves out of the canteen. Although Mr. Fortune's arrival has put a damper on the betting, I see Mr. Baxter moving through the crowd, every now and then leaning forward to let a potential customer whisper in his ear.

The three contestants stand against the far wall, Grady Fay slouching and rubbing his eyes while they draw names to see who's up first. Grady Fay groans because he has to lead off. Mr. Fortune raises his hand for the signal, and he takes his place at the head of the aisle. Mr. Baxter blows the whistle.

"If that's the best he can do," Marvin comments as we watch Grady Fay walk around the frame, "we're in pretty bad shape."

After the first bout, there's a short recess to give people a chance to get refreshments. Mr. Baxter comes striding over to Boley as if he's got something urgent on his mind. I stand close so I can hear. "Listen," he says, "you got any of them pep pills?"

"Sure thing." Boley reaches toward his shirt pocket.

"Wait a minute." Looking around, Mr. Baxter raises a finger. "Don't let nobody see you take them out." He stands there for a few seconds, chewing his cigar. "Tell you what. Go in the canteen and get me a Seven-Up. When you give it to me, slip the pills in, too. Got it?"

"Yessir."

"And for God's sake, don't mention this to *nobody.* We could be disqualified." He nods toward Grady Fay, who's lounging by the window, looking as if he's about to fold in half.

Boley returns with the Seven-Up just as Mr. Baxter's ready to blow the whistle for the beginning of the next go-around. Calling time out, Mr.

Baxter rushes the dopie over to Grady Fay. I see Grady Fay shake his head, though, and wave him away. "Well, it's up to you, son," I hear Mr. Baxter say.

Grady Fay's second try is a bit better than the first but Mr. Baxter's still not pleased. "Three minutes!" he explodes to Mr. Fortune. "Why, he can do better than that in his sleep!" And in fact—while the other contenders are up—it looks like sleeping is exactly what Grady Fay's doing, the way he's leaning against the wall with his eyes closed. Then he walks over to the window, takes a few deep breaths, and goes through a few of his exercises. Automatically, I count for him under my breath, "one and two and . . . " Turning, he rubs his injured shoulder a few times.

As he prepares to start the third doff, everybody automatically moves forward.

"Go, Grady Fay, go!" Boley yells.

I join in, walking around urging others to yell, "Go, go, go!" (All through high school, I longed to be a cheerleader, though few girls from this side of the river ever got picked.) Glancing over at me, Grady Fay smiles, and holds both hands above the spindles.

Then the strangest thing happens. At the sound of the whistle, those hands take off, flying, jerking off the full quills, throwing them into the buggy, grabbing empty ones, shoving them on, pinching the thread ends, out, up, under, twist, out, up, under, twist. All a blur.

"My God," Mr. Baxter murmurs.

Mr. Fortune's impressed, too, I can tell, because for once he forgets to flick the lint off his blue suit.

After Grady Fay finishes—two minutes and twenty-nine seconds is the count—Hoyt knows he's licked. Soon as Mr. Fortune announces the winner, all us second- shifters clap, whistle, cheer. Mr. Baxter even takes the cigar out of his mouth and joins in.

Cecil Crider's on hand to take pictures for the *News*. He takes one of Grady Fay with his hands clasped over his head like a boxer. I try to congratulate him, but can't get close for all the people around.

It's a surprise to find him at work that afternoon. Thought he'd drive back to Sawmill Mountain and stay there, but no, he's standing at Number 9 when I walk up.

"You did real good today."

"Thanks. For a while it was touch and go." I start to move on to Number 10 when he stops me. "LaVonne. You'll go with me, won't you?"

I'm so taken aback that, at first, I can't think what he's talking about. "Where?"

"To the banquet. For the winner of the second round, remember?"

"Sure. If you want me to."

"If it wasn't for you, I wouldn't even be competing."

I'm speechless. Is he inviting me out of *gratitude?* Well, gratitude's better than nothing.

The *News* puts Grady Fay's picture on the front page along with a big write-up about the contest, concluding with a mention of a banquet at the Goody Café. I cut it out, meaning to mail it to daddy, along with a letter telling him about my part in it. But the clipping remains on my vanity table, and finally I throw it away.

For three weeks, mama works on a large strip of fuchsia taffeta that she's been saving, she says, for a special occasion. The pattern—mama and me picked it out together in the women's ready-to-wear—is modeled after a dress we once saw LuAnn Sims wear on the Arthur Godfrey Show. It has a sweetheart neckline with a tiny ruffle and a full skirt that comes to my calf.

"Mama, it's beautiful," I say, catching a glimpse of myself in the mirror.

"Looks real nice," mama says, which is quite a compliment for her. "Hope Grady Fay Owens appreciates it."

When he comes to pick me up, I can't tell whether he does or not. He barely speaks a word all the way to the Café, not even when I ask about his daddy. I've never seen him so tongue-tied. Maybe it's just nerves.

He helps me out of the truck and as we walk in, I catch my breath. The Café's been made over . . . though into *what* I can't quite make out. Behind the main table is tacked the same Superman drawing, except on a larger scale, that Mr. Baxter put up on the bulletin board. Around this are taped lots of stars and planets. More stars hang from the ceiling, and in the middle of the room, a small moon dangles.

There's also a little white wooden fence strewn with roses—it looks like the same one used for the Junior-Senior banquet at the high school—that sets off the main table. The glare of the big biscuit lights overhead has been dimmed to let the candles have their effect. But the one thing that hasn't changed is the stale air smelling of cigarette smoke and scrambled eggs.

We're greeted by Mollie Sue, who's switched from her usual white uniform into a red, blue, and yellow flowered dress with puffed sleeves that leave an elastic mark around her fat arms. She leads us over to the main table where Mr. Baxter's already sitting. Immediately he stands up and pulls out a chair for Grady Fay. I seat myself and nibble on nuts from the little paper basket beside my plate while listening to the two men discuss the upcoming competition in Augusta.

The other guests are mill bosses and their wives, most of whom come in late smelling of liquor. Mr. and Mrs. Fortune are the last to arrive. Although I've had glimpses of Mrs. Fortune from time to time in the Store (though oddly enough, her picture never appears in the *News*), it's the first time I've seen her close up. Her dark hair's swept to the top of her head like Marion Marlowe sometimes does hers, and her skin has a reddish glow as if she's been lying in the sun. But the most striking feature are her eyes, which look like large bruises. When Mr. Fortune introduces us, she puts out a hand, and I take it even though it seems odd to shake hands with somebody besides a preacher.

"Please repeat your first name." Mrs. Fortune has a low, throaty voice that I have to bend close to hear.

"LaVonne." In comparison, my own voice sounds nasal and hillbilly. "LaVonne Grubbs."

"LaVonne." She takes a sip of water. "How unusual."

"Well," I blurt out, "mama likes anything with La in front of it. LaJune, LaBelle, LaNelle, LaDonna. She claims it makes things more musical." I say this as modestly as possible.

"And does your mother like music?"

"She's big on church music. And *some* popular stuff."

"Oh?"

"She likes Elvis Presley."

Taking a salted pecan out of her basket, Mrs. Fortune puts it to her lips and nibbles on it. "Elvis Presley." She says it slowly. "It sounds familiar."

"He's been on the 'Ed Sullivan Show' a couple of times."

"I don't watch much television."

I stare at her. What on earth does she do, then?

But I never have the chance to find out because at that second, the woman on Mrs. Fortune's other side—Spud Bankey's wife, June—grabs her attention away. I hear them talking about the difference between the clothes at Loveman's and Pickett's in Chattanooga, about vacations spent in some place called the Virgin Islands. And what's a conk salad, I wonder, that somebody can get so sick from it?

After an appetizer of canned fruit cocktail, Mollie Sue and her team of waitresses bring in plates of glazed ham with potatoes the size of golfballs, and a big serving of green peas. If there's one thing I *hate*, it's green peas, so I mash the potatoes and scoot the peas under until none of the green shows.

Although I try my best to stretch out the meal by taking the daintiest of bites, I've finished long before the rest of the table, who are all involved in conversations, and sit there folding and refolding my napkin.

The dessert's strawberry shortcake. I watch Mrs. Fortune push the whipped cream aside so that she can get to the strawberries, which she carefully cuts into tiny pieces with her spoon. "Where did you find these this time of year?" she asks Mollie Sue as she breezes by.

Mollie Sue beams. "Ohhhh," she says. "I have my sources."

When Mr. Fortune rises and taps on his water glass for attention, people look relieved to be able to put down their forks and listen. I glance over at Mrs. Fortune. She must be so proud of him. But she stares down at her plate and doesn't even look up.

"Friends, we are gathered here tonight for our second banquet honoring the winner of the doffing competition at our home mill. I'm very, very impressed with the young man who has come forth to represent Goody in this year's contest. His name is Grady Fay Owens, and during the next few months, you'll be hearing a lot about him." At this point, Mr. Baxter leads a tiny trickle of applause. "In second-shift spinning, Grady Fay has set a splendid example of cooperation, industriousness, and cheerfulness. This past year, fate dealt him a hard blow, but he perservered until he overcame it. I'd now like to introduce the person who will present the trophy and gift to Grady Fay—his supervisor, Mr. Frank Baxter."

While clapping, I steal a glance at Grady Fay. He looks bewildered that all this is happening to him.

When Mr. Baxter stands up, instead of snuffing out his cigar, he lays it across the ashtray so that most of the smoke curls right into my face and I have to wave it away with my hand.

"Ladies and gentlemen." Putting his hands in his pockets, he rocks back and forth on his heels. "As Mr. Fortune so ably put it, tonight is the second year of what is rapidly becoming a tradition, a tradition that promises to put us in touch, once again, with the ancient roots of cloth-making, roots that go back hundreds of years to a time of legends and fairy tales about spinning straw into gold.

"For not only does the textile industry fill material necessities, but also one of man's deepest needs: to take a raw product and transform it into something beautiful." Pausing, he glances over at Mr. Fortune, who's shifting around in his chair. "And this is simply to say that as Grady Fay Owens journeys south to Augusta and then on to Avondale—because I know he's going to win—he will find at his side countless men—yes, and women, too," here he gives a nod my way, "who over the centuries have produced materials for warmth, adornment, and a better quality of life. Ladies and gentlemen," he motions for Grady Fay to stand up, "I am honored to present this trophy and one hundred dollars to Goody's Superdoffer, Grady Fay Owens, in admiration and thanks from all of us at Goody Mills."

Grady Fay puts up a hand to acknowledge the applause, but when someone calls out, "Speech! speech!" he quickly pulls it back down. If I was in his place, I'd have thanked a few people, especially my co-worker.

"Mr. Baxter used to have a son about Grady Fay's age, did you know that?" Turning toward the voice, I'm surprised to see Mrs. Fortune's big eyes fixed on me. "He was killed in the South Pacific. His wife never got over it." She glances in Mr. Baxter's direction. "That's why she never goes anywhere with him."

"Never?" I don't know what to say.

"No." Mrs. Fortune shakes her head. "It's very sad."

"LaVonne!" I'm distracted from Mrs. Fortune by Cecil Crider calling my name. "Stand over here by Grady Fay. I want you to look up at him and smile."

That's not hard to do.

"Hold it!" Cecil shouts. "Hold it! Just like that." Moving around the table, he continues to snap at different angles.

When Grady Fay takes me home, I stand on tiptoe to kiss him. His lips are slightly dry. He makes no move to kiss me back, though. Is he missing some hormones or something? If he was Gene, we'd be rolling in the grass by now.

Two days later, one of the photographs appears on the front page of the *News*, and everywhere I go—in the Store, in the mill, on the street— heads seem to turn. Mrs. Harris over at the Inn, who's never bothered speaking to me before, suddenly makes a point of commenting on what a good likeness it is. And once, when I'm going into the post office, some teenagers run up to ask if I'm Grady Fay Owens's girlfriend.

"Well . . . " I hesitate. "I'm really his sidekick."

"Weren't you with him at the banquet?" I nod. "Then could we have your autograph?"

At first I think they must be kidding. But when it's clear they mean it, I fish around in my pocketbook for a pencil. They hand me a scrap of paper and taking it over to the blotting pad, I write in large letters,

BEST WISHES,

LAVONNE GRUBBS.

Underneath I add, PRESIDENT, THE REAL ELVIS PRESLEY FAN CLUB.

Thanking me, they back away, bowing their heads slightly as though I'm some kind of queen. For the first time I realize what Elvis knows—that us little people have finally broke out of the bottle. And now that we're *out*, we're not going back in neither.

Chapter Thirteen

AFTER THIS, ME AND GRADY FAY'RE MORE than a team. We are, as Mr. Baxter says, "indelibly linked." The whole of my mind becomes bent toward one thing and one thing only: winning. Even my Saturdays and Sundays are spent at the mill, timing Grady Fay, putting him through his paces, paying special attention to his shoulder, which still tends to stiffen up, especially when it rains. Mama doesn't like it that I don't go over to Snuffy, but I tell her the Lord will understand, and if He doesn't it's His tough luck. She warns me about being sacrilegious. Marvin warns me about something, too, but I'm not sure what. He says if I'm not careful I'll never hear again from you-know-who. "What is this you-know-who bit?" I ask him. When he doesn't answer, I go on about my business.

"Momentum" becomes Mr. Baxter's motto, and mine, too. "Do it every day," he says. "Don't slow down, don't slacken, keep the arm moving up, higher, higher, up, up." I repeat it later to Grady Fay. Afterwards we might drive down to Hookey's for a hamburger and glass of milk . . . but no french fries or fried onions, and above all, no dopies.

With this regimen, Grady Fay begins to lose the soft look he had before. His muscles harden, he grows leaner, more alert. One Saturday, in late afternoon, after two hours of what he calls "the hard grind," we get in his truck and, without any destination in mind, start driving (Grady Fay steering with one hand and squeezing a rubber ball with the other). For once, I don't worry about mama, and he doesn't constantly say that he has to get back to the farm—not even when we pass pastureland that reminds him (he says) of Sawmill Mountain, or cows that look like his own tiny herd. Instead, when we pass a particularly beautiful piece of land, he stops the car, and we get out.

It's a field with patches of winter stubble stretching all the way to a slope of woods. In the smack middle is a huge tree—probably to provide shade when the farmer's plowing—and this is where Grady Fay walks to. "Someday I'd like to have acreage like this," he says, leaning against the trunk and gazing around him. A line of mist hangs just above the ground, giving it a soft glow. I take a few deep breaths.

"Look!" Crouching, he points to a tan blur that flashes among a group of thin birches at the edge of the pasture. "And there's another." Squinting, he counts, "One, two, three, four . . . three does and a buck."

I try to follow his gaze but by the time I spot them, the does have already disappeared. Only the buck remains. He's staring back at us. "What's he doing?"

"Trying to figure out what we're up to." Grady Fay gives a low, admiring whistle. "Look at them horns!"

We wait several minutes before the buck shifts slightly and vanishes into the woods. For a second, I'm reminded of something. "My daddy loved deer," I say.

"Loves."

"What?"

"*Loves* deer. You said *loved*."

"Oh." Actually I don't know what he loves anymore. I don't even know whether or not he loves me.

Walking to the car, Grady Fay puts an arm around my shoulders, and I snuggle next to him. For warmth, I tell myself.

Neither of us say very much on the way back. Every now and then, I glance over, but he's intent on the road ahead.

> Mr. Frank Baxter of Goody, and Grady Fay Owens of Sawmill Mountain will leave Tuesday for Augusta, Georgia, where they will compete with the doffer from Peppermill Fabrics for the Superdoffer championship. . . .

Elsewhere in the *News*, Mr. Fortune in his weekly column, "From the General Manager's Desk," wishes them luck. So does Ruby Hammond in "Community Doings."

"Still got your rabbit's foot?" I ask Grady Fay on Monday afternoon. They're taking off the next morning, and although Mr. Baxter's ordered Grady Fay to stay home and rest, he's come in for a few hours of exercising. And maybe to see me?

Reaching into his pocket, he pulls it out. "Goes with me everywhere. Couldn't do without it," he says, all the time looking straight into my eyes.

Feeling shy, I touch his arm. "Be sure and keep us posted."

"Is it alright to call you at home?"

"Sure."

Then Boley comes over and leads us toward the canteen where everybody's gathered to toast Grady Fay's victory.

"Sorry this ain't the real thing," Boley says, raising his Double Cola bottle. "But we want you to know, Grady Fay ol' boy, that we're with you all the way."

"Hear, hear!" Shorty shouts.

"Don't bother coming back if you don't win," Reba Petit says, and Marvin yells a "hear, hear!" to that.

Depend on the two of them to add a sour note.

After they leave, the mill seems empty. For once, I even miss Mr. Baxter's cigar smoke. As usual, Marvin fills in for Grady Fay, but each time he gets slower and slower until I feel like we're making rounds in slow motion. I have a hard time focusing on piecing up, which causes a whole bunch of broken strings. By the end of the shift, my fingers are sore from so much pinching together.

That night, a black car comes around the plaza and stops in front of me just as I'm crossing over to Chimney Road. It's Gene. He signals me over. Usually he has his buddies with him, but this time he's alone. Soon as I get close enough, I can smell he's been drinking.

"Get in, baby," he says. "You and me're going for a ride."

"It's after twelve." I point to my watch.

"Think I don't know what time it is?" He looks at me as though I've done something terrible. "I hear you been two-timing ol' Gene while I been gone."

"What are you talking about?"

"You know." Reaching out a hand, he grabs my arm and holds on tight. "I don't like that. Don't like it one bit."

"Gene, you're hurting me."

"Wanna know if you're still my girl. Are you?"

"I guess so."

"Guess so isn't good enough. Are you or aren't you?"

I think the best thing to do is humor him so I say yes.

"Then when're you going to take a ride with me? Don't have long. Have to go back to Cincinnati day after tomorrow."

"Well . . ."

"When?"

I'm trying to back away but he's still holding on. Then I look up and see Troy's bread van heading toward us. The lights blind Gene and he puts a hand up.

"Everything alright?" Dot calls out.

At that second, Gene's hand goes limp, and I pull away.

"Come on, we'll drop you off," Dot says, and I turn and climb into the seat beside her. I'm afraid that she'll give me a lecture but instead, she talks about how great Grady Fay is and how much everybody misses him.

At home, I stay in my room with the door open in order to hear the phone ring. Whether I want it to be Gene or Grady Fay, I'm not sure.

I don't really expect Grady Fay to call Tuesday, but by Wednesday, I begin to worry about what's happening. Mr. Baxter said that the Augusta plant's much larger than Goody, and I can imagine Grady Fay being dazed by it all and not doing his best doffing. I'm so nervous that, without knowing what I'm doing, I start pacing up and down.

"What's the matter with you?" mama asks, biting a thread in half with her teeth. "Sit down! You're making me sew crooked."

But I can't sit. I can't sit, I can't stand, I can't walk around, I don't know what to do.

So I make lists of the things I'll take with me when my bonus comes through and I move over to the Inn. It's also a way of sorting out what's important and what's not, what belongs to mama and what's mine. Maybe at last I'll be a separate person.

When the phone *does* finally ring, I race to it, almost knocking over a small vase of artificial flowers that sits on a table by the living room door. Mama stops pedaling her sewing machine to listen.

"Hello," I say, slightly breathless.

But the voice on the other end is not Gene's or Grady Fay's but Dot's. "LaVonne! Come over here!"

"What?"

"Come over to the Inn. I have something to show you."

"But I'm waiting . . . "

"It's important!" she shrieks. "Hurry."

I'm torn about whether to go or not, but grabbing my jacket, I start buttoning it up. "Mama? If I get a long-distance call, tell them I'll be back in an hour."

"You expecting one?"

"Maybe. From Grady Fay. About the contest."

Reaching the Inn from the front way, I walk up the steps and through the columns, pausing for a second—but not too long because it's cold—to lean against one of them, as if I belong there.

Mrs. Harris, bent over a ledger, is at the desk, and I steal quietly by and am about to head directly upstairs when I see a small flock of mill girls near the back entrance and go over to see what all the carrying-on's about. When Dot spots me, she breaks out of the circle and runs over. "Oh, LaVonne, look! Look!" She flings out her left hand. On the fourth finger is a sparkling diamond, not very large, but big enough to see without a magnifying glass. "Troy give it to me last night. Never in my

128

whole life was I so surprised."

I squeal just like all the others. Only when Dot turns her back do I hear Reba Petit's jab to Lorene: "Did you see how small that thing is?"

"You haven't had a single call," mama says when I get back home. "What'd Dot Ledbetter want?"

"She and Troy just got engaged."

"About time. The way they carry on."

When the phone rings the next day, I'm at the table. I leap up, mouth full of food.

"LaVonne? This is Grady Fay." There's a pause while I try my best to swallow. "How you doing?"

"Good," I manage to get out. "How are *you?*"

"I won the semi-finals."

"Oh, Grady Fay! I'm so happy!"

"Uh . . . what? . . . hold on a minute. Mr. Baxter wants to say something."

"Hey there, girl!" I wish Mr. Baxter'd take the cigar out of his mouth, at least while he's talking long distance. "Your boy here's too modest. Not only did he win, but he set a new doffing record!"

"That's *wonderful!*"

Then Grady Fay comes on the line again. "I . . . haveta hang up because Mr. Baxter wants to call Mr. Fortune. I'll see you tomorrow night. Tell all the gang hello."

"I will," I say, and then he's gone. What was it Mr. Baxter'd said? Your boy? *Your* boy. I'm jumping up and down, not caring if mama says, "Sit down and eat up now," not caring if the parakeet repeats it, not caring when Miz Cowan walks in and asks what all the commotion's about and mama answers that I've just gone crazy. I'll be out of here soon, soon, soon, soon, soon.

That night when I shut my eyes, I feel like I'm gazing into a crystal ball. Grady Fay'll win the contest, be promoted to second-hand, and when Mr. Baxter retires, he'll take over as supervisor. Then he'll move into one of the big houses across the river.

And where will *I* be? Well, my future's still unsettled. "In ferment," as Preacher Crow might say.

When Grady Fay and Mr. Baxter come strolling in around six-thirty the next evening, everybody leaves their machines and runs over. Boley and Shorty pump Grady Fay's hand up and down, then grab Mr. Baxter's.

"LaVonne, we did it!" Grady Fay says, squeezing me with that strength of his until I can barely breathe. "We really did it!"

Then there's a flash, and I scream. But it's only Cecil Crider standing there, focusing his camera in every direction. He takes one of the whole group (Dot holding up her ring finger so it'll catch the light), and finally one of Grady Fay by himself, sitting in the quill buggy, his right fingers raised in a V-for-victory sign.

Though Grady Fay continues working hard—and me along with him—I'm aware, for the first time, of a lightheartedness in the way he goes about it. Or maybe he's just gotten more confident—not cocky like Gene'd be under the same circumstances, but as if there're certain things about himself that he can take for granted now. And I'm really surprised by the energy he puts out. I don't even have to nag him about exercising anymore. Just the opposite, in fact.

"Shouldn't you take a rest now?"

"Naw." He continues rowing, his arm muscles flexing with each pull. "Got to reach New Or-leens."

"New Or-leens?"

"Yep. That's where the next contest is. We're supposed to fly, but I'm going by boat." He winks at me. "Don't tell Mr. Baxter."

I stare at him. This is a whole new Grady Fay. Maybe I should introduce myself.

> Best wishes to Grady Fay Owens as he enters the semi-final round of the Superdoffer competitions. On Monday, Grady Fay and his supervisor, Frank Baxter, will be flown to New Orleans in the company plane where they will be met by representatives from Avondale Mills. If Grady Fay is successful at Avondale, the final round will take place here in Goody.

Having no idea where New Or-leens is or what it looks like, when I go to the library to return my latest Grace Livingston Hill book, on impulse I ask the librarian, Miss Howard, if she has any books on cities.

"Which cities?"

"Oh . . . Nashville, Atlanta . . . New Or-leens . . . "

"New *Orleans*," she corrects me, then leads me to a section marked "Travel" and pulls two volumes from the shelf.

I take them over to a table in the corner. The only other person around is Miss Cargle, the night nurse, who's just leaving with a big stack of books, probably all love stories to make up for what's missing in her life. I begin thumbing through the book on top of my stack, but there're not many pictures so I go on to the second.

I find out that a "Creole" is a negro who speaks French—which is hard to believe; that a "Mardi Gras" is when people dress up in funny clothes; and that a part of town called "Bourbon Street" is filled with honky-tonk joints that no doubt make Hoke Treadaway's seem tame.

On the way out, Miss Howard glances up from her desk and says something that I can't quite catch (either she speaks too low or the noise in the spinning room is making me deaf).

"I said, I hope you found what you were looking for."

"Yes, ma'am, I did."

"Are you planning a trip?"

"Never can tell," I say, and walk out.

"You are one lucky person!" I tell Grady Fay that evening.

"What?"

"To be going to New Orleans." I try to pronounce it like Miss Howard does. "Have you ever seen palm trees?" He shakes his head. "I did once when daddy took us to Panama City on vacation. They're beautiful. And there's the ocean . . . "

"I've always wanted to see the ocean," Grady Fay admits.

"And restaurants that serve fresh fish . . . "

"I hate fish."

"And old-fashioned houses . . . "

He moans. "You make it sound awful."

"You know, Elvis's making *King Creole* there right now. They're saying it's his best picture yet. I'd give anything if I could go with you."

"Me, too."

He moves on around the frame. Maybe he's heading for Mr. Baxter's office to talk to him about it. As the threads spin down, I see myself stepping off the plane.

I'm wearing a powder blue suit, my favorite color. Me and Grady Fay are immediately whisked off to a plush restaurant with three waiters standing by to deliver our heart's desires. The two of us—I saw it done once on "Philco Playhouse"—toast each other with a glass of champagne, the kind that bubbles over and spills down the front of my white blouse, not that I care, I assure Grady Fay as he rushes to dry me off. Nearby, twenty flash bulbs explode, sending up trails of false smoke. Through this smoke, I see Elvis, and he sees me. Ignoring Grady Fay, he pulls me out of the chair and into his arms, and we dance all around the floor together. . . .

Suddenly I stop. Across the aisle, I see Grady Fay's head. The whole thing's taken a wrong turn. Shaking myself slightly, I reach over to snap a thread.

On Monday morning, a group of us second-shifters stand around Mr. Baxter's car to give them a send-off. They're about to drive to the local airfield just above the Moon-lite Drive-in.

Dot's made some brownies for them to eat on the trip down, but she ends up passing them out to everybody until only one's left. Boley helps Mr. Baxter put the bags in the trunk, and when Grady Fay's falls apart (it's an old cardboard one belonging, he says, to his daddy), he also finds a rope to hold it together.

At Cecil Crider's urging, Grady Fay leans over and gives me a goodbye kiss. Though it's only a peck, afterwards my lips feel swollen.

During the week, bulletins about how Grady Fay's doing aren't hard to come by. Every evening, Spud Bankey—who's again our acting supervisor—walks through the whole spinning room announcing the day's results over a megaphone that he's borrowed from the Store manager, who uses it to announce sales.

"A victory today!" From the center of the filling section, his voice rises over the machinery roar. "Mr. Baxter just called. He and Grady Fay are in great spirits."

On Wednesday he wins again. "Terrific play!" booms Spud. "The other doffer didn't stand a chance. Both Mr. Baxter and Grady Fay asked me to give everyone their love. . . . "

Surely that's meant for me. Everybody else must think so, too, because when they pass me in the aisles, they say, "That's wonderful news about Grady Fay," as if I'm attached to him.

And I answer, "Yep, betcha Mr. Baxter's treating him to a big T-bone steak right now."

"Well, he deserves it," one woman says. "He's really *something,* isn't he?"

"*Really* something," I say.

Chapter Fourteen

WHEN GRADY FAY RETURNS, I DON'T SEE HIM until Wednesday, since Mr. Baxter gives him a day off. He comes in looking slightly sunburned. "Should be finished patching my barn by Friday," he says. "Why don't you come over this weekend and see it?"

"I'd love to."

"Pick you up on Saturday morning. Around ten."

It'll be a relief, I tell myself, to get out of the house. For the past few days, me and mama have been doing nothing but sitting in front of the television. Elvis has just been inducted into the army and we've been trying to catch all the news we can. We've seen him boarding a bus in front of the recruitment office so many times that I know every expression by heart. Not only his, but Gladys's, too.

"That woman's headed for a nervous breakdown," mama says.

"How can you tell?"

"Them big rings under her eyes, and that glazed look. Gives you away every time."

"What does *she* have to worry about?"

"Her son going overseas, that's what."

A sudden flash comes to me: a parade of trucks and tanks passing along the highway through Goody. It must've been near the beginning of World War II because I'm still so small that daddy has to lift me up so I can see. What I remember most are the tanks. I'd never seen anything so scary-looking. They made the soldiers seem puny by comparison.

"Where they going?" I ask daddy.

"Overseas . . . and some of them'll never come back."

"Why not?" I'm looking at a boy with short yellow hair that stands up on his head like corn stubble.

"They'll be killed."

"Overseas." I repeat the word under my breath but mama hears me.

"Mark my words," she says.

Though Saturday morning's gray, I'm still glad to get out of the house. Grady Fay's truck pulls up on the dot of ten.

"Why is it, every time I go to Sawmill Mountain, it's gloomy-looking?" I ask, gazing up at the sky through the windshield.

"It's supposed to rain. Radio said."

"Really?"

"Few drops of water never hurt anybody."

The longer we drive, the darker it gets. Finally Grady Fay swerves onto the rutty road that leads to his house. The second he stops, I'm out of the truck peering around. "Which way's the barn?"

"Over here."

I follow him along a path that takes us past a fence where two cows graze on brown grass. "Ouch!" I stub the toe of my ballerina slipper on a sharp rock.

"Careful." He takes my arm. "Don't you have any more shoes?"

"What's wrong with these?" Of course I know, only I'm not about to let on, not with my toe still smarting.

"They're not good for the country. You need a pair like mine."

I look down at his worn brogans and turn up my nose. "Don't like country shoes."

"Neither did my mama."

As we get closer to the barn, I can tell, from all the green lumber nailed in between the weatherbeaten planks, how much work Grady Fay's done. Inside are new stalls and feed troughs.

"How many cows you got?"

"Twenty-five. Most of them are off in the pasture." Taking my arm again, he guides me through several mounds of manure over to an inner stall where a tiny calf stands on spindly legs.

"Oh, how cute! Can I pet him?"

"Doubt she'll let you close enough."

I tiptoe over, holding out my hand. But the calf, opening its eyes wide, circles around to the opposite corner. Three times we switch positions without my ever touching him. "Tricky little devil. How old is he?"

"*She*. About six weeks."

Then he leads me up to the hayloft, recently replanked but still smelling of sweet tangy hay that's stacked in squares against one wall. Climbing down, I spy two old dusty saddles hanging crooked against the wall of the feed room. "You have horses?"

"Nope. These belonged to my mama."

"Oh."

"She brought 'em with her when she come to live with daddy. Ever ride a horse?"

"Only a mule."

"We had mules, too. But ma didn't think mules were good enough for them saddles. They're English. Which means there's nothing to hang onto. I know because I once slipped one over our old mule and took off. Near 'bout broke my neck. But that's nothing compared to the beating ma give me."

Outside the barn, I take several deep sniffs of air that smells of grass and wild onions. I also feel a few drops of rain.

"Here we go," Grady Fay says, putting out a hand.

We begin walking toward the house. By the time we reach the road, great pellets are coming down. "Didn't take long."

"Let's make a run for it." Grabbing my hand, Grady Fay pulls me along.

Although we go charging in, the man in the straight-backed chair by the stove doesn't even bother glancing up.

"Wow!" Grady Fay says, grabbing a towel and running it through his wet hair. "It's really coming down! Daddy, this is LaVonne Grubbs." Finally he looks up. "LaVonne works with me in the spinning room."

I give a real big smile. "Hidee, Mr. Owens." But he merely nods and returns to his newspaper.

"I was showing her our new barn."

"Not new," his father mutters. "Only done over."

"Done over then . . . like new," Grady Fay says, standing next to the stove and gesturing for me to do the same.

"Built it myself back in '32, year your ma and me was married." I can see how much Grady Fay resembles him—in the face, at least. Although some of that hang-dog expression has been left behind.

"Would you like something to eat?" Grady Fay asks. But remembering the state of the kitchen on my first visit, I shake my head.

Mr. Owens turns another page. "Raining you say?"

"Yessir. Pouring." Then he turns to me. "Sure you wouldn't like some coffee? Warm you up."

"Wouldn't mind a cup."

I follow him into the kitchen, trying not to make my glances around the place too obvious. It does seem cleaner than before.

The tapping noise on the tin roof suddenly turns to drum beats. "Listen to that!" For a few seconds, we're both still. There's a clap of thunder. When he opens the door for an instant, stray raindrops drift in. Then he shuts it again, gets out two cups. "After you finish the coffee, maybe we'd better head back. Sometimes these dirt roads turn to mud pretty fast. You don't wanna get stuck here."

If it was just him and me, I might not mind. In fact, it might be real cozy. But I can't see me and Mr. Owens in the same picture. "Mama'd be worried."

He pours me a syrupy brown mixture, and holding my breath, I drink as much of it as I can. I long to tell Grady Fay some of the things I've been thinking but now the timing seems wrong. I set down my cup. "Ready when you are."

Grady Fay turns on his heel like he's disappointed, too. "I'll be back," he says to Mr. Owens as he grabs a jacket off the back of the door.

"You going out?"

"Taking LaVonne home." He hands the jacket to me. "Here. Put this over your head."

The old man looks confused. "But it's raining."

"I know."

I dash out behind Grady Fay, who holds the door. The rain is now coming down harder than ever. As we back out, I can see the gullies filling up. We skid and slide up to the main road.

Grady Fay makes a swipe at the mist on the windshield. "If this keeps up, I'll have to stop." Even now we're only inching along. It's as though a curtain of water has been drawn around us. "Can't see a thing!" When he opens the door a crack, the rain comes charging in. "Least I know we're still on the road." Putting his head out all the way, he drives to the nearest turnoff. "I'm pulling over at Galloway's store. It's just a few yards away." Then I hear the crunch of gravel beneath the wheels and we come to a halt.

The rain sounds louder than ever. "Well, it can't last forever," I say.

Taking a handkerchief out of his pocket, Grady Fay wipes off his hands and face. "Sorry we had to leave so soon. You'll come back?"

I smile and nod.

"Funny. I knew it was going to rain yesterday."

"How?"

He touches his shoulder. "This thing started aching." Reaching over, he pulls me close. We sit with our heads together, not a totally comfortable position, but I don't mind. We stay this way a long time. Finally I turn my face toward him. But he's not looking at me. He's looking out the window. Following his gaze, I can make out a gas pump and beyond that, a big Dr. Pepper sign. "Reckon we can start now," he says, removing his arm, "if we creep along." For the first time in a long while, I think of Gene. He has that pinch of seasoning that's missing from Grady Fay. If only Grady Fay could be a bit more . . . grabby. But I guess that'd be the same as asking a chicken to turn into a hawk. Wonder what's happened to Gene.

If I imagined that mama might be nervous, I'm wrong. When I get home, she's laying on the sofabed, Vaseline smeared on her face, watching a wrestling match, and barely glances up. She loves wrestling. Says it reminds her of the way Miz Cowan and her husband used to fight. When the thin one knocks the fat one to the floor and then bounces up and down on his stomach, she cackles. I can hear her all the way to the bedroom, even with the door shut.

Next morning I sleep late. When I look at my watch, it's almost ten. We've missed church. I rush into the kitchen, where mama's listening to gospel singing on the radio. "What's wrong? Why didn't you wake me?"

"Pearlie B. called and said the choir was canceled. Then she called back and said the church basement was flooded and the whole thing was canceled. Anyhow, it's still pouring."

Mama fixes a big breakfast: slabs of country ham, fried eggs, and biscuits. While washing dishes, we hear a thumping noise. Mama turns. "What's that?" At the opposite corner of the kitchen, a steady drip of water's coming down. "Lord have mercy, what next!" She gets a bucket from the porch to catch it in. "Tomorrow I'll call Wormy LeCroy." (Wormy works in the maintenance department and does plumbing on the side. He's so skinny that Marvin predicts, one of these days, he'll mistake himself for one of his own pipes.)

By Monday there're *two* leaks, and two buckets underneath. Wormy says there's no point in doing anything about them, though, until the roof has a chance to dry out. "Tar just won't stick in this weather," he says . . . several times.

"What if it gets worse?"

"Then you'll have to go to the Store and buy another bucket."

By the time I'm off to work, the rain has finally stopped, though the sky has such a sultry look to it that I wear my raincoat. Mr. Baxter comes around to tell me that Grady Fay can't get in because of the muddy roads. "Had to walk two miles just to call me," he says.

Just before twilight, a downpour comes, and thunder and lightning along with it. It's such a dramatic sight that, at the break, me and Tessie leave our machines for a few minutes to stand at the windows watching. Since Tessie can't see so good, I find myself describing the scene to her. I try to make it sound like something out of *True Confessions*. "Suddenly a flash of lightning illuminates a lone figure struggling, through the torrent of rain, to reach the other side of the footbridge. Nothing, not even a storm, can keep him from her side tonight. . . . "

Marvin Cowan comes and joins us. At the next flash, I glance over; for an instant, he resembles somebody in a horror movie.

Later, when I walk in the kitchen, I almost stumble over the three buckets and two pots that are lined up across the floor to catch the leaks. One of them apparently sprang up directly over Pretty Boy's cage because mama's drying it out.

"I'm scared the whole roof will cave in," she says, frowning up at the row of large brown stains on the ceiling.

Unable to sleep, I listen to the steady drip-drip-drip in the next room. I turn and twist, knowing already that if I ever get to sleep, I'll wake up in a bad mood. Like daddy used to when he claimed to have been wrestling with the devil all night. When he left, mama said that the devil'd won. She'll probably say the same about me.

Though I do feel tired the next morning, I manage to drag myself up. Mama's standing at the kitchen stove. "It's still coming down," she says, pointing to the window. "River must be getting high."

The continued downpour causes what Mr. Baxter calls "a whirl of activity."

Mr. Fortune orders four truckloads of sandbags from an army surplus store in Atlanta. These are stacked up and down the banks between the footbridge and the larger concrete bridge. Residents of Wart Town, especially those by the river, have already moved out and gone to stay with friends or relatives. The two Goody policemen are kept busy re-directing traffic around places where the river's about to overflow.

Grady Fay's been stuck on Sawmill Mountain for a week and a half, and of course Mr. Baxter has to call both the Southeast Textile Association and Bufford Mills, where the other finalist works, to put off the last match.

On Thursday of the second week, I join mama, Miz Cowan, and Marvin in hiking up to Pleasant Hill to look at the dam. Marvin says it'll bust open at any minute, and naturally he wants to be there when it happens. Halfway up the hill, I can hear the water crashing down. At the top, a large crowd has already gathered, including Mr. Fortune, who's gesturing toward the dam.

"He's gonna have to call in the National Guard," Marvin says.

But that night the rain stops. I've grown so used to the constant dripping that the silence wakes me up. Going to the window, I pull back the curtains. Not only has it cleared up, but a couple of stars can be seen overhead. A huge doorknob of a moon shines brighter than it has in weeks.

On my way to work the next day, I can't help noticing how cheerful people look. They're smiling and making jokes, though every once in a while, someone still shoots a worried glance toward the sky.

Mr. Baxter tries to get up a betting pool on whether or not the sun'll shine for the next five days. But I reckon a lot of folks—me included—are too superstitious to test their luck.

Chapter Fifteen

EVEN THOUGH THE LAST ROUND OF COMPETITION is rescheduled, it barely gives Grady Fay a chance to get back in the swing of things. Mr. Baxter tries to delay it longer, "but the rules were against it," he reports, shaking his head. To highlight its importance the *News* prints the headline in red ink, which hasn't been done since V.E. Day. There's also a huge picture of Grady Fay, which is such a flattering likeness that I can't resist cutting it out and taping it to the wall next to my Elvis poster. The best news is that all us mill workers will be given the day off, so everybody's grateful to Grady Fay on that score alone.

Mr. Baxter gets the idea of contacting the Channel 12 news team in Chattanooga for extra publicity, and to his surprise, they call back and say they're sending down a camera crew. This throws Mr. Fortune and all the mill bosses into a tizzy. Mr. Baxter's told to get the spinning room in "shipshape order."

"Marvin Cowan'll have to do some work for a change," Dot comments on hearing this.

Fly-specks and knots of greasy lint that have been stuck to the walls for years are suddenly gone, washed off and covered over with a coat of gray paint. A notice tacked on the bulletin board asks every worker to be responsible for his or her particular section, which—as Dot mutters— means that we constantly have to be cleaning up after ourselves. Rules against taking potato chips or peanuts or crackers out of the canteen and into the plant proper are now taken seriously. Anybody seen grinding a cigarette into the newly polished floor will be docked an hour's pay.

'Course this puts a big strain on everybody. "Feel like I'm walking around on egg shells," is the way Boley puts it, and he's not far wrong.

In the canteen, we become so conscious about making a mess that it spoils our fun. Several people comment that they'll be glad when it's all over.

But the one who bears the brunt of the pressure is Grady Fay. He begins to look haggard, as if he isn't sleeping well.

"You alright?" I keep asking, seeing the circles under his eyes deepen. He's grown skinny, too. In the canteen, I watch him take a few bites out of a sandwich, then throw the rest away. As far as I can tell, he seems to be living mostly on dopies. Mr. Baxter's so busy with all the preparations that he's not able to give Grady Fay much attention, and I'm not sure he's aware of any problem. To cheer Grady Fay up, I make a banana pudding and take it in to him, but he only picks around at the banana slices, leaving Marvin and Shorty to finish off the pudding part. Dot notices this, too. "That boy don't act like hisself," she whispers to me. "I'm worried about him."

"He'll be okay."

"A lot's riding on it."

"He can handle it."

I only pray I'm right. A lot's riding on it for me, too.

On the Thursday before, I go down to Richville to buy myself a new outfit, one that'll show my figure off better than the sack dresses I normally wear.

"What's so special about this contest?" mama asks later when I model the dress in front of the living room mirror, "that you throw away good money on a bought dress. Besides, the waist is too pinched."

"But I love the color. The saleswoman called it 'electric blue.' Will you hem it up for me?"

"It's too dressy for work," mama says, then shrugs. "But if you don't mind being the laughing-stock, it's alright with me."

Since I'm moving out soon, I can afford to be nice. "You want me to look good, don't you? Television people will be there."

Mama sniffs. "What does that have to do with you? You're not one of the contestants."

"No. But I'm associated with somebody who is."

As I'm walking toward the mill on the day of the contest, I can see a huge banner whipping back and forth in the wind. WELCOME TO THE SUPERDOFFER CHAMPIONSHIP, GOODY MILLS VS. BUFFORD MILLS.

A crowd's already gathering outside and as I get closer, I see people turn and whisper to one another. Without thinking, I put a hand up to smooth my hair. A pink and black van bearing the name WSCB-CHANNEL 12, CHATTANOOGA is parked out front, and three stocky guys are carrying equipment in.

At the top of the steps, a man I've never seen before puts out a hand.

"Keep to your left, miss. We're setting up on the other side." Nodding, I continue on. "And watch all the wires," he calls out.

It's a different place I walk into . . . partly because of the bright lights, but also because of the long strips of crepe paper floating from fixture to fixture and covering the posts in the middle of the big room. Mr. Fortune, dressed in a beige suit with a beautiful figured tie, is standing in the spotlight backing off slightly from a microphone being shoved in his face. "This is a red letter day in the history of Goody," he's saying. Then, "Yes, I feel certain . . . " but I can't catch the rest for the noise of people tramping up the steps, even though the television men keep telling them to quiet down. Then someone points to me, and I let myself be pulled over. The lights are blinding. A tiny man with makeup on his face asks me about my connection with Grady Fay, and I explain, as best I can, about helping him train for the contest.

"What's Grady Fay Owens like as a person, Miss Grubbs . . . in your own words?" The man's voice is as oily as his complexion.

"He's . . . " I'm searching for something to say " . . . hardworking . . . thoughtful . . . and very nice. Very, very, very nice."

"I know you're proud of him." The man gazes into my eyes the way Preacher Crow does when he's trying to see my innermost thoughts.

Hope the camera won't catch the pink flush that I feel spreading over my face or the sweat breaking out on my forehead. Licking my lips, I reply, "Yes, yes, I am." The man waits for me to say more, but when I don't, he thanks me and moves on.

I spy Mollie Sue, who comes over to gush at my interview, and Jake Haygood from the undertaking department, and bosses from other shifts, as well as a couple of girls from the glove mill, who are wearing the same lime green uniforms that mama used to wear. Behind them come Dot and Marvin.

Dot grabs my arm. "You did real good," she says. "And only seemed a tiny bit nervous."

"I had so many butterflies," I clutch my chest, "I could hardly *breathe*."

"Want a Coke? Let's go get one."

The two of us—followed by Marvin, who's mumbling to himself about all the cleaning up he'll have to do afterwards—head for the canteen where we join the long line in front of the Coke machine.

"Never seen anything like this before," Dot says. "Where did all these people come from?"

"It's been well advertised." I look around. "Do you see Grady Fay?"

"Bet Mr. Baxter's got him under lock and key."

Near the machine, a man in a t-shirt that says BUFFORD MILLS leans against the wall sipping an Orange Crush. The drink is only a shade brighter than his hair. His face and arms are spotted with freckles.

"Wonder if he's the one Grady Fay's doffing against," I whisper to Dot.

Dot gives him the once-over. "He don't look like much."

Since the canteen's packed wall-to-wall with people, we take our drinks outside. Even the plant room's crowded. I see Mrs. Fortune strolling by with June Bankey. They're both wearing high heels and the kind of silk prints that seem to flow as they walk along. On impulse I go rushing over and put myself directly in their path.

"Hi," I say to Mrs. Fortune, who looks at me blankly, then raises her eyebrows at June Bankey as if asking for help. "I'm LaVonne Grubbs. I sat next to you at the banquet."

"Of course." She puts out a hand. "How nice to see you again. And what a pretty dress. Such an unusual color." Her eyes move down my blue taffeta from top to bottom.

"Thanks."

"You'll have to excuse us . . . " I can't hear what else she says, because they move away.

Rejoining Dot and Marvin, we make our way over to the filling section. The area around Number 9 frame has been roped off and little bunches of spectators are already straining against the rope to get a better view. "I have to find Grady Fay," I say.

"There he is," Dot points.

"Where?"

"There."

Then I spot him with Mr. Baxter, who—judging from the way he keeps punching the air with his cigar—is giving him last-minute instructions.

"Oh," I groan, almost in tears. "I won't have a chance to wish him good luck."

"Sure you will." Dot's tone is firm. "You just barge right up there."

But it's easier said than done. When I finally succeed in pushing my way to the front, one of the television men refuses to let me through the rope.

"But I have to speak to him!" I nod toward Grady Fay. "We're *partners.*"

"Sorry, ma'am, but they're about to begin." In desperation, I wave my arms up and down. Finally Grady Fay sees me, and smiles. Is he nervous? It's hard to tell from this distance.

"He seems in pretty good spirits," I report to Dot, who's been waiting for me near one of the posts.

"Let's try to find a place where we have some kind of view." She looks around. But the best we can do is over by the window. "Might as well be on the moon," she groans.

"At least we'll have fresh air . . . "

"Shhh." Dot puts a finger to her lips. "Mr. Baxter's making a speech."

It's the usual. He's *honored* to have B. J. Denton and the rest of his team from Bufford, and hopes everybody will do them the *honor* of making them feel welcome. "And in conclusion," he says, his voice rising as it always does when he's trying to be dramatic, "may the best doffer win."

"Yea, Grady Fay!" Dot shouts.

A tall man standing directly in front of us turns around and stares at us without smiling.

"He's got to be better than somebody named B. J. Denton," I whisper. Both of us are now on tiptoes.

"I'm gonna get myself a better view if I haveta bust that crowd wide open," she says. "You coming?"

But I've had enough pushing and shoving. Besides, I can *hear* what's going on. "I'll stay put," I say as she disappears into the mob of people.

The sound of the starting whistle makes my heart pump faster. Well, this is it. When it's over, I'll get my raise and Grady Fay'll get a big promotion. From now on, it's *really* onward and upward!

"Go, Grady Fay, *go!*" Sounds like Boley's voice. Some other people pick it up, and pretty soon a whole chant can be heard.

Finishing my Coke, I turn and set the empty bottle on the window-sill. For a second I glance down at the river. The drain from the dye plant is pouring red into the water. Reminds me of a song I sang with the Quartet, and for lack of anything better to do, I begin humming it in a very low voice. Maybe it'll bring Grady Fay luck.

> *Are you washed,*
> *In the blood,*
> *In the soul-cleansing blood of the Lamb?*
> *Are your garments spotless,*
> *Are they white as snow,*
> *Are you washed in the blood of the Lamb?*

Just then, I hear a round of applause. Grady Fay must have done real good. I clap, too.

Now it's the other doffer's turn. Poor fellow doesn't know he's up against not just one man but a whole team. I lean toward the man in front, who can see more than I can, and ask how it's going.

"Great. Just great."

Wonder if he's one of the new workers that Spud Bankey just hired for the third shift. Anyway, Grady Fay must be way ahead.

There's a ten-minute break between rounds. Though a few straggle toward the canteen, most people, not wanting to lose their places, stay where they are. Since Dot is nowhere is sight, I figure she must've joined Boley on the other side. There's such a buzz of voices that everything else is drowned out. From where I'm standing, the only person I could possibly have a conversation with is the tall guy, but he doesn't seem overly friendly. I do make an attempt, though. "He's real fast, isn't he?"

"Yes, ma'am." He looks at me, then past me. "Specially today. Somebody must've put something in his food." When he laughs, I notice that his front teeth are brown and crooked. "Can you smoke in here?" I shake my head, but he takes out a cigarette and lights it anyway. I back up against the window.

By my watch, ten minutes have already come and gone. Mr. Baxter's probably out among the spectators trying to raise some bets. Either that or revving up Grady Fay to make an even higher score. I turn back to the window. It's started drizzling outside, and on the pane two tiny drops are racing down the glass, side by side. I bend closer to watch. The one pulling ahead is Grady Fay. The other one swerves to the right while Grady Fay rolls all the way to the bottom.

This time when the whistle sounds, I make a real effort to see something, but the man in front keeps blocking my view.

"Do you mind," I tap him on the shoulder, "moving to one side a bit?"

"There's nowhere to move." He stays put like he's rooted there.

I probably couldn't have glimpsed Grady Fay anyway, considering the way he hunches over as he doffs. I *can* spot Mr. Baxter, though—at least I think I can—from the smoke that drifts up from his cigar. It must be seesawing in his lips, the way it does when he's nervous.

At that second, the television lights go on filming the final stretch. I hear Boley shouting again, "*Go, go, go, go. Faster, faster, faster, faster!*"

I can tell, by the way people shift positions, that he's moved around to doff the other side of the frame. The yells are deafening. I wonder if it's Dot's voice screeching, "Come on, Grady Fay, come on!" Then the lights go out, and everybody claps and whistles. If I *could* whistle, I would, too. After the other doffer's turn, the whole thing'll be over.

Except for a few stray mumbles and whispers, the guy from Bufford doffs in complete silence. Too bad he doesn't get the same kind of support. For a second, I feel sorry for him.

In the end, only a scattering of applause can be heard—and a few shouts, mostly by the man in front of me, who's jumping up and down. Wanting to find somebody to celebrate with besides him, I try to make my way through the crowd. People don't seem to be moving much at all . . . just standing around in little clumps.

Just ahead, I spy the back of Dot's head. But she's walking away, and

I can't catch up. As I get closer, the television lights come on. The glare blinds me and I put a hand up to shield my eyes. Neither Grady Fay nor Mr. Baxter is anywhere in sight. But I do catch a glimpse of Marvin Cowan and make a beeline for him, though he'd not normally be my first choice. Least he might be able to tell me where Grady Fay is. When he sees me, he throws up a hand. "Knew this would happen," he smirks as I get closer. "I predicted it."

"Yeah?" It's sad the extremes Marvin goes to just to impress people. "Didn't we all?"

"You did, too?" He squints at me.

"Of course."

"You're joking!"

Now it's my turn to stare. Since Marvin seems denser than usual, I decide to change the subject. "You know where Grady Fay is?"

"Sure." He points behind him. "Over there with Mr. Baxter."

"See ya later. Haveta give him a hug."

"Reckon he could use one."

I continue slipping through the groups who are standing around talking. Some are familiar faces, and one or two blink at me and nod. Suddenly I stop dead still, turn, and push my way back to where Marvin is. "What did you mean by that?" I ask as soon as I'm close enough.

"By what?"

"That he could use a hug."

"Couldn't you? Under the circumstances?"

"*What* circumstances?"

"You know. If you'd lost."

For a second, I'm too stupefied to speak. "Are you telling me that Grady Fay Owens *lost?*"

"Yep."

"I don't believe it!"

Marvin's grin widens. "Well, he did."

"How *could* he?"

"Easy. Fell behind. The other guy was faster."

"But all the shouting . . . "

"Didn't do one bit of good. Any more than that rowing machine did."

I'm in such a state of shock that when I find myself back by the window, I hardly know how I got there. Some of the crowd's beginning to leave, and I can see the red-headed doffer from Bufford talking into the microphone. The man who was in front of me is standing beside him, and he's asked to say a few words, too. I feel like a fool.

And what words of comfort can I give Grady Fay? What can I give myself? All that work down the drain! No bonus, no raise, no promotion, no nothing!

145

Then I glimpse Dot, a handkerchief held to her eyes, talking to Boley. "Oh, LaVonne," she cries, throwing her arms around me. "How could this happen?"

"I don't know," I answer truthfully. "I can't find Grady Fay. Do you know where he is?"

"Over there with Mr. Baxter," Boley says.

Mr. Baxter's standing near the door talking to Mr. Fortune. But I don't see anybody else.

He's so deep in conversation that he doesn't notice me until I pull at his sleeve. "Where's Grady Fay?"

"Oh." He looks around. "Think he may have left already."

"Left?"

"Yeah. He's real let down. As I was saying to Mr. Fortune here, I think it was the rain that did it. All that time out. Yessir, I think fate conspired against us again."

All the way home, I keep repeating to myself, "Grady Fay lost, Grady Fay lost, Grady Fay lost," trying to make it sink in.

When I walk in the door, mama sees by my face that something's wrong. "Grady Fay lost," I say, slumping down on the sofa with my head in my hands.

"Just what I expected," mama says.

Just what *I* expected. Not one word of consolation.

Chapter Sixteen

GRADY FAY DOESN'T COME TO WORK THE NEXT DAY, or the next. According to Mr. Baxter, he doesn't call either. Which floors me because it's not like him. Every hour that passes gets me more and more upset. Mr. Baxter, too. He tells Dot to ask Troy to go over and check on him. Troy comes back and says that Grady Fay's got a cold. Be in on Monday. Maybe. It's that "maybe" that bothers me.

On Saturday, a letter arrives, which I snatch away from mama before she has a chance to see the postmark. It's from Delphi, so I can pretty much guess Gene wrote it. The note is scribbled on the back of a flyer announcing a drag race. It says, "Just got back from Cincinnati. You looked beautiful on TV. See you soon, I hope." It's not signed. Reckon he figures a name would be a waste of time. I look around for some place to hide it, and end up stashing it under my pillow.

Monday comes and goes, and still no Grady Fay. Finally, on Friday, he straggles in. I see him stop long enough to speak to Mr. Baxter, then move on. His walk's lost that springy step and is back to the heavy-footed lope he had when he first started working here.

What am I going to say? Play it as it comes, I tell myself. I make sure to be busy. When he gets closer, I summon my most casual voice. "Tried to find you after the contest, but you were gone like a flash."

"Had to get home." He can't meet my eyes. I'd like to reach over and give him a big squeeze, but I'm afraid he'd just back away. When he finishes loading the quill buggy, he pushes it toward me. "Sorry I let you down," he mumbles. "You, Mr. Baxter, everybody."

I decide to let the threads go for a few seconds and trail after him.

"Grady Fay, it could happen to anybody." He shakes his head. "'Course it could!"

"Mama used to call daddy a loser," he says in that flinching way I thought he was rid of. "Reckon I take after him."

"Huh!" I almost spit on the floor in disgust. "There oughta be a law against mamas like that." I'm talking about *his* mama, and a few others I could mention.

But instead of answering, he just bends over the buggy and keeps going. I ache to give him some kind of comfort.

Next afternoon, I come in to find him already there. He has an axe, which he's using to chop up the Machine.

"Oh my God!" I squeal.

But he goes right ahead. The blows send splintering noises over the click of the frames. I've never seen him like this. His hair, usually perfectly in place, is all tousled, his face looks like it's on fire, and his lips are pressed against his teeth.

I rush to find Boley. "You know what Grady Fay's doing?"

"Yeah, I know."

"Well, aren't you going to stop him? Thought you intended to patent that machine."

"No sense patenting something that don't work."

I look at him. I want to answer that it *had* worked, *did* work, and maybe would work again, only I can't seem to get the words out.

I circle Grady Fay, trying to figure out how to approach him, but when I get close, he turns and gives me a snarl, not *me* directly, but *something* inside his head. I'd like to jerk that axe out of his hand, but if I did, no telling what he might do in the wild animal state he's in. So I stand and watch the contraption that brought us together being destroyed bit by bit, and I'm not able to do one thing about it.

When he finishes, and it's all a pile of wood, he takes the wood downstairs, load after load, and throws it into the big dumping barrel. Then he returns, rolls down his shirt sleeves, picks up the axe, and strides out like an angry giant. He doesn't even make a pretense at doffing.

At first, I think he's just gone off on some errand and wait for him to come back. But he doesn't.

I run over to Dot. "Grady Fay's gone." I can feel my throat tightening up.

"Gone?"

"I think he's walked off the job."

"Grady Fay wouldn't do that."

"I think he's already done it."

I wait. Every day I wait for him to turn up. I stand at the window, gazing down at the plaza, praying to see that old truck of his, which I used to joke about, drive up, and him jump out and bound up the stairs. Well, not *bound,* Grady Fay'd never do that, but take two at a time, and sometimes three, except when I was beside him. Finally, Mr. Baxter spots me moping around. Says, "LaVonne, aren't you slacking up a bit?"

I say, "Yessir, guess I am."

And he says, "Well, I sympathize with that, don't feel so hot myself, but we can't just let ourselves go. We got to keep up a certain standard."

So I return to the frames and go through the motions. But my heart's not in it, and a lot of threads break, and then I have to stop and pinch them together, and the lint flies up my nose, and I sneeze, and breathe in some of it, and have a coughing fit. As you can see, I'm a mess.

And here comes Mr. Baxter again. Won't let me alone. "Snap out of it, girl," he keeps saying. I hear him telling Dot to see if she can cheer me up. Dot says she can't do the impossible.

One morning while I'm supposed to be sleeping, I hear mama confiding to Miz Cowan that she's worried I'm close to a nervous breakdown. I can't even be bothered to reassure her. Anyway, I'm not so sure myself. I just close my eyes again.

Part of it's the heat. After several weeks of beautiful weather, the muggy stuff's come upon us overnight. I can barely gather the strength to put up the front porch awning so mama can sit out in the swing in late afternoon. Or to get down the fan from the storage shelf in the closet and hook it up. But somehow I do. Then I lay back down with an arm draped over my eyes to shut out the light. When I'm not doing this, I plop down in the living room and watch television, though I don't really see or hear much.

"Don't you ever *move?*" mama asks. But I don't even have the energy to blink, much less shake my head. "You're going to get hemorrhoids."

One evening mama's waiting for me when I come in from work, which is unusual for her these days. At first I think something's wrong, that the heat's got to the parakeet maybe, but she points to the television. "Gladys Presley's been taken to the hospital," she says. "Heard it earlier."

"What's wrong with her?" Instead of going back to my room as I usually do, I sit down a minute.

"Nobody seems to know."

"Probably just a checkup." I let out a big yawn. Once I would've got excited about Gladys, but lately her and Elvis seem so far away. Like relatives I never see. Like daddy. "I'm going to bed." And I turn on my fan and lay down on the bed, but I don't get much sleeping done. I'm still wondering if Grady Fay's okay.

Next morning, I pad out to the kitchen for my first dopie of the day. Mama's puttering about at the stove. Surely she's not planning on cooking a big meal in this heat. "Did you hear any more news? About Gladys?" I ask her before she can ask me something.

"Not a thing. Reckon you were right. Whatever it is must not be too bad."

Two days later, I'm standing at the newsstand, rifling through movie magazines, when I spot a headline in the *Chattanooga Times* saying that Elvis has obtained an emergency leave from the army to be at his mother's bedside.

I go home and tell mama that Gladys's condition must be serious. Then I pull out the radio—an old Philco that's hardly ever played except on Sunday morning when mama listens to gospel—and plug it in. Don't know which has the most static, it or Pretty Boy.

Flipping the dial from one station to another, I catch a second of Patti Page, of health news, of a Duz commercial.

"If you don't leave it in one place, we'll never hear anything," mama yells from the doorway.

" . . . at Methodist Hospital in Memphis, Tennessee . . . "

"Here we are."

" . . . where Elvis Presley's mother, Mrs. Gladys Presley, was admitted over a week ago with symptoms similar to hepatitis. Since that time, her health has deteriorated rapidly, leaving doctors puzzled about the exact cause of her illness. Although Mrs. Presley's condition is still serious, she appears to have rallied considerably since the arrival, late last night, of her famous son from Fort Hood, Texas, where he has just completed his basic training. For further news on Mrs. Presley, stay tuned to this station . . . "

"Sounds like she's improving anyway," mama says.

When I come in that evening, I switch on the kitchen light and see a note on the table.

GLADYS IS A LOT BETTER THOT
YOUD LIKE TO KNOW

Even with the fan and all the windows open, my room's stifling, and I have trouble getting to sleep. Tiptoeing into the kitchen, I open the refrigerator to see what's inside. Careful not to wake up mama, I pick the first things my hand comes to: cherry jello, a piece of chocolate pie, and some cornbread dressing left over from Sunday dinner. It's somehow satisfying to eat them in just that order.

"LaVonne?" From somewhere mama's voice floats through. I sit up with eyes still half-shut, then fall back down and put the pillow over my head.

"LaVonne?" This time she shakes me.

"Hmmmm?"

"Can you hear me?"

"Hmmmm."

"Gladys Presley's dead." I throw the pillow aside. Mama's face looks bleak. "She died in the middle of the night. And Elvis wasn't even with her, isn't that sad? They told him to go rest, and then she took a turn for the worse."

"When did you find out?"

"Just now, on the radio."

I'm wondering if she might be hearing things. I turn on the "Today Show," but they don't show much about it, only the back of the Methodist Hospital and an ambulance driving away. No shots of Elvis at all. Maybe he's gone into hiding.

Afterwards—still in my pink wrapper 'cause I can't be bothered getting dressed—I pad out to the front porch and stand for a few seconds looking up and down the street. Nothing to see, though. Not a single car or truck, coming or going. A blank. Just like my life.

Then the phone rings and, sighing, I walk inside to answer it. When I say hello, I'm shocked to hear Gene. He's the last one I expected.

"LaVonne," he says. "I want you to listen to me real careful." His voice is low and serious. "You heard the news?"

For the first time in days, I feel alert. "Don't know what you're talking about . . . "

"I mean, about Elvis's mama?"

"Well, sure . . . "

"Listen, me and my buddies are striking out for Memphis. I want you to come."

"What?" Am I hearing right?

"I said, I want you to come. You want to see Elvis? I know you do."

Is he nuts? "But I can't . . . " Then I lower my own voice and start whispering. "I can't go to Memphis with you. Mama'd have a fit."

There's a pause. "Didn't know I was dealing with a mama's girl here. Figured I was dealing with somebody who had some gumption. Figured you wanted to see the world. That's what you used to say."

"I do, but . . . "

"This is our chance, baby. Yours and mine. May be our only one. You got to grab opportunities when they come your way."

It's just what Preacher Crow always says, or something to that effect. "I suppose I could take the bus . . . "

"I'll wait for you at the station tonight. I'll wait till you get there. I'm counting on you. Don't let me down." Then the phone clicks and he's gone. Just like that. Never saying hello and certainly not goodbye.

I go back out on the porch and sit for a few minutes on the step. Across the street I see Miz Cowan shaking out her mop. Hope she doesn't come over and start jawing. Especially when I'm trying to think. If I do go, it'd be the craziest thing I ever did. But maybe it's time to do something crazy. I'm certainly not getting anywhere by being normal.

I get up, banging the screen door behind me. Mama's in the living room dusting. "Whew, it's hot," she says, taking out a kleenex and wiping her face and hands.

"Thought I was gonna faint in the mill last night."

"Don't see why you can't have air-conditioning."

"Cold air makes the threads break. They claim."

"Bet they're just trying to save electricity."

"I'll do that," I say, taking the dust rag from her. "Fix yourself something with ice in it."

So while she shuffles off, I go over to the telephone, pick up the directory, thumb through it, and dial. Turns out there's a bus leaving at 11:06. Gets into Memphis at seven with a short rest stop in Nashville. I go into the kitchen where mama's on her second glass of iced tea. "Do we have any bananas?"

"Why?"

"Suddenly I have a craving for bananas." Instead I pour Rice Krispies into a large bowl, sprinkle on lots of sugar, and listen to them crackle. They seem to be saying, "Go, go, go."

Mama notices that she's forgot to take off the cage cover. "Mama's sorry," she says to the bird in that fake voice that makes my skin crawl. "Ess she is."

As I eat the Rice Krispies, I'm wondering how to break the news. No matter how I do it, she'll be upset. Maybe I'll just leave a note and slip out. That's cowardly, I know, but it'd save a whole lot of fuss. What about my overnight bag? She'll see it and wonder what I'm up to.

Then I get a brainstorm.

I call Dot. Mrs. Harris answers and buzzes her room. It takes a few minutes, but finally Dot picks up the phone. Like Gene, I don't waste time with small talk.

"I need you to do me a favor."

"Okay."

"I got a chance to go to Memphis. To see Elvis. I'm taking a bus this afternoon. Can I tell mama I'm spending the night with you?"

"You're going by yourself?" Dot sounds like she doesn't believe it.

"Somebody's meeting me."

"Who?"

"Nobody special . . . an old boyfriend."

"Not the one who turned up at the skating rink that time?"

"Of course not," I lie.

"I don't know, LaVonne, I don't want to get mixed up in nothing that might backfire."

"Dot, you're always telling me to be more independent. Finally I am, and look what happens!"

There's a long pause. I got a hunch those words hit home.

"Well, okay. I guess so. When'll you be back?"

"Tomorrow night."

"If you're sure it's only one day."

"I'm sure."

"Be careful," she says.

Be careful! Isn't that the story of my life?

There're plenty of empty seats on the bus, in fact I have one all to myself. For the first ten miles or so, I sit there stewing. I stew about sneaking out, about telling mama a lie. But as much as I'd like to deny it, there's a definite excitement to it. Grady Fay Owens can just go . . . you know where.

Then I doze off. In my dream, daddy—dressed in his white suit—stands before me, posing for a picture. I say, "Smile, daddy," and he does. I say, "Hold it, now," and I look down and click the camera. But when I glance up, he's gone.

At Chattanooga, more passengers get on. Outside the city limits, I glimpse some hills in the distance. We pass a big lake, with a sign that says, "Property of the Tennessee Valley Authority." Two men in rubber boots and leather caps walk along the road carrying fishing gear.

That's the last spot I take much notice of until we reach a stretch called Briley Parkway. When tall, gold-tipped buildings start rising up, I realize that we must be coming into Nashville.

I prefer staying in my seat during the rest stop, but if mama was here, she'd say I should stretch my legs to get back the circulation. So I do. At the snack bar, I order a ham sandwich and a Coke. But the guy who serves it has dirt under his fingernails, which takes away my appetite.

The bus starts up again, this time with a full load. Across the aisle is a boy in a mesh shirt, the kind that Gene sometimes wears. I've been trying to avoid thinking of Gene and me, but suddenly I get a tingly sensation. I turn back to the window where dusk is on its way.

Past Centerville, past Bucksnort, past Barren Hollow Road and a house with chickens roosting all over the front porch. The man standing in the yard looks familiar—like Preacher Crow, in fact—but when I glance back, he's gone.

Past the Eye-Forty Motel, past Cuba Landing, past huge fields with ditches. The drone of the bus makes me sleepy again.

A murmur from somebody in front wakes me up. Outside I see a span of yellow and brown water lazing along. "Tennessee River," the woman beside me says, though I haven't asked. It splinters into branches that look like mama's long, bony fingers.

Then Shiloh National Park, and Forked Deer River, and beyond that, a big shopping center, jammed between two Churches of God.

Soon as the bus reaches the Memphis City limits, my palms begin to sweat and my throat feels like I swallowed a mouthful of sand. Not that I'm nervous or anything. I've got twenty-five dollars in my pocket—part of it Christmas money I've saved—so what's to be nervous about? Oh, dear Lord, don't let mama find out what I've done!

Stepping off the bus, I'm stunned by the heat. It's worse than at home. I look around, but there's no sign of Gene. What if he doesn't show up? It'd serve me right for fibbing and conniving. Walking over to an empty seat, I plunk down my bag.

I wait for over half an hour. I'm thinking I've been made a fool of. Got me here to Memphis when all along, he had no intention of showing up. Probably sitting in Delphi right now laughing his head off. But why would he play a trick like that? Because he hates mama? Because of Grady Fay? Doesn't make sense. Anyway, I have to find a place to stay. If only there was someone to ask. I glance around without seeing a single soul whose opinion I'd trust.

Hanging from one of the pay phones is a thick directory, which I flip open. First I try a motel. My hand's shaking as it moves down the page. There're three with the name of the city. I dial the Memphis Motel and wait. But when the man finds out I just came in on the bus, he says he doesn't have any vacancies. Next I dial the New Memphis Motel, and am careful not to mention where I'm calling from. The woman says she has one room left and gives instructions on how to get there. She says she'll hold the room for an hour. I'm afraid to ask how much it costs.

In the meantime, somebody's taken my seat and I have to stand. My feet are swollen and my shoes are killing me. Must've rubbed a blister. I'm in a sorry state, but I'm not going to cry about it. I can take care of myself. My chin's up all the way.

Grabbing my suitcase, I go outside to get a taxi. If I have to walk far, I'll faint. And who should be coming in as I'm going out? Talk about fate. He grabs me, holds me close.

"Hon, sorry for being so late. Had car trouble outside Nashville." He pauses a second. "Where you going? You wasn't going to wait for me?"

"I thought. . . . " I fling my arms up. I *am* glad to see him!

"You thought I was pulling something over on you? You thought that of ol' Gene?" He takes my chin in his hand. "You know better than that, baby."

We're standing there blocking up the entrance so I start to pick up my suitcase and move on, but Gene stops me. "Runt'll carry that for you." He turns and gestures to a weasely-looking guy standing behind. "Runt. Get the lady's bag." Then he pulls me out the door and toward a car that's parked in front. "Runt needs to build up his muscles. That's why we let him do all the legwork."

We crawl into the back. He introduces me to Bear, the big fellow behind the wheel. Looks like the same one who shoved Grady Fay into the seat at the skating rink, which makes me feel a bit funny about riding with him.

"Heard a lot of talk about you, ma'am," Bear says.

"Well . . . hope it was good."

He grins. "Sure was." I giggle. I'm so used to mama's insults that I'm out of practice when it comes to compliments.

Runt puts my suitcase in the trunk, then gets into the front seat. Gene takes my arm, squeezes it. "Baby, you call the shots. What'll it be? Something to eat or drink? Drive around a little bit? Go out to Graceland?"

"First I need to see about my motel room. Or they might give it away."

"You got a room already?" He looks surprised. "Ol' Gene was gonna take care of that." I tell them the address, and Bear says he thinks he can find it. "This guy's got a perfect nose for directions," Gene says. "He could make his way to the moon, if he had to." I can tell he really likes Bear. And Bear likes him. Wonder what that makes Runt. Runt seems a bit sulky, as if he's "lifted up the wrong foot to piss," as Grandpa Jess's fond of saying.

I have to admit that Bear's a pretty good driver, because he goes straight to the motel without one hitch, as if he's lived in Memphis all his life. Must be a gift, coming to a new place without being a stranger.

Telling the boys to wait in the car, Gene takes my bag and marches with it right up to the front desk. "We got a reservation in the name of Grubbs." I step up and pay for it in cash, then she gives me the key.

"Y'all together?" she asks. "'Cause if you are, you have to pay double."

"I'm just visiting," Gene says, and winks at me.

The room has blonde furniture, a blue rug, mustard-colored drapes, and a peculiar smell . . . like a refrigerator that hasn't been defrosted for a long time. I go into the bathroom and stare at the fresh blue towels placed neatly side by side on the rack, at the tiny bars of soap. If mama was here, she'd say, "Don't forget to put paper around that toilet seat before using it."

"This is pretty nice," Gene says, sticking his head in. Then before I have the chance to wash my hands, or *anything*, he's got me by the waist, rubbing his face against mine until I can feel all the stubbly places. "Baby, baby . . . " he whispers. Gives me goosebumps.

At the same time, I'm about to pee in my pants. He sees me twisting around, and lets go. I close the door, and after doing what I have to do, including giving my face a quick once-over and my lips a fresh coat of lipstick, I go out. He's sitting in front of the TV. Moving closer I can see Graceland lit up with an eerie blue glow. All kinds of big cars line the driveway. And hundreds of fans! Gene pulls me into his lap.

"What do you think, baby?" he murmurs into my right ear.

"Think we'd better get going, otherwise we'll miss the party!" It's supposed to be a joke, but he doesn't laugh.

"Okay. But afterwards we'll have our own little party, right?"

Reckon Gene has trained the boys well, because they don't seem at all impatient as we come walking out.

"Okay, Bear. Graceland. Hit it."

"Right, chief."

"Chief?" I turn to Gene. "He calls you chief?"

"I'm chief honcho, hon. Don't you know that?"

Runt says traffic's going to be a mess, and of course it is. But Bear makes some quick moves, like driving on the shoulder of the road, that put us ahead. I'm busy staring out the window at all the hamburger joints and used-car lots. "Just think. Elvis passes these things every day," I say to Gene, hearing myself use the kind of worshipful tone I usually save for church.

As we draw nearer, crowds swarm in and out of the traffic. Gene leans so close I can feel his breath against my cheek. He puts an arm around my shoulder. "You can get a glimpse of Graceland from here if you look quick. See. Between them trees."

I scrunch down. Sure enough, there it is. Something out of a fairy tale. Every window lit up. And Elvis somewhere inside.

The farther we go, the more the crowd thickens. Bear sits on the horn but they seem deaf.

"This is it," Bear says.

"Then we'll get out and walk." Gene grabs my hand. "Come on, baby."

Bear turns around. "Where'll we park?"

"You see to it. It's your car."

I think Bear has every right to get pissed off at this remark, but it doesn't seem to bother him. Gene tells Runt to go with Bear, and we'll meet up with them by the main entrance.

So we step into what an insane asylum might be like if they released all the inmates at one time: a couple hundred people bent on the same thing—getting a glimpse of Elvis. A few of us secretly think we might even go a step farther and talk to him. Least that's what's in my head as Gene and me push and claw through the multitude. I say "multitude" because it reminds me of Preacher Crow talking about the crowds that come to see Jesus. He called them "the multitude." And he described Jesus performing miracles, like multiplying food from scraps when they got hungry. I still got the leftover ham sandwich in my pocket. In a pinch, maybe I could give it to Elvis and he could multiply it. Always did think he had some Jesus in him, though no doubt Reba Petit'd say I was blaspheming.

We finally reach the back of a line that twists and circles like a long snake that turns in on itself and swallows its own tail. (Preacher Crow has preached on this, too.) As we move forward, a man in front of me shouts, "the gates of Heaven," and I realize we're not far from the big iron doors with the musical notes that I've seen so many pictures of. Six guards with billy clubs stand on each side to keep order. But order's hopeless. Sometimes a car turns into the driveway, and when this happens, the crowd is pushed back.

Several people get trampled on. A little girl in front of me has lost her mama, and is bawling hard. Then somebody picks her up, and her sobs turn to hiccups.

All the time Gene's holding my hand, sometimes rubbing my palm with his thumb, but mostly just hanging on so we don't get separated. After awhile, his impatience begins to show. "Hate standing in lines," he says over and over. "Only suckers stand in lines." Tightening his grip, he pulls me along.

I try to dig in my heels, but he's stronger. "We'll lose our place!" I say. As we make our way through the crowd, I feel a little like Moses walking through the Red Sea. Only I bet the people whose toes we step on don't consider it that way, otherwise they wouldn't cuss at us. Gene tells me to ignore it. He says this is what happens when you go after what you want. Something I never heard from Preacher Crow.

At the gate, he marches straight up to one of the guards. "Sir," he says, "we got friends waiting for us inside there. Would you be nice enough to let us pass through?"

The guard shakes his head. "Buddy, you're the fiftieth person who's asked me that. Looks like you could think up something new."

"My girlfriend here's sick." He gestures toward me. "She needs to stretch out on the grass."

"Heard that one, too. Tell her she oughta go home."

"We're a long way from home, sir."

"Then I'd say you're up to your neck in shit."

There's a pause. Gene studies the guy. Then he gets right up in his face and whispers. Guess I'm not supposed to hear, and I pretend not to, so I won't have to be shocked. "Listen, dog-breath, you let us in there or I'm gonna jerk off your dick and ram it up your ass, understand?" I can see the man bristle, put a hand on his billy club, lift it out of his belt. "After that I'm gonna slip you ten dollars so you can get the best blow job in Memphis." He looks at the man and grins. The man looks at him, and after a few seconds, grins back, then signals us to pass on through.

"How in the world did you manage that?" I ask Gene, all innocent-like, as he's putting away his wallet.

He takes a few swaggering steps. "When you're with me, baby, you're in the big time." Spreading his arms, he turns to me. "What'll we do, now? Have a peek at the ol' lady? I think she lies thataway." He points toward the front door of Graceland, where another line has formed.

"Aren't we supposed to wait for Bear and Runt?"

He snaps his fingers. "Almost forgot." Putting an arm around me, he kisses the top of my head. "What would I do without you, baby?"

"Same as you always do." When Gene gets cocky, I turn shy and don't know what to say.

He looks around. "Now, whatta you suppose is keeping them boys?"

While we're waiting, an older couple, a white-haired woman and a man with a cane, keep glancing in our direction. They seem to be arguing about something. Finally they come over.

"Hope we aren't disturbing you folks," the man says. "My wife here's got a bee in her bonnet, and won't be satisfied till she's rid of it. I keep telling her she's making a fool of herself, but she won't listen."

As the woman steps forward, white tufts of hair rise from the top of her head. She gets so close to Gene, I'm sure he must be able to see the blue veins underneath her face powder. "I told Sonny that you *must* be one of the Presleys. There's a *remarkable* family resemblance."

I'm about to put my two-cents' worth in when Gene stops me.

"You're a very sharp lady, ma'am." He touches his forehead with his finger. "Very sharp. Matter of fact, I'm Elvis's brother. Pleased to meet you." He sticks out a hand.

The woman touches her crepey throat and gasps. "You're not!"

"Yes'm, I am, I truly am."

"I didn't know Elvis had a brother," the husband says, staring at Gene with something close to suspicion. "I don't believe he does, either." Pulling out a handkerchief, he wipes his brow.

"Sonny, hush!" the woman says.

"More than a brother." Gene gets right up in her face and whispers under his breath. "His long-lost twin."

"His twin wasn't 'long-lost,'" the woman says. "He died."

"Don't you believe a word of it, little sister. They give that baby out for adoption quick as it was born."

"Gladys wouldn't have done that."

"Anybody would if she had two mouths to feed and not enough worms. Oh, I don't blame her one bit."

"You poor thing!" The woman looks like she's about to cry.

"I admit it wasn't easy but I managed. Sad part is, just when mama and me was reunited, she up and died. Luck was against us, you might say." He gestures toward the front door where people are viewing the casket.

"Well, I'm sure happy to meet you." She turns to her husband. "Sonny, give me your pen."

"What for?"

"For just a minute." Searching through her pocketbook, she locates a scrap of paper, holds it out. "I wanna get your autograph on this so I can show it to people at home. Otherwise they'll never believe me."

"Be happy to oblige, ma'am." He takes the pen and writes GENE HANKINS.

Sonny looks at it and grunts. "Thought you were a Presley."

"Gene Hankins's the name my adopted parents give me. Wouldn't be right to turn my back on them."

"I certainly wish y'all luck," the woman says, taking me in for the first time.

"Appreciate that," Gene says and starts yanking me away. "Bye now."

"Hey, wait a minute!" The man follows us, puffing hard. "What about my pen?"

"Oh. Sorry." Gene tsks a couple of times. "Slipped my mind." He holds it up. "Mmmm. Silver. Present from your wife, I betcha."

The man snatches it back without answering.

As we walk away, Gene pulls me close again. "That pen was gonna be our meal ticket. Now I haveta think of something else."

"You are *shameless,*" I say. I don't say how I'm feeling about it.

"Well, baby, nobody ever said I was an angel. You wouldn't want an angel, anyway, wouldja? Too boring." When he starts tickling me, I get hysterical. "Wouldja?"

"No, no!" I'm laughing so hard I can hardly get my breath.

Then we hear somebody calling Gene's name, and when we turn around Bear and Runt are both standing at the gate. Gene tells me to wait, and goes over. I don't know what he says to the guard, but whatever it is makes him open the gate and let the two in. He clasps both around the shoulder, and the three of them stroll back, joking together.

"Okay, boys," Gene says, "you ready to view the corpse?"

"Not me," Runt mumbles, shaking his head.

"Now, Runt, don't tell me you're afraid of a dead body?"

"That there'll bring bad luck," Runt says. "I had an uncle who touched a dead person, and he got warts all over his hand. They never would go away."

"We ain't gonna *touch* nothing, we just *looking.* Ain't no harm in that."

159

"Lookin's worse," Runt says. "They don't like to be looked at. Sooner or later they get back at you for it."

"Believe this feller's scared, don't you, Gene?" Bear snickers.

"Go ahead, laugh," Runt says. "You'll see."

"Come on." Bear gestures to Gene and me. "Let him stay here."

He and I walk toward the front entrance, with Gene following slightly behind. I'm surprised the line's not longer. We take our places and inch up bit by bit. I stand on tiptoe, but there're too many people in the doorway to see anything. Gene's beginning to look uneasy, like he's getting cold feet. "Uh, listen," he says, "I think I'll go keep Runt company. No need him standing there all by himself. When y'all finish, just come on back."

So Bear and I are left alone, not quite knowing what to say to each other. Finally I ask him how long he's known Gene.

"Oh, 'bout a year and a half. Me and him worked in the same place."

"Where's that?"

"Service station outside Chattanooga. He stayed there awhile, then him and the owner had a run-in, and Gene quit. When he left, I left, too. Then we both got jobs at this auto mechanic's shop up in McMinnville. When that didn't work out, we moved on to Knoxville. That's where we met Runt. You may not believe this, but Runt can take a whole car apart and put it together again. He just ain't too good with people."

As we get closer to the casket, I'm feeling a combination of excitement and dread. "That's where you work now?"

"Me and Runt do. Gene got fired. Then he went up to Cincinnati. A few weeks ago, his granny died and left him a little money, so he come back home."

I start to ask why he was fired, but Bear probably wouldn't tell me, and I'm not sure I really want to know anyway.

Just as we reach the steps, two men dressed in dark blue suits come out and close the front doors behind them, shutting off any view of the hall and casket. One of the men's carrying a megaphone, and he walks to the edge of the porch.

"Folks, can I have your attention for a minute? Folks, will you please quiet down?" After a few seconds, he goes on. "Due to the enormous turnout to pay last respects to Gladys Presley, we've decided to move her body to the Memphis Funeral Home, which has the facilities to take care of such large numbers. I'm sure you can appreciate the strain this situation has put on the immediate family. But if you'll bear with us, you and all those still waiting outside the gate will have a chance to view the body tomorrow. The doors will open at nine in the morning. I want you to know that we appreciate your cooperation."

"You mean, we waited in line for *nothing?*" Bear bellows out. "That ain't fair." Other people shout their agreement.

160

The men in the blue suits huddle together. Then the guy with the megaphone steps forward again. I think he must like talking on that thing because he spends a lot of time switching it on and off, testing whether people are hearing him or not.

"Folks, Mr. West here is going to pass among you and take your names. If you show up tomorrow, you can just go right to the front door, and the guard will let you in without waiting in line again."

You wouldn't think it'd take so much time for people to simply sign their names to a sheet of paper, but every one of them gets into a long conversation, leaving the rest of us shifting from foot to foot.

Finally Bear can't stand it any more. Signaling for me to follow, he starts walking away. I'm too tired to do anything else. By this time, it's completely dark, and hard to recognize faces. "Where are they?" I ask Bear. Since he has such a good sense of direction, I let him guide me. Pretty soon we come upon two figures sitting on the grass with cigarettes dangling out the sides of their mouths and a butane flip-top supplying enough light for them to play mumblety-peg by, the way boys in school used to. I start to say something, but Bear interrupts me. "Shhhh," he whispers, "Don't disturb Gene during his shot."

I don't call flipping a penknife off your shoulder "a shot," but when it sticks upright in the ground, he sure seems proud of himself. I hear Bear chuckle.

"Your turn, Runt," Gene says, passing the knife over. Runt gives it a good flip, but it hits the grass, falls over and lays there. Gene lets out a yell. "Ya-hoo! Owe me two dollars." Jumping up, he grabs me and gives me a smack on the cheek. "You're my good luck charm, hon."

"Hear my stomach growling?" Bear says.

"That what that roaring is?" Gene turns to me. "You hungry, hon?"

I could tell him I'm starved, that I haven't had anything all day except a bowl of Rice Krispies and a few bites of a ham sandwich. But I just nod.

"Where's the car, Bear?"

"Thataway." He points down the road in the direction we came in. "I backed as far as I could on the shoulder and stuck her in somebody's driveway."

Gene grabs my hand and we walk out as though we live here and are just taking an evening stroll. When we pass the guards at the front gate, Gene throws up an arm and they wave back. Grady Fay would never do such a thing. In fact, if I'd come with him, we'd still be *outside* the fence. I let Gene swing my hand as we walk. He only lets go to take a couple of swigs out of a pint bottle he's brought along. He's in great spirits, and, except for being tired and hungry, I reckon I'm in great spirits, too.

After we pass through the crowd—a lot of people are still standing around talking although they've been told to go home—Gene empties the last of one bottle and takes out another. "Brought us along a little liquid refreshment." He hands it to me. "Taste this, baby, it's high octane. Warm you up."

I start to say that I'm plenty warm already, hot, as a matter of fact, but I suspect this is not the kind of heat he's talking about. Before I can utter a word, he's holding the bottle to my lips, and I swallow what comes out. Oh, Lord! I struggle to spit it out, but it goes down my throat all the way. Liquid fire, Grandpa Jess'd call it. Hitting my empty stomach, it feels more like wild fire! Then Gene lifts it to his own lips and takes a couple of healthy swigs before passing it on to Bear. By the time we reach the car, he's finished it and has started in on a third.

As we walk up, a man's sitting on the hood, holding a shotgun. "This your jalopy?" he asks. You can tell he's not too happy about it being there.

"Yessir," Bear says. "Sorry 'bout leaving it in the driveway, but I didn't know what else to do."

"Drive it back to town, put it in a parking lot."

"I was headed toward Graceland."

"I know where you were headed, I know where *everybody's* headed. But you don't park on somebody else's property. Me and my wife have been waiting a hour and a half to get outta here."

"Let me handle this, Bear." Gene steps up to the man. "Buddy, he apologized. Ain't that enough?"

"You owe me three dollars. That's what parking in Memphis costs."

"That's highway robbery."

"Listen, you saved yourself money. You could've had a fifteen dollar traffic ticket."

"What if I said we ain't got three dollars?"

He spreads out his hand. "Simple. I'll call the police. They'll be here in two minutes. Might even run you in. We don't like strangers here in Memphis."

"Well, you sure got a lot of them now," Bear gestures over his shoulder.

"Get in the car, Bear," Gene pipes up. "We're wasting time."

"You're going to stay right here till the police come," the man says, pointing the shotgun at Gene.

A woman appears at the front door of the house and calls out, "Bill! What's going on?"

"Phone the police, Martha, and tell 'em to hurry."

"Listen." Gene starts walking toward the man. "Nobody threatens me when I ain't done nothing."

"Stand back now."

"You know that gun's just for show anyway."

"I said, don't get any closer."

"Why, I bet it ain't even loaded." As he keeps walking, the man backs away slightly, then, without warning, turns and lights out for the house. In a flash Gene tackles him to the ground, sits on top of his chest, and pummels his face. Taking out his penknife, he opens it and puts it to the man's throat. "Mister, you be careful who you pick on next time."

But the man still has some fight in him. He puts a hand up to one of Gene's eyes. For a second, it looks like he might gouge it right out, but Gene wrestles his arm down. The next thing that happens turns me sick. Holding the man's hand to the ground, Gene hits him a thudding blow that knocks his head to one side. After that, he lies quiet.

The woman's looking out the window trying to see what's going on, but is too scared to come out. I'm scared, too.

"Let's get outta here," Gene says.

I'm thinking that maybe we should tell the man it's all been a terrible mistake, and drive him to the nearest hospital, but Gene shoves me into the back seat and Bear takes off like a bat outta hell, almost hitting another car. Once we're on the highway, Gene tells him to slow down and he does, which is a good thing because pretty soon we meet a police car with the siren on going in the opposite direction, and I know it must be headed for the man's house.

"Find us a good place to eat, buddy," Gene says. "A nice, out-of-the-way drive-in."

After that, it's real quiet, even Gene is quiet. He takes out what's left of the third bottle of whiskey and drains it all, not even offering any to Bear and Runt. Guess everybody's busy with their own thoughts. Certainly I am. I'm wishing I'd never come.

Bear drives way to the other side of town and turns into a place that doesn't look much different from Hookey's on Highway 27 back in Goody. Bear orders three hamburgers, Runt and Gene a barbecue pork, and I get another ham sandwich. But when the food arrives, nobody eats much, except Bear, who finishes his, then takes whatever the rest of us can't finish. Now I'm worried about what might happen with the police.

"I'm getting tired," I say, giving a big yawn that's half-real, half-fake. "I think I should call a taxi and go back to the motel."

"By yourself? We can't let you do that." His words are slightly slurred. "Can we, boys?" Runt and Bear shake their heads.

"I don't . . . "

"This is a big, wicked city, hon. You could get into real trouble." He's stopped smiling now, and is frowning at me. He takes my hand, and holds it so tight that I can't pull away. "I'm ready to leave, too," he says into my ear. Then to the front seat: "Okay, Bear. Step on it."

Bear stops in front of the New Memphis Motel. I get out, and Gene gets out, too. "See y'fellows later," he says, and slams the door. As we walk into the tiny lobby, I'm hoping the young man at the desk will stop us, but he doesn't even look up from his book. So there's nothing to do but turn the key, then say goodnight to Gene and try to shut the door. But before I have the chance, he's pushing me inside, straight toward the bed. It seems like something out of *True Confessions* when he falls on top of me, hitching up my skirt. "I been waiting, baby," he says. "I been waiting for this a *long* time."

"Oh God!" I whisper, as he begins kissing my neck. Pulling him closer, I run my fingers through his hair. I feel his body on top of me, his hips pushing against mine. He tears off my blouse, ripping some of the buttons, fumbles with my bra, growing more and more impatient, until finally it springs open and his hands cup my breasts. At this point I'm moaning out loud, especially when he starts rubbing his chest against me in a kind of frenzy. I'm pressing against him, too, as if I can't get close enough. He moves his hand over my breasts, vibrating one nipple, then the other. "Oh, God," I moan again. My eyes are closed. I'm breathing hard. This is the moment I've been dreaming of.

But when he pinches my nipples real hard, my eyes fly open and I push his hand away. Raising up, he takes me by the shoulders and kisses my face, my lips, until gradually, I begin to relax again. Then he sticks his tongue in my mouth. As soon as I taste the alcohol, I draw away. This time his grip tightens, his fingers dig into my skin and I squirm around, trying to get out from under him. "Cut that out!" he says.

I can't see his face, but the tone of his voice is scaring me a little. I tell myself that the best thing to do is lay there as still as possible and let him do what he wants. So I stop struggling. But instead of calming him down, this seems to make him more angry. His hand touches me, not in the soft, tender way I'd imagined, but rough and bullying. He kneads my breasts as though they're rubber. The pain makes me wince, but I try not to make a sound. The worst thing is his stale whiskey breath. I don't intend to do it, but when I feel his hand close to my lips, I bite one of his fingers deep enough to draw blood.

He yelps and jerks his hand away. "Goddammit!" Spitting the word out, he smacks me so hard across the cheekbone that my head spins. I get ready for him to do it again, but instead he puts his mouth next to my ear and whispers. "Don't be this way, baby. Just be still . . . real still. . . . "

Holding my arms at the wrists, he yanks my skirt off, and my panties, and struggles out of his pants, which is not easy because now I can see how drunk he really is. I feel something ropy brushing between my thighs, rubbing and chafing against them. His breathing turns wheezy as he tries to push it into me, but it's too soft and won't go in. I feel him sliding up and kneeling over my face, his knees pinning me down on each side. He holds his thing to my lips. "Suck it, baby, suck!" At first I resist, then he hits me again, harder than before.

Forcing my mouth open, he puts his slimy thing inside. With him threatening to choke me again, I try to pump on it with my tongue until it gets a little hard and he rushes to stick it in even though I keep crying, "Please don't! Please don't!"

"Just relax, baby. Relax." He's breathing so fast, he can hardly get the words out.

Then it's all the way in, and he's pushing back and forth. I'm trying to pull away, but he's too strong.

His face looks awful—more like an animal than a human being. I look away from him and try to hold my breath, but even so, a few yells escape. Finally—it seems like an eternity—he shakes all over. I feel something gush inside me and a second later, he lets go. His hair's wet with sweat, and so's his face. I lie very still, my head turned to one side.

About that time, I hear knocking, and then the door's flung open. Two policemen are standing there. Gene jumps up. I try to cover myself as best I can.

They drill me with all sorts of questions, but all I can do is stare down at the spread. The main thing they want to know is whether I'd like them to take me to a hospital. I still can't speak. I just shake my head. They ask if I want to press charges. Pulling the bedclothes higher, I glance over at Gene, who's looking at me as though his eyes could bore right through mine.

Again I shake my head, and mutter, "Please just make him leave." The words are hard to get out because my mouth is so sore. They keep harping on the charges until finally I say okay. But when I find out that I'd have to stay in Memphis for a few days, and even come back if the case goes to court, I tell them I can't, I'd get fired.

So they take him away. I don't know what they plan to do with him, but as they drag him out, he's smirking. I know I haven't seen the last of him. After he's gone, I turn and catch a glimpse of myself in the mirror. My right cheek's beginning to swell, my upper lip looks like it's been stung, my nipples are sore, my insides hurt. I wonder if they'll ever be the same again. One of the policemen returns and asks if I'm sure I don't want to see a doctor, but I whisper "no." I'm too ashamed to let anybody see me in this shape.

Dragging myself up, I catch hold of the mustard drape—which now seems the color of puke—and leaning against the wall with one hand, I creep into the bathroom. Then I slump down beside the toilet and suddenly I feel so sick. Everything comes up. After that, I lie on the floor, resting my head on my arm. When it begins to clear a little, I turn on the tub faucets and, after a few minutes, lower myself into the hot water. I scrub my skin until it's almost raw, and sweat seeps from my pores. I begin to feel a little better. Then I turn on the cold water, push down the shower knob, and let the water douse my face.

It hurts too much to dry off. I go back in the bedroom and, still wet, lie down crossways on the foot of the bed, and just breathe a while. What would mama say if she knew? I keep reliving the whole awful scene over and over in my mind, wondering how it turned out this way, and how I could have changed it to make it come out different.

Next morning is no better. I lay there thinking, am I ever going to be able to get up and face myself again, much less the person at the desk or the people in the lobby or all the unknown multitude who'll be flocking to the funeral home? All I want is to be back home in my own room. I call the bus station to find out what time the bus runs, hoping I can leave right away, but there's nothing until three in the afternoon, so I have a whole morning to kill. At first I think about staying in bed, but the longer I lay there, the worse my thoughts get. I turn on the television, but they still don't go away. I think I might go crazy if I don't get out of the room.

I take another bath. I stay in the bathtub for the longest time, scrubbing myself over and over.

After that, I put on some Max Factor makeup I've brought, adding extra over the bruises, wincing because they're real tender, and when I've finished I look okay. Not great, but good enough to get by without being stared at.

The plump woman behind the desk in the lobby sits filing her nails. Her face is like a page from one of my old coloring books—lipstick smudged and blue wedges painted way beyond the corners of her eyes. "Hear you had some trouble last night," she says. "Coulda predicted it."

A conversation with a stranger is the last thing I need at this point, and I try to dodge it with a question that I need the answer to anyway. "Is the Memphis Funeral Home far from here?"

"Three blocks down Union Avenue." She points the file in that direction. "Remember, you have to be out by eleven."

"Can I leave my bag in the lobby?"

"As long as I'm not responsible for it."

I walk out into a sun that's so strong, it makes everything a little wavy. I'm still trembly so I hold my pocketbook over my head to shield my face from the hot rays.

The line's not as long as I thought it might be, which gives me some hope for being able to stand in it. It moves along at a pretty fair pace, too, and it seems no time at all before I reach the steps of the funeral home. A man in sunglasses and a white suit stands by the door with folded arms, ordering people to put out their cigarettes and spit out their tobacco. As I get closer, I can hear organ music. "Just As I Am," sounds like.

Then I'm standing in a long hall, faintly lit by hanging lamps of blistered-colored glass. Against one wall, a man sits holding a walkie-talkie. "No picture-taking," he says over and over. And if anybody's rude enough to speak in a loud voice, he comes over to them. "Now let's show some respect, folks, let's show some respect."

Beyond the arched doorway, I can see a casket surrounded by enough flowers to fill three or four whole yards. Though a red velvet rope keeps us from touching anything, one woman does brush her fingers across the lilies to see if they're real or artificial. "Thought so," she says, but I don't know what she thought. When she gets close to the casket, she whispers to her husband, "Right pretty, isn't she?"

"Pretty" isn't the word I'd use. Her face is as puffy as mine, except it doesn't have any bruises. The heavy makeup can't hide the wrinkles and dark circles under her eyes. But the thing that gets me most is her grey skin. Like people's skin on the TV back at the motel.

A guard gestures for me to move on, so in one second I try to memorize everything so I can tell Dot and Tessie.

We leave out the back door into a space that must have been a parking lot, but is now filled with hundreds of fans. I look around to make sure that Gene and his buddies are not among them, but probably they're still at the police station. Or, if they're smart, keeping a low profile.

A big Cadillac swings into the driveway and a shout goes up. "Elvis! Elvis!" Several girls scream.

Then other cars arrive . . . a procession of long limousines that all look alike. Suddenly a white Buick turns in, its brakes screeching. "That's the Blackwood Brothers," a man beside me says. "I'd know that long nose of James Blackwood anywhere." A murmur goes up. People begin streaming through the door: men dressed in seersucker suits with string ties; women in dresses scooped out at the neck, and heels as long and thin as nails. One wears a straw hat so big that it flops on the sides as she walks. Next come the casket and pallbearers, led by a fat man who comes out, looks around, and signals to somebody inside. That must be Lamar, I think to myself, proud to recognize one person at least.

When the casket moves into the sun, it looks like it's caught fire. The crowd gets so quiet that I can hear the pallbearers' footsteps crunching on the cement. A woman kneels down, moaning and praying.

What happens next takes place with such split-second timing that I keep thinking, "This must be a movie I'm in, it must be. . . . "

The driver of the pink Cadillac jumps out and runs around to open the back door. By standing on tiptoe, I can see that two men, one young, one old, are now making their way through the line of guards.

Is that really Elvis? I have a quick glimpse of him ducking his head into the back seat. Then the grey-haired man climbs in. Must be Vernon. The driver gets in behind the wheel and slams the door.

Oh God, I pray, please let him look up. Please! Look!

And he does. He looks up and right through me, as though I'm not really standing here, as though I'm some kind of fence post, just like daddy did on the morning he left. Suddenly my whole body starts to shake. I want to rush at him, tear apart that carefully combed wave, wrench open those sullen lips, pinch those nostrils until he understands that I'm somebody, too. *Somebody.*

I can't push the sobs back any longer. Reaching blindly into my bag, I grab the first thing my hand comes to: a compact, which I throw as hard as I can against the Cadillac's rear window as it drives off. It misses and falls, the small mirror breaking into pieces on the concrete. People turn to stare. I should be embarrassed, but I'm not.

I walk back to the motel to pick up my suitcase. Now all my energy's gone, and I just feel depressed.

Hailing a taxi, I head for the bus station and home.

Chapter Seventeen

It's on the bus that I start wondering what I'm going to say to mama. How can I explain the bruises? I also worry about Gene turning up. But after the Memphis police finish with him, surely he wouldn't have the nerve to show his face again.

By the time I reach my front yard I have a few excuses lined up. Good thing, too, because mama and Miz Cowan are sitting in the porch swing fanning themselves, although it's a bit cooler than when I left. Feels like I've been gone months instead of overnight.

"What in the name of Jesus happened to you?" As I draw closer, mama stands up to peer at me. Thank God it's dark, and she can't see too well. Naturally Miz Cowan's peering too.

"Had a little accident," I say, heading for the front door with my suitcase. "Over at the skating rink last night."

"Told you that place was dangerous. You alright?" mama says, looking at me as though she's not quite sure.

"I'm fine. Gonna run me a cold tub. Then I might go right to sleep." I say this so she won't come in and try to talk to me.

I *do* run a cold tub. And I *do* lie down on my bed, and snuggle up with my teddy bear, and before I know it, I've dozed off. And I sleep so sound that, for once, even mama's banging around in the kitchen next morning doesn't make a dent. But I wake up with a start. I must've been yelling because mama's standing over me, asking what's wrong. I tell her I had a nightmare though I can't remember anything about it. Now she's really staring at me. Guess I must look worse in daylight.

"What kind of accident put you in that shape?"

"Actually I was skating real fast and lost control and hit a whole bunch of chairs on the sidelines." I'm sure Grady Fay won't mind my taking over his story. Especially since I'll never see him again.

"You're lucky you didn't bust something. Hope this teaches you a lesson."

"It *did*. It did." The way I say it seems to satisfy mama, and I'm grateful for small favors.

When I go into the bathroom, I'm surprised to see that I'm beginning to look halfway human. But I still have to do a makeup job before going in to work.

At the mill I meet Dot on the stair. "Did your mama tell you that she called up to check on you? I didn't know what to say so I told her that you were in the bathroom, and we were about to go out. What happened to you anyway?" she asks, looking at me closer.

I ignore her question. "Did you say where?"

"No. She asked, but I changed the subject."

"That's good, 'cause I told her we went over to the skating rink."

"Was the trip worth it?"

"I appreciate what you did, Dot."

"What's the matter with your face?" Tessie asks, at that moment walking up and turning her Coke-bottle glasses in my direction. When she does that, it makes me feel like one of them bugs we used put under the microscope in biology class.

"Got trampled by the crowd."

"Trampled!" she says, shocked.

"There were a lot of people pushing and shoving. Especially when Elvis came out."

"You *saw* Elvis?" Tessie gasps.

"I got to go in now. Tell you 'bout it later."

Of course if you're going to tell a story, you've got to make it a good one. And I do the best I can, giving a description of Gladys in the coffin, and one of Elvis winking at me before he gets in the car. After they ooh and ah and carry on, I swear them to secrecy so mama won't find out, which is a shame, Dot says, because I deserve a wider audience, especially the fan club members. Then I say something that really surprises her. I tell her that I'm turning the fan club over to her and Tessie, that somehow I don't feel the same way about it anymore.

"Maybe you're just growing up, LaVonne," she says, and I answer that maybe I am, and if it's true, I admit it's about time.

I don't think much about Gene at all, except every once in a while, he pops into my mind as I'm piecing up and I wonder if he feels any regrets. When I go home, I'm careful to hitch a ride with Marvin, and ask him to see me to my door, even though it probably seems a little odd to him since I generally turn down his offers.

But I have trouble getting to sleep, and do a lot of what mama calls tossing and turning. She says I scream out some, too, but I don't remember much of that. Though one dream hangs on. I'm walking along a dark alley, and a man's coming toward me. It looks like daddy so I'm not the least bit afraid, but when I get closer I see it's a stranger. By then it's too late to run, but I try anyway and he ends up chasing me.

When I wake up, I thank God that it's just a nightmare and I'm okay. But that's not all I do. To make amends for all my lying and scheming, I try to get up a new Sunshine Quartet, still using Bobby Echols of course, and a baritone who Pearlie B. knows from Sandy Creek and—this is my last resort—Ettie Mae Tucker, who might be loud but she does sing a pretty good alto. Sunday afternoon, we practice for a long time, and by four o'clock we're beginning to sound a lot better. Some of Ettie Mae's flatter notes are now more or less on target, thanks to Pearlie B. taking her back over the bad spots. Pearlie B. says that after a couple more rehearsals, we'll be ready to go.

In the mill, it's the same old boring routine, except I'm not complaining about it anymore. Over at the library, I take out a couple of Grace Livingston Hill books, but after reading a few pages, I put them aside, like some food you get turned off from. I'm feeling bloated, too, but that'll be alright once I get my period. I tell myself that being two weeks late is not enough to lose sleep over.

Then one Monday afternoon, just as I'm getting ready to walk out the door so I'll have time to stop in at the Store before work, the phone rings. If mama'd been there, I'd've asked her to get it, but she's over at Miz Cowan's helping her make blackberry jelly. So I answer. The pause I hear gives me a chill.

"LaVonne?" I don't say a word. "Before you hang up, I want to apologize. I know I did some bad things, and I don't have any excuse for them, except some people shouldn't drink, and I guess I'm one of them. Paid for it though. Spent a whole night in jail."

What am I supposed to say? That I'm sorry? I let a long pause go by before I answer. "Gene, I think we ought to leave well enough alone."

"What does that mean?"

"Just what I said."

"I can't do that, LaVonne. You mean too much to me. You mean *everything.*" His words sound like he's been into the Karo.

"Sure didn't seem that way in Memphis."

"Told you, I was *drunk.*"

I start to say something, then realize there's no point. He doesn't really sound sorry, and even if he is, what's done is done. "I got to go to work now."

"Okay, baby. But we'll get together soon, right?"

I hang up and rush out the door. For a few seconds I stand on the porch holding on to one of the posts. His voice brought that time back so clear. *Too* clear.

I have to get out of the house real fast so I walk to the Store and buy myself a big banana split at the soda fountain. Pretty soon, Tessie comes by, and I ask for an extra spoon so we can share it. "Tessie, you're so dependable. You're about the most *dependable* person I know. You're almost as dependable as Dot."

"Is that good?" Tessie asks, and I start laughing. She's puzzled because my laugh's a bit too loud, and what she said wasn't that funny, but anyway, as we go into the Grey Mill, I feel better.

The second we get inside, Dot comes running up. "You'll never believe who's here! He's in right now, talking to Mr. Baxter."

"*Who?*" Tessie and I ask at the same time, but Dot won't tell us because she says she wants it to be a surprise. But I can make a guess, and if I'm right it's enough reason for rushing into the ladies room and making sure my lipstick's straight and my nose's not shiny.

It takes every ounce of will power to return to Number 10 frame as though nothing's happened. I wouldn't say I'm excited, because I'm not sure yet. I work one side of the frame, and start up the other side when I see him standing at the end waiting. He's not smiling, though. Maybe he's not glad to see me. Maybe he doesn't even *care*.

He watches me like one of them checkers who come around once in a while to see if we're keeping up with production. At the moment, my production's not great, because my hands have turned to putty. The threads get twisted when I lift them up and when I pinch them together they don't stay. I get to the end of the frame, and my fingers try to catch a stray thread, but I miss it. Grady Fay has to reach out and hook it for me.

"Come to ask Mr. Baxter for my old job back." His face is fleshier than I remember, as if he's been eating too much and not getting enough exercise, but he looks good to me. "First I want to apologize." I just stare at him. Reckon today's my day for apologies. "For walking out like that."

"I could see you felt real bad."

"I did. It was the low point in my life."

I'm tempted to ask if it was worse than when his mama left, but I don't have the heart. "I'm glad you're back," I say. And this seems to hit the mark, because he smiles for the very first time.

Everybody in the department, including Reba Petit, comes up to him and grabs his hand or hugs him (like Dot). Even Mr. Fortune drops in to welcome him back, which is unheard of. As for myself, it's like getting to know somebody all over again. I'm aware of the strangest things: the big veins running up and down his arms, or the tilt of his head as it bends over the spindles.

By Sunday, I'm in such an up mood that I tell Pearlie B. that the New Sunshine Quartet will soon be ready to make our first appearance, and she should ask Preacher Crow to schedule it. Of course I have it in the back of my mind to invite Grady Fay over.

But after the practice, I'm not so sure. Ettie Mae is still missing notes even though Pearlie B. goes over them with her again and again. Maybe she's tone deaf.

This is also the week that Elvis leaves for Germany. He holds a TV press conference just before getting on the ship. Mama puts her face right up to the screen, so she won't miss any little detail. I go into the kitchen so I won't have to listen.

"Better come see this," she calls out. "Elvis is walking up the gangplank. Oh, it's so sad!"

When I don't respond, she comes to the door. I'm sitting at the kitchen table, my head in my hands. "What in the world's wrong with you?"

How can I describe my feelings? How can I say that I want to put Elvis out of my life, along with someone else? Instead, I hold my stomach, and complain of cramps (maybe this will bring on my period) so I can disappear into my bedroom and shut the door.

Later, mama comes and tells me about it. When she gets to the part where a reporter asked about Gladys, she chokes up. "Somebody called it the end of an era," she says.

"Could be the beginning," I say.

During the following week, Mr. Baxter comes over to ask if me and Grady Fay'll be willing to work overtime on Saturday. It's a rush order, he says, and we'll be paid double-time for it. Shorty and Boley are coming in, too, he says. I leap at the chance and so does Grady Fay. We're working opposite sides of the frame. Sometimes I wonder whether we're running away from each other or trying to catch up.

Saturday is weird. The place is so deserted that I have a tough time concentrating. In the first half-hour, my threads break six times, which sets some kind of record. Part of it's worry about my period. My breasts are beginning to get hard, too. If I didn't know better, I'd be paralyzed. But the Lord wouldn't deal me such a low blow. Under my breath, I pray harder than I ever have before.

During supper—shorter tonight than usual—we sit in the canteen watching Mr. Baxter do his card tricks. He pulls aces out of Grady Fay's pockets and coins out of his ears. "You don't wash none too good, do you, boy?" Boley teases. After Mr. Baxter leaves, there's a long silence.

Finally Boley raps the table with his knuckles. "Hey! The four of us oughta go somewhere after this. To celebrate."

"Celebrate what?" Shorty wants to know.

"Making all this extra money."

"We could pile into Grady Fay's truck and drive up to Hoke Treadaway's," I say.

"Doesn't Hoke close at twelve?" Shorty asks.

"Not for his special customers." Boley stretches his long arms. "He'll let me in."

All this time Grady Fay hasn't said a word. "You goin'?" Shorty turns to him.

"You bet," Grady Fay says, and looks at me.

"Meet you at the top of the steps, then." Boley gets up. "Mr. Baxter won't mind if we take off five minutes early."

In the truck, I sit in Boley's lap with Shorty squeezed in between him and Grady Fay. Boley asks me if I haven't filled out a little, but I don't answer. When we reach Hoke Treadaway's, the neon sign has already been turned off.

"Looks dark, doesn't it?"

"Naw." Opening the door, Boley pushes me out, then steps down himself. "He's got the curtains drawn to keep out the state patrol. I know Hoke."

We walk up to the door, and Boley knocks on the door. "Hoke! You in there?"

Then we hear footsteps, and the door opens a crack. "Who's that?" a voice calls out. "Can't you see we're closed?"

"It's Boley Westbrooks and a few buddies from the spinning room. We been working hard and we're real thirsty."

The door opens another crack, and this time a face peers out, the eyes squeezed together as if trying to see our shapes in the dark. "Boley? Hi, boy." He swings the door open. "Come on in, but be quick about it."

As we file past, I get a glimpse of a stooped man with a few stray hairs smoking up from the top of his head. I'd never have recognized him as the Hoke Treadaway I knew as a child.

"So, fellers . . . and gals, excuse me, ma'am . . . want something to wet your whistle, huh? Well, follow me." He shuffles toward the counter, and past it, into the back room. "Why you working on Sat-dy night?" Drawing a mug of beer from a barrel, he hands it to Boley, who's already blowing the foam off when he grabs it back and hands it to me. "Sorry. Ladies first."

I shake my head.

"Oh, come on," Boley says. "If you're worried about your mama smelling it on your breath, you can blame it on me. I'll even come in and apologize. I'll say, 'Miz Grubbs, it's my fault, I plied your daughter with alkyhol, I admit it . . . "

Hoke stares at me. "Grubbs? You're not Jim Tom's kid?"

"Yessir, I am. I used to come in here with daddy and play your punchboard."

"Lord, gal, that must be at least . . . " he rubs his chin, " . . . thirteen years ago. You've changed a bit since then." He chuckles. "Your dad sure could put 'em away. Don't know how he did it and drive that ambulance at the same time. He did steer it into a ditch once. His ol' lady cussed him up and down." He finishes filling the fourth mug and wipes his hand across his dirty t-shirt. "Ever hear from 'im?"

"Not lately." I stare down at the foam on top of my beer. "I used to."

"Didn't he move north?"

"To Detroit."

"And marry again?"

"Yessir. They got two boys."

"Two boys. Well, that must please 'im." He chuckles again. "He was some rounder."

When I glance up, I see Grady Fay looking at me.

"What are we standing around for?" Boley asks, gesturing toward the other room. "Been doing that all night. Let's go sit."

Hoke follows and begins gathering up the empty glasses on the pine bar and tossing them into a dishpan.

"You got anything to eat, Hoke?" Shorty calls out, settling himself into a booth.

Hoke takes a bowl of pretzels over to the table.

"Hell, these are stale," Shorty says. "Aincha got no barbecue left?"

"Might be able to scare up enough for one sandwich if y'all wanna split it."

"I'm not hungry," I say. I'm trying to eat as little as I can so my stomach won't stick out any more than it already does.

"Me neither," Grady Fay says.

"Then me'n Boley'll take it."

Hoke disappears into the back.

"Come on, Shorty," Boley nudges him. "Let's us have a go at that." He points to the pinball machine on the other side of the room.

Grady Fay and me sit there sipping our beers, not talking much. I'm reminded of the last time I came to Hoke's place. Mama'd had to work late in the glove mill—like I did tonight—and daddy was looking after me. After supper he took my hand in a way that made me uneasy. Like he was being *too* nice.

"Tell you what, hon. You and me're going out on the town. It'll be a secret between us, okay?"

"Where?"

"Ohhhh. Lemme see . . . how's about Hoke Treadaway's? While I get myself a brew, you can play the punchboard. How's that?"

I shake my head. All I want is to go out in the back yard and finish making mudpies.

"I'll buy you a pack of Dentyne," daddy says. "Whatta you say?"

When I don't answer, he promises me a chocolate moon pie, a bag of M&M's, and an R.C. Suddenly I feel real powerful. But scared, too.

"Will we stay long?"

"Naw. A few minutes, that's all." And he half-drags me out the door as if afraid I'll change my mind.

"Wanna play the juke box?" Grady Fay leans across and sticks a dime in the slot. "Pick out something."

I lean my head against the back of the booth. "You do it."

In a few seconds, "Love Me Tender" comes on.

Daddy settles me on the stool next to his, orders me a R.C. and himself two homebrews, which he downs one after the other. When he finishes, he wipes the foam from his mouth. "Boy, I needed that! Gimme one more, Hoke." Then he turns to me. "You alright, hon? Wanna try the punchboard now?" I nod. "Hey, buddy!" He waves to a man at the other end of the bar. "Slide that board down, will ya?"

The little papers inside each hole are folded up like a pleated skirt. When I punch one out, I can read the numbers on it. Daddy says that if I hit the lucky combination we'll win a brand-new Plymouth. I don't much want a Plymouth, but winning's winning. I'm on my fifth try when a woman with the blackest hair I've ever seen slides onto the empty stool on the other side of daddy. He seems to know her, and for awhile he's so busy talking that he forgets about me being there. Finally he shifts around. "This here's my little girl." He squeezes my shoulder. "Right, LaVonne?" The woman looks at me, but doesn't say anything.

While I drink my R.C., I can hear the two of them whispering together, and once in a while, the woman laughs. It's a real soft laugh, different from mama's. I start to wonder when we're leaving, and am about to ask when daddy turns around and flips a quarter on the counter. "Here, hon, get yourself some peanuts. I'll be back in a few minutes." I start off the stool after him. "No, you stay here. I won't be long. This lady has a dead bat-try and I'm gonna try to help her out." He waves from the door. "Hoke, give LaVonne whatever she wants and I'll pay you when I get back."

Hoke sets out a package of peanuts and tells me I can punch some more numbers if I want to, but I don't. All I want is to go home.

The minutes drag on. I occupy myself by making wet patterns on the bar with my drink. On the wall in front of me is a clock. Wish I knew how to tell time. I watch the long hand move slowly down, past four, past five, past six. Still daddy doesn't return. I get off the stool.

"Hey!" Hoke calls after me. "Where you goin'?"

"To find daddy."

He comes rushing out from behind the counter. "Now, listen. You don't wanna go out there in the dark." I try to wrench my arm away. "A bear might getcha." He pulls me back to the stool. "You stay in here with Uncle Hoke where it's nice and safe. Your daddy'll be back soon."

Finally, when the big hand gets to eight, the door opens and daddy walks in smoothing his hair. The black-haired woman's not with him. I notice a line of sweat on his forehead and upper lip.

"Sorry it took so long, hon. Hoke been taking good care of you?" He slaps down a half-dollar. "Hey, Hoke, gimme one more homebrew before we cut outta here."

"Boy!" the man at the end of the bar snorts as he watches daddy gulp down the beer. "Fixing bat-tries must give you a powerful thirst."

Listening to the music, I'm feeling completely relaxed. "Couldn't get up now if I had to," I say to Grady Fay. Under the table, our legs are touching.

We sit there in a silence that's only broken by Boley swearing as he misses a point over at the pinball machine.

Finally Grady Fay leans over, smiling. "You look like you're half asleep. Is that what beer does to you?"

I nod. "Makes me mellow, I guess."

When the next round arrives, Boley and Shorty join us. Grady Fay takes a few sips of his, then pushes the glass away.

"Aren't you gonna drink the rest?" Boley asks.

He rubs his eyes. "Afraid of dozing off while I'm driving."

"I'll finish it, then. No point in it going to waste."

Wonder if Grady Fay'll take me home last.

Saying goodnight to Hoke, we drift outside. I stand for a minute stretching my arms and taking deep breaths. The sky is so clear. "Look. There's the Big Dipper." I point overhead. "And that's Venus."

"How do you know?" Boley asks, opening the door of the truck.

"My daddy told me."

We pile in. Everybody's real quiet, even Boley. I'd give a lot of pennies for Grady Fay's thoughts right now. When I see him turn into Wart Town to take Boley and Shorty home first, my insides start boiling up. Call it a premonition, or something.

"What street is it again, Boley?"

"Cemetery Road."

"I'll get off here, too," Shorty says.

He lets them out, and circles back through the plaza toward Chimney Road. When he pulls up in front of my house, he sits there a minute, then steps out and comes around to open the door on my side. As he helps me out, it seems the most natural thing to walk right into his arms. He holds me so tight that I can feel the metal buttons of his old denim jacket. Then, turning my face up, he kisses me very softly. I'm the first to pull away.

"When you and me gonna get married?" he asks, still holding on to my hand.

"Who said we were?"

"Well, aren't we?"

"Reckon there's nothing else to do," I say as he draws me close again. But would he feel the same if he knew the truth?

Chapter Eighteen

FOR THE NEXT FEW DAYS, I'M SO HAPPY THAT I push all thoughts of Gene Hankins to the back of my mind and concentrate on Grady Fay. Mostly I'm puzzling over how to break the news to mama. Grady Fay wants to be there when I tell her. "It's only proper," he says. "Like asking for your hand."

I explain to him that mama's peculiar. "No telling how she might react," I say. "Maybe it's better if I do it by myself."

I try to choose a good time. Probably on Thursday, right after "Arthur Godfrey and His Friends." Arthur always puts her in a good mood.

So the next Thursday, I beg off from work, asking Dot to tell Mr. Baxter that I feel feverish. After supper, I pave the way for my big announcement by offering to wash the dishes.

"Uh-uh." Mama shakes her head. "You scatter water everywhere. Besides, I thought you were sick."

"I feel better. Want me to dry?"

"They'll dry theirselves."

But I do anyway. There're not many. Two plates, two glasses, two forks and spoons, Pretty Boy's food and water dishes. And all the time I'm wiping, I'm wondering how to lead into it. Finally I say, "Mr. Baxter's talking about entering Grady Fay in the doffing contest again."

"Don't know why," mama says. "He'll just lose."

"Not this time, I bet."

Mama grunts. "Well, he did before. What's changed about him?"

That's when I come close to blurting out, "*Me,* that's what!" But I check myself. No sense in letting the cat out of the bag too soon.

Just before Arthur Godfrey comes on, we watch a commercial for life insurance that shows a big family—grandparents, children, grandchildren—all sitting around a big table together. The grandmother is dandling a baby on her knee.

"Bet you can't wait to have grandchildren, mama," I say as a lead-in.

Her head snaps around. "Are you trying to tell me something?" Her fierce glance goes right through me. "I hope you haven't gone and done something you'll regret . . . "

"What are you talking about?"

"You and that piece of trash from Sawmill Mountain . . . "

"Mama!"

" . . . so you have to get married."

I feel a whole stomach-load of guilt backing up. "I haven't . . . "

" . . . Because that would be the end of me. *The end!*" She slaps her palm down hard on the arm of the chair.

I sink further back into the sofa cushions. It's beginning to look more and more hopeless. After a while, I get up and go into my bedroom. I can hardly stand to look at my body in the mirror anymore. I'm almost tempted to punch my stomach to try and make the bleeding start. I'm almost asleep when I hear a knock at the door. "LaVonne, you awake?" mama calls out.

"No," I say.

Opening the door, she stands there looking very small and frail. "The reason I said what I did," she says, "is so you won't make the same mistake I did."

Now I'm wide awake. I stare at her. "What mistake?" I ask.

"I just want you to have a better life, that's all." I can see her chin start to quiver. Drawing a kleenex out of her pocket, she wipes her eyes. "That's all I want in this world."

I can't stand to see mama cry. I reach over and take her hand. "It's alright. Come on, now. Everything's alright." But of course it's not.

When Grady Fay asks the next day in the mill if I've broken the news, I have to admit that I haven't.

"Why not?"

"I just couldn't."

"But *why?*"

"Because I *couldn't*, I told you." I turn back to piecing up. He follows me.

"LaVonne?"

"What?"

Now he's giving me that soulful gaze of his. "You still want to, don't you?"

"Want to what?"

"Get married."

"'Course I do." I feel so much like confessing, but I stop myself.

"'Cause I wouldn't want to push you into anything. My mama was pushed into marrying my dad. So she said."

"Grady Fay." I step up and kiss him on the cheek. "Nobody's pushing me. I just think the first thing is to win mama over." This is also the best way I know to stall for time.

"Win her over? Thought you were just going to tell her."

"By winning over, I mean talking to her, taking her places, getting her to like you."

"She hates me, huh?"

"She doesn't *hate* you . . . she just doesn't know you, that's all."

He disappears around the other side of the frame. But in a few seconds he's back, scratching his head. "Uh . . . what do you think your mama would like to do?"

This takes a bit of thought, which is hard with the machines cranking beside me. "Well . . . she loves wrestling."

"She does?"

"Bet she'd enjoy seeing a live wrestling match."

"I'll ask Marvin. He goes to those things."

A week later, I mention the idea to mama. "Grady Fay has three tickets to see wrestling up at Delphi. He wants you to come."

Mama looks at me suspiciously. "Me? Why me?"

"I told him you liked it."

"Well, I ain't going nowhere in that ol' truck."

But after dinner, she appears at my bedroom door. "Who's wrestling?"

"Lemme think. He told me . . . Genghis something or other. Some funny name."

"Not Genghis Conn?"

"That's it!"

"Mercy Lord!"

"What's the matter?"

"He's the best. I'd sure like to see him."

"Then come on."

All the way to Delphi, I worry about mama complaining about the truck. Instead she keeps her mouth shut and hardly says a word.

The match is held at a sports arena outside town—which isn't really an arena at all but just a bowling alley with an attached room that's been roped off in the middle with rows of benches placed around the sides. I start to sit down on one of them, but Grady Fay pulls me up. "This section's for colored people," he says. "See the sign?"

By eight o'clock, most of the seats are taken and some of the men in the back, impatient for it to begin, start whistling and stamping their feet. Grady Fay says they're rough customers, and when I look around to see if he's right, I catch sight of Gene and his two buddies sitting there. He's looking right straight at me. He grins and waves.

Jesus Christ, what's he doing here! Does he have spies? But maybe it's only a coincidence. Anyway, I don't let on.

J. W. Spriggs, a local boy, makes his entrance in what looks to be an orange bathing suit under a blue flannel bathrobe. He's a real contrast to Genghis, who struts in wearing red trunks studded down the sides with rhinestones; thrown around his shoulders is a red cape lined at the top and bottom with some kind of fur. "Looks like he skinned a couple of cats, don't it?" mama comments. When he turns around in the center of the ring, bowing and waving his arms, I can see GENGHIS printed on the back of his cape in purple sequins.

"His real name's Lenwood Conley," mama whispers.

"Why does he call himself Genghis?"

"Have you ever heard of a wrestler named *Lenwood?*"

"No."

"Well, then."

Genghis is such a showman that it's hard *not* to look, even though I'm worried about Gene. Right now Genghis is twisting J. W. Spriggs's neck around until I'm sure he's going to screw it right off. Reminds me of the way mama kills chickens.

"How can we *watch* this?" I ask, putting a hand up to my eyes to block the sight of J. W.'s face being pushed around like it's a rubber ball.

"They ain't really hurting each other," mama explains. "It's all show."

But I'm not convinced. And when Genghis takes hold of J. W.'s hair and yanks at it so hard that his eyeballs practically pop out of their sockets, I can't help moaning. Grady Fay reaches over and puts an arm around me. The worst, though, is the kick to the groin that sends J. W. writhing to the floor while the referee's standing over him counting. "Get up, J. W.," mama shouts. "Get up!" On the final count, J. W.—looking half-dazed and still in pain—manages to struggle to his feet.

"Betcha Genghis kills him next time," mama cackles.

I groan again. "I'm not sure I can stay here to see it," I whisper to Grady Fay. He takes one look at my face and leads me out to the snack bar for a Coke. I feel that Grady Fay deserves some encouragement so I say, "Mama's warming up. I can tell." About that time I see that Gene's stationed himself against the wall watching me. I don't think Grady Fay spots him, though. Trouble is, we can't get back inside without passing by him.

"So what about our unfinished business, baby?" Gene calls out.

I look away and don't say a word.

"You know what I'm talking about. That business in Memphis. When we were in the motel together, remember?" He turns to Grady Fay. "Bet you didn't know about that? LaVonne here lets on to be a real goody-goody. But I can tell you what she really likes."

Grady Fay's standing there dumbfounded. There's a long silence. Finally he manages to get some words out. "That's enough of that kinda talk. You don't say things like that around ladies."

Gene glances around, then looks straight at Grady Fay. "Where's the ladies? I don't see none."

Grady Fay stares at him. I grab Grady Fay's arm. "Come on," I say. "Don't pay any attention." As we walk away, I can hear Gene laughing.

Grady Fay stops. He looks pale. Says he can't stomach any more wrestling. Says he'll be outside.

Nothing else for me to do but go back in and take my seat. I'm just in time to see Genghis put a foot on J. W.'s head and roll it back and forth. His eyes are wide open and begging for help. I've seen a kitten being mangled by Miz Cowan's dog wear the same expression. After the third pin, the umpire stops the match and declares Genghis the winner.

"Where's what-his-name?" mama asks, as we get up.

"Waiting in the truck. He's not feeling so good. Well, did you enjoy it?"

"I did, but you know what?" I'm holding her coat so she can find the armholes. "Think it's better on television."

On the way home, Grady Fay's so quiet that I'm sure it's all over. When he stops in front of the house, he gets out and walks mama to the door. Then he says goodnight—if he'd had a hat on, he would've tipped it—and zips right off.

That night, I don't sleep a wink. I lie there wondering what to do.

Next morning, I think about it some more. That afternoon, I'm waiting on the steps when Grady Fay comes in. I suspect he means to sidestep me, but I don't let him.

"Can we talk about last night?"

"Guess so."

"We can't do it *here*. We have to go some place private."

Turns out the best spot is the one where we always talk—right beside the machines because the noise is so loud, only someone whose ears are used to it can hear anything.

"Gene Hankins was my boyfriend in high school. But I hadn't seen him in a long time until he turned up that night at the skating rink."

"Why didn't you tell me you knew him?"

"I was afraid Mr. Baxter would fire me."

"I wouldn't have let him."

"He's the boss."

"What about Memphis?"

"When you left like that, I was beside myself. So when he called and asked me to meet him in Memphis, so we could see Elvis, I did it."

"Yeah. And what happened?"

I've been dreading that question. If I tell him the truth, I might never see him again. "Nothing."

"Not according to him."

"Less than nothing."

"You swear?"

"May God strike me dead if it's not the truth." Is it my imagination, or do I feel a sudden twitch in my stomach?

"What's *less* than nothing?"

"A zero minus," I say, trying to remember my algebra.

"I guess that's good enough," he says, but doesn't seem quite sure about it. He gives me a long look before taking off around the frame at lightning speed. I think he must be even faster than before. I stand there hugging my arms to my body. Right now, I wouldn't much care if God did strike me.

The main test for mama comes when Grady Fay invites us to have Saturday night supper at the farm. He drives over and fetches us in late afternoon so that mama'll have the chance to see something before it gets dark. It's a cold, blustery day, but at least the sun's shining. At first I'm worried about mama being too critical, but I can see she's playing her "gracious lady" role. She nods ever so slightly to the dirty-looking kids standing in front of the trailers along the road.

The first thing we do is walk across the field to the pond so that Grady Fay can show us his prize heifer, bought with the hundred dollars he won in the doffing contest. The cow stands, still as a statue, knee-deep in water.

"Don't its legs get cold?" I ask Grady Fay, my teeth chattering every time the wind swoops down inside my thin cotton jacket.

"Naw, cows don't feel it none."

"Sure is a pretty animal," mama says. I give her a sharp glance to try and tell her she's on the verge of overdoing it.

By the time we get back to the house, it's almost dark. Grady Fay's daddy's on the porch.

"Think we weren't coming?" Grady Fay scrapes the mud on his brogans off on the bottom step.

"Supper's getting cold," Mr. Owens says. He nods towards mama. "Looks like rain, don't it?" He turns and goes inside, and we follow.

I can tell that somebody—most likely Grady Fay—has made a great effort to clean up the place. He's even thrown an afghan over the back of the sofa to cover up some of the worn spots. Should've hung some pictures, too, but I can advise him later about this. Except for a red felt pennant that says SOUTHEASTERN WORLD'S FAIR, ATLANTA, GEORGIA, 1950, and over in the corner a sampler with the words JESUS WEPT on it, the walls are completely bare.

"Who did that?" I ask, pointing to the sampler. I didn't notice it before because the room was so dark.

"Mama. 'Bout the only thing she left behind. It and the English saddles."

The kitchen looks better, too. The wide plank floor's been scrubbed clean.

Without bothering to remove his old felt hat, Mr. Owens sits down at the head of the table. We've barely had the chance to pull our chairs closer before he starts in. I watch his whiskery jaw move up and down and wonder what mama thinks of him. Not much, I bet.

"Mr. Owens, do you have any close neighbors?" mama asks, picking up her fork daintily.

"Not within shouting distance."

"Don't you miss them? I'd die if I didn't have Miz Cowan across the street."

Mr. Owens shakes his head and continues chewing. "Been my experience," he says, "that all neighbors is good for is tending to other people's business."

After that, we eat in silence.

"I never seen such manners in my life!" mama says, once we're back inside our own door. "They didn't even use napkins! Can you imagine? No napkins!"

Listening to her, I feel more and more discouraged. About everything.

"We'll try once more," I tell Grady Fay at the mill on Monday. "And if it doesn't work, we'll call it quits." I don't say quits about what.

He sighs. "I've run out of ideas, LaVonne."

"I have one."

"What's that?"

"Mama's always wanted to have Thanksgiving dinner in a restaurant and not have to cook. She says she's tired of collecting turkey bones. We could take her out."

"Where?"

"Well, there's the Café. I hear Mollie Sue makes good dressing."

On Thanksgiving, mama wears her best shoes, her best stockings, her best dress. "If it's an occasion, it ought to be one from the bottom up," she says.

I try to match her mood, but my heart's just not in it. There's a cramping in my stomach, too. I hug myself to try and ease it. Sooner or later, Grady Fay's going to have to be told, and I dread to think what'll happen.

Mollie Sue—who remembers Grady Fay from the banquet—leads us over to a table in the center of the room. "You can see everything from here," she says.

'Course there's not much to see—only Cootie Bledsoe sitting over in the corner with a huge napkin tucked in his collar, and Willie Ruth Teems who rushes in from the telephone office on her lunch break.

Mama orders the holiday special—turkey, dressing, candied sweet potatoes, peas, mashed potatoes—and asks Mollie Sue if she can have an extra helping of cranberry sauce on the side.

Grady Fay's next, and he wants fried chicken.

"*Fried chicken!*" Mama's shocked. "On *Thanksgiving?*"

"I don't get to have it much."

Mama sits there with her mouth turned down staring at Grady Fay.

When it's my turn, I clear my throat. "Waffles," I say. Even Mollie Sue is surprised. "And a side order of bacon." Mama's mouth is hanging open. "Oh, and a lot of syrup."

"That comes with it," Mollie Sue says, writing it all down.

While we're waiting for the food to arrive, mama takes her napkin and carefully wipes her knife, fork, and spoon, and the rim of her water glass.

After the main course, we order mincemeat pie for dessert. "Just think," mama says. "I been hearing about mincemeat pie for years but I've never actually tasted it."

When it arrives, she takes a big bite and chews it slowly. "Don't know what all the fuss is about," she says, putting down her fork.

"It's different," I say, my mouth full.

Mollie Sue comes around to refill our water glasses and notices the pie left on mama's plate. "Try vanilla ice cream on top," she says. "Kills the taste."

While we're sitting there, I feel something funny happening. Excusing myself, I rush into the bathroom. There's a big stain on the back of my skirt, but I'm too relieved to be embarrassed. Leaning against the wall, I whisper, "Thank you, Lord" over and over. Then I wash off my skirt as best I can with paper napkins, stick several more inside my panties, and go back and announce to Grady Fay that I gotta get home right away. As it is, I'm almost doubled over.

While we're driving back, he suddenly slams his fist hard enough against the steering wheel to make me jump and says, without any lead-in at all, "Miz Grubbs, LaVonne and me wanna get married."

As I tell Dot later, I'm sure *this* is the ballgame, and that mama'll start screaming and carrying on. But she doesn't. She just looks straight ahead. "I figured," she says.

"You did?"

"Well, I'm not an idiot."

"We'd like your permission."

"I reckon you have it."

He turns to her as though he can't believe what she's just said. "We *do?* I thought you didn't like me."

"I don't know where you got that idea. Bet LaVonne put it in your head." She leans over close to him. "Hope you've thought it out good, though. She ain't the easiest person in the world to live with." I glance at her. Is she smiling? I could swear she is.

"Well, Miz Grubbs," Grady Fay says with a straight face, "everybody can't be perfect, can they?"

Listening to the two of them laughing together, I sit there speechless.

Chapter Nineteen

BOTH ME AND GRADY FAY WANT TO GET MARRIED without any fuss or bother, but mama has other ideas.

"Only do it once," she says. "Oughta be an occasion."

So we decide on a small wedding, just for the family and a few friends—which includes all the people on our shift and the entire congregation of the Church of God of the Prophecy. We settle on December 31st, but since the church is holding a Watch Service that night, it has to be postponed until January 8th, which coincidentally is Elvis's birthday. Funny how Elvis keeps popping up, even when I thought I was finished with him.

Once the date's set, things begin to snowball.

First, Cecil Crider takes our picture for the *News.* When it appears the next week on the Social Happenings page, I cut it out and send it to daddy, along with a short note saying that I hope he'll be able to come. Actually, I'm doing more than hoping. After one miracle, why not pray for another?

Next, Dot, with Tessie's help, holds a shower for me over in the dining room of the Inn. Tessie bakes a big coconut cake with green and red cherries stuck to the top and this, together with boiled custard and Cokes, serves as refreshment. The entertainment is a take-off on "This Is Your Life," with me as the subject. Dot has volunteered to be master of ceremonies, and she brings out Pearlie B., who tells about my singing in church and organizing the New Sunshine Quartet (which hasn't quite got off the ground *yet,* but maybe it will), and Mr. Baxter, who describes how nervous I was when, fresh from high school, I first came to work in the spinning room. He bet Marvin Cowan I could do it, he says, and won. The highlight, though, is Shorty Toles' imitation of Elvis singing

"Heartbreak Hotel" with Tessie (without her glasses for once) pretending to be a swooning fan.

"I never acted like that," I say, half in protest.

At the end I open the presents: a set of pots and pans from second shift spinning; a tiny hostess apron from Pearlie B.; a mixing bowl from two of the fan club members; a trash can with a picture of a dog on it from Miz Cowan; guest towels from Boley's wife; and four coasters with pictures of Rock City from Reba Petit. Everybody leaves about eleven so Dot and Tessie can clean up. Marvin Cowan, who's come to pick up his mother, gives me and mama a ride home. As I'm getting out of the car, he whispers out of the corner of his mouth, "Somebody's wanting to see you."

"Who?"

"You know."

I just stare at him for a second and go on inside.

"That was so nice of Dot," I say as I turn on the living room light.

Mama scowls. "Bet she just did it so you'll do the same when she gets married—if she ever does."

The days before Christmas seem to fly. There's the usual party at work, only this time Mollie Sue—claiming it's in my honor—bakes a big ham instead of the usual fried chicken. On Christmas Day, Grady Fay and his daddy drive over to eat turkey and dressing with us. Mr. Owens sits at one end of the kitchen table, and Grandpa Jess sits at the other, eyeing one another. "Don't that old man ever say nothin'?" Grandpa Jess mutters later.

"Old? He's younger than you," mama says.

"Ain't you ever heard of age being all in the mind?"

"Yeah? Well, I'll remember that the next time you start complaining."

Me and Grady Fay are saving up for our honeymoon trip so we only give each other token presents—a puzzle, a pair of stockings, a tie, a tiny Santa Claus pin. We plan on driving down to Panama City, Florida. I'm real excited about seeing it again. I've told Grady Fay all about it, how daddy would hold me up whenever a big wave came close. "It's the prettiest place," I tell him for the tenth time. "Palm trees everywhere."

He says he's looking forward to seeing the ocean. Isn't one of the best things in life being able to show the person you love something new?

It's on Christmas night that panic begins to set in. Grady Fay and his daddy have gone home, and mama puts Grandpa Jess on the road while he's still sober enough to drive. Me and her are in the living room—which is dark except for the light from the television and our old artificial Christmas tree—watching the "Fred Waring Show." When the choir begins singing "I'll Be Home for Christmas," it suddenly dawns on me that soon I'll be leaving for good. I glance over at mama—who's sitting in the platform rocker with her head thrown back listening—and wonder if she's thinking the same thing.

Just before bedtime, the phone rings. When I answer it, heavy breathing's coming from the other end. I slam the receiver down hard.

"Who was that?" Mama opens her eyes.

"Some pervert," I say, then give her a goodnight kiss and go into my own room. It's hard to get to sleep, though. I'm not sure whether it's because I ate too much dressing, or heard that song, or got that phone call.

Mama's making my wedding dress out of a white satiny material called "sateen." It has a pinched-in waist, a flared skirt, and a "sweetheart" neckline above two tucks. The tucks are the hardest things, she says.

Each day I try it on. In the beginning, it's only pieces of pattern pinned on and shifted around. Then gradually, bits of the dress begin to take shape—a sleeve basted together, a back that starts at the shoulders, a waist that's too tight for me to bend over in and has to be taken apart, and finally the skirt without any band to it at all, just gathers, first one side, then the other. Sometimes I get tired of standing while mama pins, unpins, rearranges.

"Be still," she says, the straight pins moving up and down between her lips. "You're going to make me get this wrong."

At night when I come in from the mill, I glance over to see how much has been done. Sometimes it looks like nothing at all; then the next evening a whole finished piece appears, as if by magic. I try it on, standing on a chair so I can get a glimpse of myself in the mirror that hangs above the mantelpiece. "Wish I could see better," I say, twisting around. "Do you think the skirt's too full?"

"Looks just right to me." Mama comes over and tugs at one side. "Any less would make it skimpy."

And I nod. "You're probably right," I say. I'm in a mood now to be carried along, to bend to someone else's wishes, to be told what to do and what not to do. My main hope is for the phone to ring and for it to be daddy calling long distance.

On December 28th—which is the day before my birthday, only nobody ever celebrates it because it's so close to Christmas—Marvin Cowan comes over. I think he's going to ask me something about filling in the week that Grady Fay and I are on our honeymoon. Turns out, he's not asking, he's *telling*. "Gene needs to talk to you," he says. "He'll be in front of the Store at two o'clock tomorrow afternoon."

"I have nothing to say to Gene Hankins." I give him a hard look. "What's your connection with him?"

"His mama and my daddy were first cousins. I didn't know it, though, till he called me up about a year and a half ago. He fixes my car for nothing."

"Did he ever ask you about me?"

"A little, but I didn't tell him much." Marvin looks so uncomfortable that I'm sure he's lying. "Listen. He feels real bad about what happened. He just wants . . . to wish you luck and all."

"Luck! Oh, sure."

"Trust me, that's all he wants."

But I *don't* trust Marvin, and I don't go near the Store . . . not even when mama asks me to get her some rat cheese. I wait till three-thirty—when I'm sure Gene'll be gone—before I mosey over to the Grey Mill.

As I'm walking through the plaza, I see him ahead of me, leaning against the doughboy statue, smoking a cigarette.

"Oh Lord!" I say under my breath, and move away from him. He follows me, walking fast. I turn in another direction. He turns, too. He could easily catch up with me if he wanted to. As I dash in and around the parked cars, I see him watching me. Finally I run toward the Grey Mill without once looking back to find out if he's following.

Mr. Baxter spots me coming in, glances at his watch, shakes his head. I just keep on going. But instead of heading directly to the machines, I take a detour into the ladies room to wash my face and compose myself. When I reach the frames, Grady Fay looks up. "Where you been?"

"Had to run an errand for mama. Took longer than I thought."

Thank goodness for piecing up. I have so much catching up to do that I don't have time for conversation. When the others take their break and go into the canteen, I say I'm not hungry and stay at the machines.

The more I think about all this, the more I feel like jumping into a bucket head-first. As it is, I go around like I'm a zombie. "Cheer up," Dot says. "This is the happiest time of a girl's life."

Mama says my face is so long, I look like I'm going to my own funeral. But Grady Fay's the most concerned.

"LaVonne? What's the matter?"

"Nothing."

"Something is."

"Tired, that's all."

"Everything's gonna be alright." And when he puts his arm around me. I rest my head on his shoulder, feeling that maybe it will, after all.

When I get off from work, I always look around to make sure Gene's not hanging around outside. To be on the safe side, I also ask Dot and Troy to drive me home, even though I feel pretty silly doing it.

Then one night, sure enough, he's standing outside the main door as the shift changes. Doesn't make a move to come near me. Doesn't say a word. Just looks. Gives me the creeps.

I begin to see him everywhere, even in places where he's not, which is maybe his intention. I even examine my bedroom before stepping into it. And make sure all the doors are locked up tight. That's how spooked I am.

On the day of the wedding, I wake up before daybreak and lie in bed, my knees drawn up to my chest. The TV weatherman said we'd have a light snow, but it hasn't happened yet. If it snows really hard, Grady Fay won't be able to drive down from Sawmill Mountain and we'll have to call the whole thing off. This might be the best thing that could happen. As Preacher Crow says, leave things in God's hands. But I'll tell you a secret. Sometimes I don't trust God.

As light begins to seep in, I look around my room. Soon it won't be my room anymore. If only I could be twelve again! But being twelve wasn't too good either. On the floor, a suitcase lies open, waiting for a few last-minute things to be placed inside. My white dress hangs from the closet door. In the half-dark, it looks like some kind of haint.

Hearing a noise, I get up and creep into the kitchen. Mama's standing at the oven door, warming her hands. "What're you doing up this early?"

"Couldn't sleep."

"Well, you better go back and try. Otherwise you'll have big rings under your eyes."

So I crawl under the covers again, spending the time praying for daddy to show up at the last minute. He can handle anybody, even Gene Hankins.

When I wake up the second time, it's snowing—not hard, but enough so you can tell it's more than pieces of lint floating through the air.

"Oh, no!" Mama stands at the kitchen window groaning. "Look at that! Just our luck! Won't be anybody there!"

But it soon stops, although the threat still hangs in the air.

Why do I keep imagining that daddy *will* come? Why do I keep imagining that he'll really care?

He tears open the envelope, unfolds the clipping, stares at it for a second, then says to his wife, "Lookee here," pointing, "this is my baby girl, all grown up. She's getting married. I don't believe it!"

And during the ceremony—just as Preacher Crow gets to the part about "if any man can show just cause . . . let him do so now or forever hold his peace"—he comes striding in, calling out from the back of the church, "Hold on! Just a minute now! Let's not be hasty here. I haveta look this boy over, make sure he's right for my little girl."

Or will it be Gene who stomps in, breaking things up, making a scene? Wouldn't put it past him. "O daddy, daddy, please help me!" I whisper.

"You look right pretty," mama says when I get the wedding dress on, and the tiara veil in place—one of the few compliments she's ever paid me. "A tiny bit of rouge," she says, "will take away that peaked look." I put on a dab, and a little eye makeup, too.

Bub drives us over to the church. Says he's cleaned the back seat especially for me, but mama insists on covering it with a sheet anyway. When he lets us out, she glances around to be sure Grady Fay's nowhere in sight. I'm looking around, too—to make certain Gene's car is not parked somewhere nearby.

Don't think I've given up on you, daddy, I say silently as I'm walking toward the door. Right this second, you could be getting off the Grey-hound. Somebody at the station'll give you a ride over. You'll be just in time to give me away instead of Grandpa Jess doing it.

At the door, Dot and Tessie are waiting to hustle me to the back.

"You look just like a blonde Debra Paget," Dot whispers, which reminds me of Elvis.

I still feel bad about Dot not being my maid of honor, but she says she understood it had to be mama. Over in the corner, Pearlie B.'s rehearsing the Sunshine Trio (which is what it's been called since I resigned two weeks ago) in "Always," trying as usual to keep Ettie Mae on target and as usual not quite succeeding.

Then it's time. Reckon daddy isn't coming after all. Reckon it's just as well. But I can't help feeling disappointed walking down the aisle on Grandpa Jess's arm—smelling whiskey on his breath everytime he leans close—instead of somebody handsome, somebody I'm proud of. When I pass Marvin Cowan, who's sitting at the end of the aisle beside his mother, I give him the Evil Eye, which I shouldn't do in church, especially on my wedding day.

Then I glimpse Grady Fay watching me walking toward him, a big grin on his face. "Oh, daddy, if you could just see all this!" I'm thinking, as we stand in front of Preacher Crow. I'm thinking about it so hard that I barely pay attention to the voice droning on . . . "be your lawful wedded husband, to love and to cherish" . . . and, during the long pause when I'm supposed to say "I do," I just stand there until Preacher Crow has to repeat it. "I do," says a crackly voice that doesn't sound like mine at all, but like some ventriloquist's dummy.

And all through the exchange of rings, through the peck that Grady Fay plants on my lips, through the cutting of the cake with the little figurine of the bride and groom on top, I keep waiting for the door to bang open, to hear footsteps. When I change into my maroon gabardine suit that's my "going away" outfit, I make an excuse of forgetting something in order to turn back and look around to be sure I haven't missed anybody. But finally, Grady Fay helps me into the truck. Mama—her eyes big and raw-looking—clings to the window and sticks her head in.

"Call me the *minute* you get to Panama City, hear? And you," this to Grady Fay, "you drive careful. The roads'll be slippery."

I wave and blow kisses, then toss the bridal bouquet in Dot's direction.

"Well, how does it feel to be Mrs. Grady Fay Owens?" Grady Fay asks once we're on our way. To tell the truth, I'm feeling a bit of a let down so I say it's not the right time for such a question.

Once in a while I look out the back window to make sure we're not being followed—which I realize is overly dramatic, but why take chances?

We inch our way over the Georgia border and down to the lower end of Alabama, passing places with one or two stores that I'm sure don't appear on any map. When we reach Eufala, the flurries of snow turn into raindrops. At any minute, especially as we get closer to the Gulf, I tell Grady Fay, the sun'll come out and palm trees'll begin to spring up. I even open the window in hopes that a warm breeze will blow through. But it doesn't. It's still freezing.

Instead of the tropical paradise I remember, Panama City looks gray. The boats in the harbor, covered in canvas, rock back and forth at the end of heavy ropes. We ride around trying to find a motel that hasn't been shut up for the winter. Driving down one deserted street after another, we finally spot a neon sign that's turned on—at least, some of it is. It says THE O AN VIE , and for a second, I wonder if it might not be some foreign language. Behind the sign, I see a chain of run-down stucco cottages snaking off the road.

The proprietor, a woman in her sixties with leatherish skin and a cigarette dangling between her lips, tells us we're lucky because she was just about to close for the night. "You'll have to put up with an unheated room," she says, "but it's better than nothing." She says she'll bring in a small heater to take the chill off.

While we're taking our suitcases out of the truck, Grady Fay reminds me that I promised to call mama.

"It's too cold," I say. "I'll do it in the morning."

"Won't she be worried?"

"Probably asleep by now."

The moment I've been dreading has arrived. Shivering, I crawl between damp sheets next to Grady Fay. I've brought, as part of my trousseau, a

195

low-cut red nightgown with two thin straps and lace at the top, but end up wearing two layers of sweaters over it so my teeth will stop chattering. Grady Fay clings to me, while I lie stiff as if I'm locked inside a big cake of ice. I keep thinking, This is not fair to him, it's not fair, but I can't get the memory of Gene's pounding out of my head. "I'm so tired," I say, as some kind of excuse. He looks disappointed but keeps on hugging me anyway, and I drift off to sleep.

The next thing I know, it's still dark. Turning on one side, I see Grady Fay looking at me, the whites of his eyes catching the moonlight outside. He doesn't reach for me, though, he just keeps staring, and I stare back. Then he smiles, and at first I don't smile, then I do. One of his fingers twists around mine, and my cold foot seeks out his warm one, until finally I nestle against him. By the time he leans over to kiss me, the thawing out process has already started.

When I awake, Grady Fay, now fully dressed, is peering through the dirty slats of the venetian blinds.

"Can you s-s-see the ocean?" I ask, a blast of cold air hitting me as I sit up.

He turns around and gives me a shy grin. "Nope. Nothing but the backs of houses."

Feeling a sudden modesty, I go into the bathroom to put on my clothes. My breath makes curls over the sink as I brush my teeth. Two dead spiders lie beside a dirty soapdish.

"How far's the ocean?" we ask the woman at the desk.

"Block and a half." Taking a long drag of cigarette smoke, she lets it out in a steady stream. "*That* way."

Leaving the truck, we strike out walking. A cold breeze blows from the direction we're heading in, and we tuck our heads into the collars of our jackets.

"What's that fishy smell?" Grady Fay turns up his nose.

"That's the ocean."

After climbing three sand banks, we come to it. I remember it as bright green, but today it looks brown. The waves are huge, and they crash onto the beach with a thud.

"My gosh," Grady Fay says, staring at the scene.

"When we used to come here on vacation, daddy would lift me up above the waves. He wouldn't let them touch me."

"He didn't want anything to happen to you."

"No," I say. Then I'm quiet.

"We could walk apiece," he says.

"Well."

As we step over the loose sand, Grady Fay kicks at it with the toe of his shoe. Suddenly I can't go on. "I'm too cold," I tell him.

I wish it was summer so we could run and jump into the water. Seeing it now only makes me shiver more. "I'm really *frozen.*" We start back. At the edge of the beach, we turn and take one more look. "Well," I say after a couple of seconds, "aren't you glad we came and saw it?"

Nodding, he takes my hand, and we stroll back to the motel.

During breakfast, I try to talk Grady Fay into driving on to New Orleans. I keep telling myself it doesn't have anything to do with Elvis, either, because he's clean out of my mind. "It's a spot everybody should see," I say. "Especially since we're so close."

Finally he agrees. While he checks us out, I put in a call to mama. I let it ring nine or ten times, but there's no answer.

"Musta gone over to Miz Cowan's," I tell Grady Fay. "I'll try again later."

We're eighty-two miles due west, in a tiny Mississippi town called Lackalutchie, before I think of it again. Grady Fay pulls over at the next diner.

"Still not there," I say, while we're waiting to be served.

"Maybe she's at your grandpa's."

"Not unless there's some special church doings."

Our plates arrive, heaped with hamburger patties, cabbage, and mashed potatoes.

"I know!" I look up between bites. "Bet she's over at the church cleaning up the social hall after the reception."

Grady Fay smiles. "Now, you see." He's got a whole mouthful of potato. "Knew you'd figure it out if you thought about it hard enough."

"She's sure to be back by four. That's when she takes Pretty Boy out of the cage to give him some exercise."

I'm in charge of looking at the map and telling Grady Fay which road to take. As long as it's a four-lane highway, I do all right. But once we turn into narrower roads, it's hard to keep track.

"Why don't these places put up some signs?" I say, as we drive around trying to find our way out of Bogalusa, Louisiana.

Exasperated, Grady Fay pulls over to a gas station to ask, while I go to the ladies room. When I come back, he's gunning the motor. "What time is it?" I ask him. "My watch has stopped."

"Twenty after four."

"I should call again." I nod toward the pay phone inside the station.

"I don't believe this!" I say, climbing back into the truck.

197

"No answer?"

"None."

Grady Fay waits for his chance to pull out into the traffic. "The guy in there said we take 90 all the way, so look for the sign. He said it'll be on the main drag."

We drive on . . . slowly . . . stopping at two red lights.

"LaVonne, do you see it?"

"What?"

He groans. "You haven't even been watching."

"I want to call Miz Cowan." I turn to him. "Probably it's nothing . . . but I just don't feel right."

Holding out an arm, he swerves into the other lane just in time to avoid being hit by a big moving van coming from the other direction.

Miz Cowan's voice sounds like she's inside a hole in the ground.

"This is LaVonne. Can you hear me?"

"Thank God!"

"Where . . . "

"We didn't know *how we were gonna find you!*"

"I couldn't . . . "

"Your mama had another attack."

"Oh Lord!" Was it on account of I didn't call? "When?"

"Not long after supper, we think. Marvin went over to take an umbrella she'd left in his car, and found her. She was unconscious."

I want to ask, "Why?" "How?" Instead, I stand there letting the phone dangle until Grady Fay comes up and takes it out of my hand.

"Miz Cowan? . . . Yes. What happened? Oh, no!" He glances toward me. "We'll turn right around. . . . Yeah, but it's gonna take awhile, we're in Bogalusa. . . . Never mind, we'll be there as soon as we can." He hangs up. "Don't worry, hon," he says, patting my shoulder. "I'll get us back in no time at all."

"Bet it's nothing much anyway," I mutter a few minutes later as we're passing the Bogalusa city limits. "Probably just a way of getting us home. She can't stand me doing something that she's not part of."

By the time we reach Alabama and are heading north, I've talked myself into the notion that mama's fine. I even know what I'll say when I walk in. I'll say, "Well, you did it again!" I'll stand there with my hands on my hips. "Can't even have a honeymoon without you spoiling it!"

Chapter Twenty

Except for pausing once or twice for a Coke or cup of coffee, we drive back nonstop, pulling up in front of the hospital at 3:12 A.M.

"Strange hour to be awake," Grady Fay says, helping me out of the truck, then stretching his arms.

We go in the back way. I've been sitting so long that I walk in a jerky, zigzaggy way as if my muscles are being pulled in several directions at once.

The hospital's almost totally silent. Our footsteps seem to clang and echo as we climb the steps into the small lobby on the second floor.

Miss Cargle's sitting at the front desk. "Well, finally!" she says as I move toward her. "I'll take you to the room." She stands up, pulling at the skirt of her uniform. "You have to be prepared for your mama not knowing you."

"Not *know* me?"

"This attack is a lot worse than the first one." She gestures down the hall. "Follow me."

The corridor seems longer than before. Each step we take is marked by the squeak of Grady Fay's brogans. Hearing the noise, Miss Cargle turns and stares at his feet. He tries to walk in the quietest way possible, but this only makes the squeaking worse.

"Here we are." She stands aside and waits for us to enter.

The door's pulled to, but not completely shut. I'm so afraid of what I'll see that I push it open very slowly. The only light's coming from a small lamp on the bedside table, but it's enough to make out a figure under the oxygen tent and to see the equipment surrounding her. Mama's deformed hand hangs from the side of the bed. I tiptoe closer and take hold of it. It feels cold and lifeless.

"Mama?" I whisper. She's lying face-up, her eyes closed, her mouth slack. "Mama?" I say it louder, expecting her eyes to pop open, but they don't.

"Oh my God!" I turn to ask Miss Cargle if mama was like this when they brought her in, but she's already gone. Grady Fay tries to take me into his arms, but I shrug him off. Comfort's not what I want now. I want her to stir, to show some signs of life.

As I sit there, Grady Fay paces back and forth, back and forth until I can't stand it any longer. "Why don't you go home?" I realize that the tone of my voice sounds a little sharp, so I put a hand on his arm. "No use in both of us staying."

"What about you?" He looks ready to drop.

"I can sleep in that." I point to the chair by the side of the bed. "Go on now," I say, half-pushing him toward the door.

"I'll be back later."

Returning to the bed, I pull the chair close and take hold of the hand again. The longer I sit there, the more it begins to feel like the lifeline binding the two of us together. I stay that way for hours. One time I doze off, and wake up with a start only to find that our hands have come apart. I clasp it again, this time tighter than ever, and promise mama that I'll stay awake.

When morning comes, people begin appearing. Dr. Henderson looks in to check on mama's condition. On the way out, he pats my shoulder. A nurse brings in a breakfast tray and sets it down.

"Mama can't eat that," I say.

The nurse shrugs. "She gets it anyway." At the door she turns around. "Why don't you have it?"

I glance at the orange juice, the dish of Cream of Wheat, the slices of toast (burnt at the edges) and cover them with a napkin. Dropping the hand long enough to pour myself a cup of coffee from the small pot, I drink it as quick as I can, then rush back to the bed.

Later Miz Cowan sticks her head in the door. "How is she?"

"The same." She doesn't venture inside. "You have any idea what happened?"

"All I know is that when Marvin went over, she was lying on the floor . . . clutching the phone. He told me not to tell you that, but I think you ought to know."

"Phone? You mean she was talking to someone?"

"'Pears that way. You'll have to ask Marvin. He called an ambulance right away." She stands there a few more minutes. I ask her to sit down but she shakes her head and says she'd better be going.

Dot's next. I'm sitting there with my eyes closed and don't even hear her come in. "LaVonne?" She walks over and puts a hand on my shoulder. "Is there anything I can do?" I shake my head. "If there is, you call me now, y'hear?"

Though I know they all mean well, it seems like everybody, even the doctors and nurses, are trying come between mama and me, trying to put static into the silent messages we're sending each other through our fingertips. Sometimes I hold her hand so tight that my own hand turns damp and sweaty. I can feel this sweat seeping into mama's skin, bringing her back to life.

As the day goes on, I keep waiting for Grady Fay to return. Then I decide that he's probably gone over to the farm to check on his daddy. But he'll surely be here by nightfall. And a few hours later, he does walk in. He doesn't say much, though. He still looks tired. But I'm too distracted to offer any sympathy. Besides, I'm the one needing sympathy, if anybody does.

"Where you been?" I ask. "I was getting worried."

"I overslept," he mumbles. "How is she?" He nods toward the bed.

"The same."

"Why don't you go home for awhile, and let me stay?"

The idea fills me with horror. "I can't leave mama!"

"Doc Henderson says this might go on . . . for a long time."

"You talked to him?"

"Just now."

"Isn't there anything he can *do?*"

"He claims not."

"Call in one of them specialists or something?"

"Wouldn't do any good. I asked him."

I squeeze mama's fingers even tighter.

He pulls something out of his pocket and hands it over. "Almost forgot," he says. "This letter came while we were gone."

Recognizing the handwriting on the envelope. I tear it open.

Dear Lavonne,
   Sorry not to make your wedding.
Can't take off from work right now.
But I want you to know I'm very
happy for you, and wish you the best
of luck. Enclosed is twenty dollars,
which I hope you'll use to buy something
you need.
                    Love,
                    Jim Tom

I read it over and over, trying to picture what was in his mind when he wrote it. It's the word "love" that haunts me. Love, love, love. But why did he sign his name "Jim Tom" instead of daddy? Maybe it's his way of saying "you're grown-up now." I think so hard I make myself tired.

While I'm sitting there with my eyes shut, Grady Fay lounges near the window. He's still looking gloomy. Every now and then, he comes over to my side of the room. "Here, drink this," he says. My eyelids feel so heavy. When I make myself lift them, I see him standing there holding an R.C. I take it and down the whole thing. But when he steps behind me and tries to massage the back of my neck, it annoys me.

"Please don't." I pull my head away.

"Thought you liked me doing that . . . "

"Yes, but . . . "

"What?"

Knowing that I'm on the verge of tears, I try to hold them back by taking deep breaths. But they come anyway and the breaths turn into sobs.

"Aw, hon." Grady Fay pulls me up out of the chair, but our embrace is awkward because I refuse to let go of mama's hand or leave her bedside.

"I need . . . to be by myself," I say between heavings.

"You don't want me to stay with you?" He looks so crushed that I almost change my mind. But it's got to be just mama and me. That's the only way I can save her. So I shake my head.

"Well, in that case . . . " He stops at the door and turns with a long pause. "Be seein' you."

Even as he's leaving, my eyes are already closed again, shutting him out. I know I probably hurt his feelings, but at the moment I'm too tired to care. I stroke mama's knuckles, each one jutting out like a separate knob, trace the scar-line that zigzags over two of her fingers and down into the fold, touch her thumbnail, ragged at the edge as if it's been torn off, examine her cuticle and the tiny half-moon that she polishes around. It seems strange that the same fingers that were always so clutching and grasping are now limp, their strength gone. I rub them along my cheek.

I think about Elvis, too. Not the old way, but more grownup. I think about how he sat at his mama's hospital bed, just as I am, now. For long hours, never leaving her side, waiting, waiting, waiting. I can sense his presence near me. This thought gives me strength.

During the evening of the second day, mama begins to stir. At first I think it might simply be a reflex to the nurse jiggling the catheter while she's emptying the urine bottle. But after the nurse leaves and I stand up, stretching my body to relieve some of the numbness from sitting so long, the fingers jerk slightly. Peering through the oxygen tent, I see mama's eyes wide open and staring directly at me.

"Mama!" I cry. Then bending over, I whisper, "Mama! I knew you'd get better. I knew you'd come to yourself." I wait for her to say something but seconds and minutes go by with nothing but that unblinking stare. "It's me, mama," I say. "It's LaVonne." The next time I say it slower, turning it into two names, "La-Vonne," and wait. That stare becomes her whole face. I squeeze her hand.

"You feeling better, mama?" I can hear the hysterical edge in my voice. "Is there anything you want?"

Suddenly the face changes . . . not changes, but shifts: the lips clamp together, the eyes open wider, the pupils dilate, the hand tries to pull out of my grasp.

"Mama, don't do that!" This time I yell out. "Don't *do* that!" I bend closer. "Mama! I'm afraid!" If anything'll bring her around, it's those words, they've always worked before. "I'm afraid," I say again.

But the fingers beat against my palm like a trapped bird. I don't want to let go, but I have to. I can't hold them against her will. The second I release her hand, it flies up to the crumpled mound of sheet and settles on her chest where it trembles, then lies still. The eyelids flutter and close.

"Mama!" I scream. I look at her for a second, then turn and run down the hall yelling for one of the nurses. Miss Cargle, who's at the other end, comes quickly, followed by another nurse waving a stethoscope. They race into the room. Meanwhile I'm leaning against the wall outside, my lips moving, saying, "Please God, please God, please God," over and over. I hear them shove the chair aside and raise the oxygen tent. Dr. Henderson rushes in. I hear their strains and grunts, hear Dr. Henderson murmur, "It's no use."

When I walk back in, I see Miss Cargle rearranging her hands, crossing them, one over the other.

It's Marvin Cowan who shows up to drive me home.

"Where's Grady Fay?" I ask, confused that he's not here by my side.

"He took off." Marvin says. "Reckon he's gone over to the farm."

"He doesn't know about mama?"

"Probably not."

I'm puzzled more than worried. But to tell the truth, I'm not much of either, because Dr. Henderson's given me a shot and I can already feel its effect. Can barely phrase the questions I need to ask Marvin.

"Why was mama holding the phone?"

"What?"

"When you found her?"

"How do I know?"

"Think you do."

But my mind seems to slip away, and I have to let the subject go . . . for now anyway. By the time I reach home, Marvin has to lead me inside, and Miz Cowan helps me into bed.

At first I sleep real sound. Then the dreams come. In one, I'm wandering through a broken-down house, walking through room after room, searching for something, someone, but the place is completely deserted. Next, I find myself—me, who can't swim at all!—diving with the greatest of ease into green water. As I swim through this water, I see pieces of seaweed and bright orange coral and birds the same color as Pretty Boy. It's the first technicolor dream I've ever had, and I wake up ready to tell it to Grady Fay. Except Grady Fay's still not here. It's Dot who's standing in the doorway. So I tell her.

"*Birds?*" she says.

"Isn't that weird?"

"What's coral?" She sits down on the bed beside me.

"A plant that grows underwater. That's what daddy said. He's the one who showed it to me." I close my eyes.

"LaVonne?" Dot takes my hand. "You gotta get up now." I don't say anything. "Jake Haygood called. You have to pick out a casket. He's waiting."

"Ohhhhhhh." Groaning, I put the pillow over my head the way I used to when mama nagged at me. I try to get back the dream, but it's no use. The green water's gone, the coral's gone, the birds are gone.

Nobody's seen Grady Fay since he took off for Sawmill Mountain. "Is this any way to be treated?" I say to Dot.

Dot's avoiding my gaze. "We'll talk about it later," she says. "Important things first." As she's helping me dress, I'm wondering what could be more important.

Friends and neighbors have already started bringing in food. Dot, who doesn't know where to put all the dishes, plates, and casseroles, sticks as much as she can in the refrigerator and leaves the rest lying covered on top of the table and cabinets. Pulling aside wrappers, I see fried chicken, meatloaf, fried green tomatoes, two angel food cakes, butterbeans cooked in bacon drippings, biscuits (cold by now) with slices of ham inside, Miz Cowan's Coca-Cola cake, Waldorf salad with too much mayonnaise, a huge bowl of wilted green beans, and other dishes that I don't even bother looking at.

Dot insists that I take a few bites of the bananas and Post Toasties that she's fixed. "Come on," she keeps saying after every bite. "Eat a little more."

"You sound just like mama," I say. Then the tears begin welling up. "I haveta make a phone call." The idea has just occurred to me.

"Let me," Dot says. "You go ahead and eat."

I shake my head. "This is something *I* have to do."

In the living room, Grandpa Jess is stretched out on the platform rocker with a huge plate of food in his lap. When I come in, he stops long enough to mumble something that I don't catch.

Picking up the phone, I dial O, and Willie Ruth Teems comes on the line. "Willie Ruth . . . "

"Is this LaVonne?"

"Yes . . . "

"I was real sorry to hear about your mama, hon. But at least she didn't suffer. What place are you calling?"

"Detroit."

"And the number?"

"I don't know . . . can't find it . . . used to know it by heart . . . "

"I'll ring information." I hear a buzzing noise, then a voice comes on that sounds like it's from another planet. "Detroit information. What party are you calling, pul-lease?"

"Jim Tom Grubbs."

"Spell the last name please."

"G-r-u-b-b-s."

"One moment."

I think she must be turning pages but I'm not sure. "Sorry. I don't find a Jim Tom Grubbs listed." Suddenly I panic. Has he moved away without telling me? He could be anywhere. I'll never see him again. "There's an Ernest Grubbs, Grover Grubbs, James Grubbs, Mary Grubbs, S.T. Grubbs . . . "

"Try James."

It rings seven times. I'm about to give up when I hear a click and a woman's voice.

"Can I speak to Jim Tom Grubbs please?"

During the pause that follows, I hold my breath. "Who's this?" the woman asks.

"This is LaVonne. His daughter." I could say his long-lost daughter. I wonder if the woman's hair's still as black as it used to be.

I wait and wait. In the background I can hear the rasp of conversation, but it's muffled, like someone's holding a hand over the phone.

"LaVonne?" I recognize daddy's voice immediately. He sounds just the same. I bet he *is* just the same. "Where are you?"

"Goody."

"Oh." He sounds relieved. "How are you?"

"I'm alright. Thanks for your letter."

"Oh. Well . . . You okay?"

Has he forgotten that he asked me that before? "I am but . . . " I can feel the catch in my throat. "Mama died yesterday."

"What?"

"She had a heart attack."

I can't make out his next words because a crackling noise comes over the line. "What did you say? There's a lot of static."

"I said I thought sure your mama would live forever."

Biting my lip, I plunge in. "I was wondering if you could come down . . . "

"Come down . . . ?"

"The funeral's set for tomorrow afternoon."

"Do you know how much that'd *cost*? I'd have to fly. I mean, if there was anything I could do, it'd be different, but . . . "

"Just thought I'd ask."

"I just don't have the money."

I take a deep breath. "What if I pay your way?"

"You could do that?" He sounds suspicious, as if I've just robbed a bank or something.

"I saved up a bit of money for my honeymoon, which we had to cut short because of mama, so I have some left."

"Oh." There's a pause. "I appreciated your sending me that clipping from the *News*. Looks like a nice fellow . . . " If I say anything more than "mmmmmm," I'll be sure to cry. "I have to think about all this, you know . . . it's come out of the blue."

"You can call me back later."

"Yeah, lemme do that. Uh . . . better give me the number again. I have it here somewhere, but . . . " I recite it slow-like so he won't miss anything. "Alright. See what I can do."

I hold the receiver until I hear the click on the other end.

When I put down the phone, I realize that Dot's been standing there listening. Now I *am* crying and she puts her arms around me. "Where's Grady Fay?" I ask again.

"He'll be back soon."

"But I need him to go with me to pick out a casket."

"I'll go," Dot says.

As we climb the steps to the undertaking department, Jake Haygood stands waiting for us at the top. "You're here," he says, putting a round gold watch back into his vest pocket. "I was beginning to wonder."

"LaVonne slept late," Dot says.

"Come right this way." He points us toward a side door with a panel of blistered glass that's impossible to see through. I remember being in here a long time ago with daddy. But now the room seems a whole lot smaller.

"Let me show you my recommendation," Jake says, leading us over to a slate gray casket. "This is our most popular model."

"I like bronze better." I turn to Dot. "Gladys Presley's casket was bronze." And then to Jake: "Is it very expensive?"

"Depends on the weight. The heavier ones cost more. But since we don't have them in stock anyway, you'd have to take the lighter model, and it's about the same price. Do you want to see the inside?"

"No . . . we'll . . . it's fine."

I hand him the life insurance policy. He examines it and fills out the forms. "We'll have her back home by five o'clock," he says, as if mama's a child who's playing over at somebody's house for the afternoon.

Then Dot drives me down to Richville where, for an hour and a half of rifling through dresses, I almost forget my troubles. The salesgirls keep trying to fit me into bright-colored wool smocks, and the temptation's hard to resist.

"No," Dot says, doing the talking for me. "She needs something in black."

I choose a dress of a filmy crepe material like the ones Mrs. Fortune sometimes wears. If daddy comes, I want him to think of me as something more than a mill girl.

"Are you sure that's *appropriate?*" Dot asks, frowning as I model it for her.

"I think it suits me," I say, studying my reflection in the three-way mirror.

When I walk into the living room, I'm startled to see the casket already standing there with the top up. Even from the door, I can see how mama's face has turned to stone. To steady myself, I put a hand out to the wall.

"Easy, hon." I feel Dot's arm around my waist. "Easy."

"Looks just like herself, don't she?" I hear Miz Cowan cry out.

In the kitchen, Tessie's directing the food traffic. Mollie Sue Morton—"bless her heart," Tessie says—has sent over a ham and a dish of macaroni and cheese from the Café. Tessie has brought a big platter of deviled eggs, and Reba Petit comes bearing two bags of potato chips.

I keep wondering where Grady Fay is.

Then Marvin Cowan sticks his head in. I catch him as he eases back onto the front porch.

"You never answered my question."

"'Bout what?"

"'Bout that phone call. Was it Gene Hankins?"

The fact that Marvin turns sulky is a dead giveaway. "Why doncha ask him?"

"I'm asking you. What did he say?" He hangs his head. "*What* did he say?"

After pawing the cracks in the floorboards for a few seconds, he looks up. " 'Spect he told her about your meeting him that time in

Memphis. Said he was going to, anyway. To get even."

"To get even about what?"

"You getting married." There's another long pause. "Might as well tell you. He called Grady Fay, too."

This information takes more wind out of my sails. I stand there, completely deflated. Marvin looks like he's waiting for me to lash out at him, but I have no energy left. I turn and walk back inside.

Dot—who's standing by the door—helps me to bed.

I close my eyes. Wish I could turn back the clock. And for a few minutes, I do. I think about the time it snowed so much in Goody—the biggest snowfall we ever had.

I beg and beg mama to go out in it. Finally she gives in but not before dressing me in so many layers I can hardly move. "Now follow me," she says. "Step right where I do." And we walk round and round the house, me stepping right in her tracks. Just before we get back to the steps, I strike out in another direction to make my own tracks. I don't get very far before she jerks me up and drags me back inside.

That's what the pull and tug has always been about: making my own tracks. Poor mama.

I lie down and put the covers up over my face. Underneath the blanket and the hum of voices in the next room, I hear a phone ringing. I look at my watch: it's eleven-ten. Daddy wouldn't be calling at this hour.

"LaVonne." Tessie sticks her head in. "It's long distance."

Before rushing in to pick it up, I have to cross my fingers. "Hello," I say, trying to stay as calm as possible.

"Okay." It's like daddy to get right to the point. "Be there on the twelve-fifteen Eastern flight. Who'll meet me?"

I try to think quickly. "Maybe Grady Fay . . . my husband." The word sounds strange. "Maybe Bub's taxi. How'll they find you?"

"I'll be waiting by the information desk."

"I'm so glad."

"You're sure you can afford it? I'm borrowing the money to buy the ticket and I have to pay it back."

"I'm sure."

"See you tomorrow then."

When I hang up, everybody from Mr. Baxter to Preacher Crow seems to be looking at me. Dot comes in frowning, and I whisper into her ear. "Daddy's coming! Hope Grady Fay'll pick him up. They can get to know each other. Isn't it wonderful!"

"Shhh." Dot draws me back to the bedroom door. "Come on. You're getting all worked up. Take one of them sleeping pills Dr. Henderson gave you. That's what they're for."

But even with the pill, it's a long time before my mind shuts off.

Before the blinds come down, as mama says. *Said.* Reckon the hardest thing is getting used to the past tense.

The next morning, I wander around, feeling sick to my stomach, not quite knowing what to do. "Has Grady Fay come back?" I ask Dot, who must've spent the night.

Dot shakes her head. "He'll be here soon," she says. But I'm not so sure.

A few last-minute stragglers—people who for some reason or other can't make the funeral—stop by to view the body and sign the guest book. Each one mumbles something, but for the life of me, I couldn't begin to tell you what.

I'm talking to a woman named Gladys Dover who used to work with mama in the glove mill and wants to reminisce about some of their good times (though according to mama, there weren't any). In the middle of her speech, I hear Dot give a little yelp, and turn around.

"Where've you been?" I say, then stop. Grady Fay's face looks all red and pulpy, like it's been through a meat grinder. There's a cut on his lip, too, so it's hard for him to answer. "I mean, I was concerned about you."

"Up to Delphi," he says. "Taking care of some unfinished business."

I can only stare, knowing—without him telling me—what business he's talking about. "You should see the other party." When he tries to smile, I can see that he's chipped a tooth.

I grab him so hard, I practically knock him over.

Then I break the news about daddy coming. He says he'll pick him up, I say he's in no condition to drive anywhere, he says he'd better leave now, I say I'm calling Bub, he shakes his head, and in two seconds flat is out the door.

"That man is a continual surprise," I say, half to myself and half to Dot, who follows me into the bedroom to help me dress. "Wait'll you meet daddy," I tell her while she's brushing my hair. "Betcha anything he'll be wearing a white suit. Always did for funerals."

Then I catch a glimpse of my own face—pale and wild-eyed—in the mirror. "Do my eyes look puffy?" I ask Dot. Before she can answer, I've already started smearing on more make-up.

At one o'clock Jake Haygood and his assistants arrive. I'm in the kitchen trying to get Pretty Boy to take a few nibbles (funny how he seems to sense that something's wrong) when I hear my name called.

It's Miz Cowan. "Better get in there." She points toward the living room. "They're taking your mama out for the last time."

I walk up to the casket, knowing that people are waiting for me to do something . . . cry, shout, *anything*. But I can't.

Easing me aside, Jake closes the lid, and he and his assistants heave it up.

When they're gone, the room looks empty, as if the most important thing about it has fallen away.

Riding with Grandpa Jess to mama's funeral is my worst nightmare come true, even though we're in a Cadillac and Jake's assistant is driving us. I do my best to ignore him by thinking positive thoughts.

Elvis is beside me, holding my hand. He hums a spiritual— "The Old Rugged Cross"—for my benefit. And in between verses, he tells me he knows exactly how I feel because he's been through the same thing, that I just have to take a deep breath and bear the pain. Never, never, have Elvis and me been so close.

Then Grandpa Jess begins belching, and I lose the whole picture.

"Got the hiccups," he says.

At any moment, I think I might have to open the door and vomit.

Suppose I oughta tell Grandpa Jess about daddy. Instead I stick a loose curl back into place.

When we get to the church, I think: only a few days ago I was walking down this aisle with a wedding dress on. What funny tricks life plays.

The seats are almost filled. Have to remember to thank Dot for reminding me to phone in the date and time of the funeral to the Richville radio station. My hope is that some of mama's old friends from the glove mill heard it.

Jake guides us into the front pew, and Grandpa Jess plops down next to me. I lean over and whisper, "Leave a space between us."

"For Grady Fay? He can sit on the end."

"For daddy."

His mouth drops open and he gapes at me. "Jim Tom's coming?"

"Any second now."

He starts to rise, but only gets a few inches off the seat before I catch the edge of his jacket and pull him back. "If you make a scene," I hiss, "you'll regret it."

He sinks down like he's got a slow leak somewhere. "Who asked him anyway?" he mutters.

"I did."

"Well, your mama wouldn'a wanted it."

As he says this, Jake and his assistants are settling the casket into place, raising the lid and arranging the wreath of roses on the end. Pearlie B. sits down at the piano and voices in the church grow quiet.

I can feel a tingle on the back of my neck, as if the whole congregation has its eye on me. With this in mind, I hold my head high, trying to be as dignified as possible, in contrast to Grandpa Jess, who's busy snorting and blowing his nose.

After Preacher Crow's prayer comes the special number, sung by Bobby Echols, the only member left from the original Sunshine Quartet. It's mama's own request. Hope she's listening somewhere.

> *Rock of ages, cleft for me,*
> *Let me hide myself in thee;*
> *Let the water and the blood,*
> *From thy wounded side which flowed. . . .*

Hearing a slight bustle in the back, I can't help turning around, though I realize I'm not supposed to. I let out a gasp, for there, in the door of the church with the sun spreading a fiery glow behind his head is a figure that I'm sure must be daddy, although at the same time, I know he's not that tall. Then the man lifts his head and starts down the aisle, and I see it's only Troy Wiggins, looking for Dot.

I push down my disappointment by telling myself that Grady Fay'll be here soon. I ought to be feeling sorrowful, but all I can think of is daddy and me being reunited again.

> *While I draw this fleeting breath*
> *When my eyes shall close in death. . . .*

I spend the next few minutes trying to come up with something to say: "It's so good to see you," or "You look exactly the same."

> *When I rise to worlds unknown*
> *And behold thee on thy throne.*
> *Rock of ages. . . .*

Putting my attention back on the hymn, I hum along, remembering how mama used to sing it when she was working in the kitchen.

At the end of the aisle, a fat man is standing, hesitating about whether to take a seat or not. At first I ignore him, but when I see Grady Fay coming up behind him, I look again, and this time I stare.

Surely not! Surely to God not! I'm confused enough to bow my head and only glance up out of the corner of my eye when I see him pressing past Grandpa Jess. As he plops down beside me, I hear him wheezing dangerously. I'm aware that Grady Fay is watching me with a smile on his face and I try to smile, too, but it's not easy. The pompadour I once admired so much has been leveled to a few strands of sandy-colored hair. He reaches over and pats my hand, as though to reassure me.

Before I have the chance to say anything, he's shifted his attention to Grandpa Jess. Can't hear what's said, but whatever it is makes Grandpa Jess grunt.

I'm so busy taking in all this that I only half listen to Preacher Crow's words. Behind me, someone—Miz Cowan probably—is doing the kind of crying that should be coming from me.

When Pearlie B. starts "Just As I Am," Jake beckons me to step forward and lead the procession down to the casket. The whole pew stands. Daddy's last because he has a hard time pulling up.

Though it's the final time I'll ever set eyes on mama, I can't summon any tears. Not even when I pinch my eyes together hard. I can just hear Miz Cowan saying that she didn't detect one iota of grief on my face.

Daddy's dry-eyed, too, but that's not surprising. I see Grady Fay sniffling, which is mighty generous of him considering all he's had to put up with.

The cemetery's right behind the church so the whole congregation puts on their coats and troops out to the grave. Jake has set out a row of spindly chairs for the family, though daddy's is so tipsy he can practically rock back and forth. I can't take my eyes off him. It's as if I'm adjusting to all those absent years. His pudgy fingers are folded together across his stomach. His black overcoat looks worn and shiny, as if someone poured a coat of shellac over it.

Mama used to look in the mirror and say, "Well, this is what the years have done to me." Wonder what daddy thinks about those same years.

At a nod from Jake, Grady Fay leads me away so I don't have to witness the casket being lowered. Daddy's right behind us. Everybody clears a path and we head straight for the road where the truck's parked.

Just before reaching it, we stop a second to let daddy get his breath. His face is so red that I become a little alarmed. So does Grady Fay. "You alright, Mr. Grubbs?"

Daddy nods. Taking a handkerchief out, he wipes his eyes. Maybe he's genuinely upset. Not about mama surely. Maybe about me. I can feel myself beginning to soften toward him. He is, after all, my closest living relative. Stepping up, I take his arm. He doesn't pull away exactly, but there's not much response.

"I . . . uh . . . should be getting on to the station if I'm to make my bus." Folding the handkerchief carefully into a small square, he sticks it in his pocket. It's a gesture I've seen him make a hundred times, and it triggers other memories: daddy taking me on his lap and tickling me, daddy buying me Dentyne chewing gum, daddy holding mama back from giving me a switching, daddy singing "Little Brown Jug" whenever he'd had a few too many homebrews. . . .

"You're not going back already?" I give his arm a slight squeeze.

"Just up to Delphi." He stares at something beyond the bare trees. "I'll stay with my . . . wife's folks overnight, and they can drive me to the airport in the morning."

"Thought you might head back home with us." I try to make the invitation sound offhand, light as dust.

"I think this is best."

Then Dot comes up, and Tessie, and Reba. They stand shifting and eyeballing one another until I can no longer put off the introductions. "This is my daddy," I mumble. There's a chorus of murmurs and nods.

Only Dot steps forward and puts out her hand. "Pleased to meet you, Mr. Grubbs. Heard a lot about you." Daddy blinks at her. "LaVonne thinks the world of you. How long'll you be here?"

"Well, I . . . "

"He's leaving right now," I say, pausing to see if daddy will contradict me, but he doesn't.

"Come back soon," Dot calls out as we walk away.

Daddy turns and waves. "That's a real nice girl," he says as Grady Fay opens the door of the truck. "She a good friend of yours?"

"My *best* friend."

All the way to the station, I hold myself rigid. We pull up on the other side of the highway and sit there a second or two. Then daddy pushes down the handle. "Reckon I'd better get my ticket."

"Oh, here . . . " Reaching into my pocketbook, I take out my billfold and hand over several crisp new bills. "This should more than cover your fare."

I pray that he'll refuse it, but he holds out his hand. "This'll do nicely. I appreciate it." Leaning forward, he slides the money into his pants pocket. "Well . . . "

It's hard for me to do anything other than stare out the window, but now I turn to him. "Do you remember the time you took me to the Tivoli?"

"Tivoli?"

"The Tivoli Theater. In Chattanooga. You showed me all around the lobby and explained what everything was."

He looks thoughtful, then shakes his head. "Musta been your mama." Heaving himself up, he grabs his suitcase. "I was away a lot, you know. On calls."

I stare at him. *Had* it been mama?

There's a slight pause. "Well . . . Grady Fay . . . " he sticks out a hand " . . . it was real good to meet you." He turns to me. "If the two of you are ever up our way . . . "

"Don't imagine we will be," I say. My breath feels icy, my face hard.

Leaning over, he brushes my cheek while I pull a tiny piece of lint off my coat. Wish he'd hurry up and go. I have no more words for him.

Through the mud-splattered windshield, I watch him slowly walk to the edge of the highway, where he stops and glances up and down before crossing.

I touch Grady Fay's arm. "Let's go," I say, then shut my eyes.

All those years, I held mama responsible for what happened between them. Now she's not even here to say "I'm sorry" to. Preacher Crow says that the first part of your life's made up of hope, and the second of regret. Looks like I've entered the regret part. I'm feeling nauseous again.

Grady Fay leans toward me. "Don't you wanna wait?"

"For what?"

"Till the bus comes?"

"Why?"

Shrugging, he reaches for the starter.

At the house, I see that someone's left the screen door open. "Mama'll have a fit," I say. Then I think: mama's dead. She will never be alive again. She will never again tell me what to do. We will never yell at each other, or laugh together. The tears begin to come. Once they start, I can't stop them. I lie down on the sofa and sob into the pillow cushion. How will I manage without her?

Grady Fay puts a hand on my heaving shoulders. But this just makes things worse, and I cry harder. After awhile, the hiccups begin, and I make an effort to let up. Every time I take a breath, I breathe in a whiff of the funeral flowers.

"Open . . . some windows . . . " I tell Grady Fay, holding my nose.

When he finishes, he comes back and kneels beside me. "Why don't we pack up some stuff and go over to the farm for a few days? Staying here'll just make you gloomy."

"*Gloomier,*" I say. I feel I'll never be the same.

"What will you do about the house anyway?"

"We could stay in it during the week." I'm still sniffling, and trying to mop up my face. "Or sell it to buy that piece you liked so much up on the Delphi highway."

Entering my bedroom gives me a shock. Clothes are tumbling out of suitcases; slips, bras, and blouses are draped over the backs of chairs. Several items lie in a heap on the floor. For some reason, I pick up my old Elvis records, look at each one, and re-stack them. Then I put my teddy bear on top as if it's part of a display.

I empty one of the bags and start tossing a few things in. Snapping it shut, I move into the kitchen. Somebody's put the food into neat piles in the refrigerator and wiped the table and cabinets clean. At that second, my stomach starts heaving and I run into the bathroom.

When I come out, I'm feeling so much better that I think I might live after all . . . might even be able to make it to Sawmill Mountain. I gather up a few boxes of seed. "Leave the windows open to air out the inside," I tell Grady Fay. Am I already sounding bossy?

"We taking Pretty Boy?"

"Mama'd haunt my dreams if we didn't."

He makes a face at this, and holds the cage while I climb into the truck. I take it and put it on the seat between me and the door. Immediately it sets up a furious squawking. Between the squawks, I can hear mama's voice saying, "Eat up now, eat up now, eat up now."

I don't know whether to laugh or cry. Grady Fay reaches over, draws me next to him, and holds me tight. The bird does it again, and this time I smile. Grady Fay does, too. We sit there chuckling for a minute or two before he starts the motor.

"Shhh, Pretty Boy, shhh. Come on, now." I lean back. "Shhh now. Hush." Then I try whistling like mama used to. I'm not much good at it, but after awhile, I get better. I keep on till finally it calms down and all I can hear is the noise of the truck.

Susie Mee grew up in Trion, Georgia. After attending the University of Georgia and Yale Drama School, she became a professional actress, appearing on Broadway, off-Broadway, and television. She began writing at the same time, publishing poetry, fiction, essays, and reviews in magazines including *The Georgia Review, Poetry, American Poetry Review, The Drama Review, The New York Times Book Review, Smithsonian, European Travel and Life,* and *Redbook* (where THE GIRL WHO LOVED ELVIS first appeared as a short story called "Mama Won't Budge"). She is also the author of STORIES OF THE POETS, a book of essays on contemporary poets; and THE UNDERTAKER'S DAUGHTER, a collection of poetry.

Affiliated with Teachers and Writers Collaborative, Mee has received grants from the New York State Council on the Arts and the New York Foundation. She lives in New York City, where she teaches writing at New York University. She is currently working on her second novel.